THE POWER OF DEATH

THE POWER OF DEATH

Contemporary Reflections on Death in Western Society

Edited by Maria-José Blanco and Ricarda Vidal

berghahn

NEW YORK · OXFORD

www.berghahnbooks.com

First edition published in 2015 by
Berghahn Books
www.berghahnbooks.com

© 2015, 2017 Maria-José Blanco and Ricarda Vidal
First paperback edition published in 2017

Library of Congress Cataloging-in-Publication Data

The power of death: contemporary reflections on death in western society / edited by
Maria-José Blanco and Ricarda Vidal.
    pages cm
Includes bibliographical references and index.
    ISBN 978-1-78238-433-5 (hardback: alk. paper) — ISBN 978-1-78533-510-5 (paper-
back) — ISBN 978-1-78238-434-2 (ebook)
    1. Death. 2. Death in literature. 3. Funeral rites and ceremonies. I. Blanco, Maria-
José. II. Vidal, Ricarda.
    BD444.P69 2014
    306.9--dc23

                                                                          2014016169

British Library Cataloguing in Publication Data
A catalogue record for this book is available from the British Library

ISBN 978-1-78238-433-5 (hardback)
ISBN 978-1-78533-510-5 (paperback)
E-ISBN 978-1-78238-434-2 (ebook)

CONTENTS

ILLUSTRATIONS

Notes on Contributors

Julia Banwell is Lecturer in Hispanic Studies at the University of Sheffield. Her research interests lie generally in the field of Latin American visual cultures, with a specific focus on Mexican photography and contemporary art. She is writing a monograph on the Mexican contemporary artist Teresa Margolles (b.1963), is involved in a project on the photography of the Mexican Revolution, and also has an interest in the reporting of injury and death in sports.

Diana York Blaine, Associate Professor at the University of Southern California, teaches rhetoric, feminist theory, and literature. Her work focuses on representations of death in American culture, examining the ways in which gendered and raced narratives about mortality produce normative subjectivity in the United States. She has published on William Faulkner, Thomas Pynchon, the Jon Benet Ramsey murder case, the Dr Phil show, and Michael Jackson's memorial service. Her current project examines the stories that we tell about death in mainstream American culture.

Maria-José Blanco is a Lecturer and Language teacher in the Department of Spanish Portuguese and Latin American Studies (SPLAS) at King's College London. She is the author of Life-writing in Carmen Martín Gaite's Cuadernos de todo and her Novels of the 1990s (2013), and the editor of a special issue of Journal of Romance Studies, "Airing the Private: Women's Diaries in the Luso-Hispanic World" (2009) and the forthcoming Feminine Singular: Growing up through life-writing in the Luso-Hispanic World (2014).

Marina Cap-Bun is associated professor at Ovidius University of Constanta, Bucharest University and Indiana University. She teaches Romanian Culture and Civilization, Literature, and History of Theatre. She was Fulbright Postdoctoral Scholar at University of Washington, Seattle (2001–2002), and has been invited professor at Indiana University, SWSEEL since 2009. She has authored *Mirrors within Mirrors: A Study on I.L. Caragiale's Works* (1998); *Between the Absurd and the Fantastic: Voyages in the Mirage Waters* (2001); *Critical Essays* (2003);

Great Classics of Romanian Literature (2003); *Criss-Cross: Essays in Romanian and Comparative Literature* (Munich, 2004, 2006); *Junimea* (2007); *Romanian Literature under the Sign of Modernity* (2009).

Briony Campbell is a documentary photographer and filmmaker. In 2009 she graduated from London College of Communication's Masters in documentary photography. The same year, 'The Dad Project' became a formative chapter for her personally and professionally. The Project was exhibited, published and awarded internationally. Briony's work has been published in the UK's *Guardian*, *The Observer*, *The Independent*, *The Financial Times*, Spain's *El Mundo* and Germany's *Die Zeit*. Recent clients include London's Southbank Centre, The Photographer's Gallery and The National Health Service. She is currently studying Britain's contemporary relationship with Africa, through the lives of mixed nationality couples in East Africa.

Corina Crisu is a Lecturer in American Studies and Comparative Literature at the University of Bucharest. She has researched on contemporary African American authors (especially their rewriting of the literary tradition), and on the works of Eastern European immigrant authors who write in English as a second language. A recipient of prestigious grants (a Soros-Chevening Scholarship at Oxford University and a Fulbright Fellowship at Oregon State University), she has participated in numerous international conferences and joint projects, and contributed to academic journals and anthologies worldwide.

Eleanor David (née Parker) is Stipendiary Lecturer in Italian at St Anne's College, University of Oxford and an Associate of the UK Higher Education Academy. Educated at Christ Church, Oxford, she holds a B.A. in French and Italian, an M.St. in European Literature and a doctorate on the poetics of loss and mourning in the later work of Giuseppe Ungaretti. She has taught Italian language and literature at the University of Oxford since 2007 and has published articles on Ungaretti's commemorative poetry, ageing and creativity in twentieth-century Italian poetry and on pedagogical practices at Oxford.

Bel Deering completed her PhD 'Over their dead bodies: a study of leisure and spatiality in cemeteries' in 2012. Alongside her interests in graveyards, dark tourism, heterotopia, and enchantment, she manages a wildlife centre, nature reserve and education centre for the RSPCA and is currently researching the relationship between people and wildlife. Previous publications include 'From anti-social to X-rated: exploring the social diversity of the cemetery' in *Deathscapes: Spaces for Death, Dying, Mourning and Remembrance*, ed. A. Maddrell and J. Sidaway (2010, Ashgate) and, as B. Browning, *Just the Facts: Animal Welfare* (2002, Heinemann Library).

John Horne is a PhD student at the University of Birmingham, researching representations of torture. John holds an MPhil from the University of Birmingham entitled 'Representations of Dying in Contemporary Visual Culture and the Ethics of Spectatorship'. He has a chapter on 'Visualising the Dying Individual and End of Life Care Reform' in *Envisaging Death: Visual Culture and Dying* (2013). He is also a member of the research and advocacy organisation Bahrain Watch.

Lala Isla has a degree in Anthropology from the Universidad Complutense of Madrid. She is the author of *Londres, pastel sin receta*, a cultural and social comparison between London and Spain which explores themes such as the family, birth, education, and housing problems. Her latest book examines the silence in Spain about what happened there during the Civil War, centred on two towns in the province of León. She has co-produced two documentaries about the Spanish Civil War: *Extranjeros de sí mismos* (*Foreign to themselves*) and *El exilio* (*Exile*). She is currently working on a book about food, death and racism.

Fiorenzo Iuliano works as a lecturer in American literature at the University of Cagliari (Italy). He recently authored a book on the representation of the body in American fiction of the 1990s and a monograph on the work of Gayatri Ch. Spivak. His research interests include contemporary American fiction and graphic novels, cultural studies and theories of the body and corporeality. He is currently working on the cultural scene of Seattle in the 1990s.

Catherine Jenkins is a PhD candidate in Communication and Culture, a joint program at Ryerson-York Universities in Toronto, Canada. She teaches Professional Communication at Ryerson University. She has authored 'Aberrant Decoding: Dementia and the Collision of Television with Reality' in *The Intima: A Journal of Narrative Medicine* in Fall 2012, and 'The Message in Medical Imaging Media: An Analysis of GE Healthcare's Vscan™' in the forthcoming publication *Marshall McLuhan in a Post Modern World: Is the Medium the Message?* (2014, University of Regina Press). Her research explores the impact of medical imaging technologies on patient-physician communication.

Natasha Lushetich is an artist and researcher. Having received her PhD in 2011, she is currently Lecturer in Performance at the University of Exeter, UK. Natasha is a regular speaker at international conferences and has published with *Performance Research, TDR, Text and Performance Quarterly, Babilonia, Theatre Journal* and *The Total Art Journal* as well as in a number of edited collections. She is currently working on two monographs: *Fluxus the Practice of Non-Duality* (Rodopi) and *Interdisciplinary Performance Practice* (Palgrave).

José **Mapril** is an invited lecturer at the department of Anthropology, New University of Lisbon and an associate researcher at CRIA-UNL. He specialises in migration/transnational studies, Islam and subjectivities with research in Bangladesh and in Lisbon. He is the author of 'The dreams of middle class: consumption, life-course and migration between Bangladesh and Portugal', *Modern Asian Studies* (forthcoming) and *Islão e Transnacionalismo* (2012, Imprensa de Ciencias Sociais). He has also co-authored (with Ruy Blanes) *The Sites and Politics of Religious Diversity in Southern Europe: The Best of All Gods* (2013, Brill).

Wolfgang **Marx** is Senior Lecturer in Musicology and Head of the School of Music at University College Dublin where he also leads the Research Strand 'Death, Burial and the Afterlife'. His main research interests are the representation of death in music (with a special focus on requiem compositions) and the music of György Ligeti. Among his recent publications are articles on the requiems of Dvořák and Stanford and on the role of death in Ligeti's œuvre, the latter published in *György Ligeti: Of Foreign Lands and Strange Sounds*, edited by Louise Duchesneau and Wolfgang Marx.

Clara **Saraiva** is senior researcher at the Lisbon Tropical Research Institute, Professor at the Department of Anthropology, Universidade Nova de Lisboa, and researcher at the Centre for Research in Anthropology. She was Michael Teague invited Professor at Brown University (2001–2002 and 2008). Her research deals with death and funerary rituals (USA, Portugal, Guinea-Bissau, immigrants in Portugal), and transnational religions. Recent publications include: '*Pretos-velhos* across the Atlantic – Afro-Brazilian cults in Portugal', in *The Diaspora of Brazilian Religions*, ed. Manuel Vasquez and Cristina Rocha (2013, Brill); and 'Transnational Migrants and Transnational Spirits: An African Religion in Lisbon', *Journal of Ethnic and Migration Studies*; she also co-authored, with José Mapril (2012), 'Le lieu de la "bonne mort" pour les migrants guinéens et bangladais au Portugal', *Revue Europeéne des migrations internationales*.

Lynne M. **Simpson** is Professor of English at Presbyterian College in Clinton, South Carolina, where she teaches Shakespeare and British literature. Her work on grief and mourning has appeared in journals including *Shakespeare Studies* and a special issue of *The Humanities Review* on death in the Renaissance. At PC she was appointed an inaugural Student Life Fellow and has chaired the Women's and Gender Studies Program. She served as Program Chair for the Southeastern Renaissance Conference (2009–2011). In 2011 she was elected for a three-year term to the national Board of Directors of the College English Association.

Rebecca **Shillabeer** graduated with an MA in Publishing from Oxford Brookes University in 2010. Her dissertation 'Raped, mutilated, dismembered and strewn across the landscape: Are female crime writers of the twenty-first century com-plicit or subversive?' went on to inform her research into the fascination with torture and death in twenty-first-century crime fiction. She is currently working as a Textbook Development Editor for an academic publisher.

Ricarda Vidal is a lecturer, curator and translator. She holds a PhD in Cultural Studies (Birkbeck University of London) and teaches at the department of Culture, Media and Creative Industries at King's College London. She has pub-lished on urban space, the legacy of Modernism and Romanticism, speed, the car and driving as cultural phenomena and society's fascination with death and murder. She is the author of *Death and Desire in Car Crash Culture: A Century of Romantic Futurisms* (2013).

INTRODUCTION

Ricarda Vidal and Maria-José Blanco

In the most general terms death is defined as the final and irreversible cessation of the vital functions in an organism, the ending of life. However, the precise definition of death and the exact time of the transition from life to death differ according to culture, religion and legal system.

The essential insecurities and doubts over the nature and state of death have affected cultural production since the beginning of civilisation. Likewise our attitude towards death is characterised by anxieties and ambiguities. Death can be 'a consummation devoutly to be wished' in the words of Hamlet, or 'a wonderful gain' to quote Schopenhauer. While philosophers and poets explore the dark attraction of death, in everyday life we tend to push all thought of it aside. Death, and above all our own death, must not impinge upon the living. And yet death is everywhere: it vies for our attention on blood-splattered posters advertising the latest blockbuster films or on grisly crime fiction book-covers announcing graphic descriptions of violent death and murder. Death, it seems, is rather entertaining – at least as long as it is confined to fiction. But even when it manifests itself in all its gruesome reality in the daily news reports on wars, murders, natural catastrophes and fatal accidents, death to some extent resists reality. Shocking though it may be, it is mediated through radio or television, controlled by the framework of the news story and kept at a safe distance. It is something that happens to others, somewhere else. However, besides the mediated violent death of news broadcasting and besides the ostentatious celebration of brutal and essentially fictional death in popular culture, we are also haunted by the undeniable presence of a much more real and frightening death – death by cancer or heart disease or the often protracted dying process of old age, which is becoming more and more common in the ageing societies of the West.

As Ariès (1981) and Dollimore (1998) have shown, amongst others, these contradictory notions of death have always been part of society. However, where they have earlier been subsumed and to some degree resolved in religion, the increasing secularisation of society combined with advances in medicine, which allow an almost infinite prolongation of life (often in stark contrast to quality of life), has led to a situation which is very specific to contemporary times.

As Kellehear observes, '[d]ying – now far far away from its otherworld beginnings – has become a set of this-world trials and tests' (Kellehear 2007: 8). In his extensive study *A Social History of Dying* (2007), which spans the customs, practices and experiences of dying from the Stone Age to present times, Kellehear diagnoses a deep confusion and sensation of being adrift within contemporary approaches to death and dying. Indeed, he argues, that the process of dying has become separated from death itself by having been institutionalised to such a degree that it is almost negated:

> In our modern world, deaths do indeed occur in nursing homes, in poverty or in modern detention centres, but not dying. Dying – as a shared set of social exchanges between dying individuals and those who care for them – is increasingly unrecognised in institutional settings outside hospital or health service settings in both global or domestic contexts. Public recognition, even some personal recognition of dying, has become an abstract political affair now severed from its earlier biological, psychological and interpersonal moorings. (Kellehear 2007: 253)

However, this disappearance of the dying process has not gone unnoticed nor without protest from those nearing the end of life or those accompanying loved ones on their final journey. In fact, it has been the subject of a variety of cultural responses in recent years, such as, amongst others, Derek Jarman's *Blue* (1993), which deals with the artist's coming to terms with his own death from AIDS, Isabel Allende's autobiographical *Paula* (1994) which narrates the author's taking leave of her dying daughter, the TV drama *Wit* (2001) which follows the protagonist's journey from her cancer diagnosis to her death, Joan Didion's autobiographical *The Year of Magical Thinking* (2005) and *Blue Nights* (2011), which trace the author's mourning process after losing first her husband and then her daughter, or, most recently Michael Haneke's award-winning film *L'Amour* (2012), which charts the slow deterioration of old age and the inability of the dying protagonist's immediate family to accept her death and accompany her in her leave-taking. These personalised stories of death and loss answer to a demand within society to re-examine our approach to the process of dying and leave-taking. In January 2012 this demand was met by a four-day festival at the Southbank Centre in London, *Death: Festival for the Living*, which included poetry readings, music performances, art installations, philosophical debates and hands-on workshops in all matters relating to death. Amongst the presenters were obituary writers, funeral directors, philosophers, writers and artists, but also a group of terminally ill children. As obituary writer Harry de Quetteville remarked in a review of the festival: 'those most intimately acquainted with death are the least bashful discussing it', but all too often, we are too squeamish to listen to them. The hugely successful festival gave the dying as well as the bereaved and the 'as-yet-to-be-bereaved' the opportunity to confront and overcome this squeamishness in a genuine dialogue which was embedded within the wider framework of cultural approaches to death.

Within the interdisciplinary field of death studies a number of scholars have explored this search for a more humane, intimate (and perhaps communal) death further (amongst others Morris and Thomas 2005; Grainger 2006; Madrell and Sidaway 2010; Walpole 2011; see also the chapters by Jenkins, Blanco, Horne, Lushetich, Isla and Campbell in this volume). Madrell and Sidaway's edited collection *Deathscapes: Spaces of Death, Dying, Mourning and Remembrance* (2010) focuses on the importance of space in the process of dying, mourning and memorialisation. As the collection shows, the space of death reaches far beyond the site of its occurrence and transcends institutional limitations, thus opening ways to resituate death and dying within the community.

Kellehear suggests that stepping back and looking at the social history of death and of past ways of dying may help us to reconnect and reclaim our own final departure and that of our loved ones from over-institutionalisation (2007: 8). The popularity of the *Festival of the Living* or of exhibitions such as *Death: A Self-Portrait – the Richard Harris Collection* at London's Wellcome Collection in winter 2012/13 indicates that many of us already turn to past customs (our own and those of others) in search for alternative (and perhaps better) ways of dealing with death and dying. Showcasing around 300 works from medieval images of the German dance-of-death via nineteenth-century Victorian death photography to contemporary Mexican artefacts for the Day of the Dead, the Wellcome exhibition aimed to provide an international and cross-cultural overview of 'our enduring desire to make peace with death' (Wellcome Trust 2012).

At the outset of our introduction we mentioned the spectacular side of death. While *Death: A Self-Portrait* certainly asked its public to reflect on death and dying rituals and customs across cultures, the exhibition also included a decisive element of sensationalism. Death was not only represented but also tantalisingly present. Mediated through art and the exhibition setting, it could be consumed both with the critical distance of the (art) historian and with the intimate thrill of the spectator. Just as the Southbank Centre festival, Harris's extensive collection of artefacts and artworks from across the globe made it clear that death is not only a universal occurrence that needs to be dealt with by culture and society but also a potent source of entertainment.

In the last decades several books have been published which analyse death and its perception in the contemporary world from different points of view. The great majority of these explore contemporary death, dying and mourning with a focus on the customs, rituals and processes involved (e.g. Hockey et al. 2010; Maddrell and Sidaway 2010; Rotar and Teodorescu 2011), while a smaller number look at the purely sensationalist and spectacular aspects of death (e.g. Goldstein 1998; Piven 2004; Schmid 2006). The present volume aims to combine the study of the contradictory aspects of death as entertainment with death as the natural end of life. Like the essay collections edited by Kellehear (2009) or Madrell and Sidaway (2010), our volume cuts across a wide range of disciplines combining the arts and humanities with the social sciences. Music, the visual arts, exhibition practice, the media, literature as well as serial killers, longevity, euthanasia, cemeteries, and bereavement are explored. From their various vantage points (which in some cases are intimately personal experiences) but always with reference to Western society, the authors reflect on the response of institutions and individuals, and how death is part of our day-to-day lives even if we don't want to confront it.

The essays in our collection are organised into five broad themes which interconnect with each other: Death in Society; Death in Literature; Death in Visual Culture; Cemeteries and Funerals; and Personal Reflections on Death.

The volume begins with Catherine Jenkins's thought-provoking and at times chilling exploration of the effects that medical progress has on our quality of life as we approach death. Reiterating Ariès's (1981) and Kellehear's (2007) observations on the disappearance of death into institutionalisation, Jenkins focuses on the many contemporary cases in Anglo-Saxon societies, where death and dying are confined to the hygienic, clean and sterile spaces of hospitals, hospices and morgues. As mentioned above progress in medical science has led to an increase in life expectancy in the Western world, resulting in an ever ageing population, and it seems as though we have almost found a cure for death. However, as Jenkins shows, the flipside of a longer life expectancy is an increase in long-term illnesses and a longer dying process. With medical apparatus allowing us to keep a body alive and prolong physical existence even after the brain has died, it becomes increasingly hard to differentiate life from death. What then, Jenkins asks, does it mean to be human and how can we die in a humane way?

The next chapter shifts the focus from the dying to those left behind. Focusing on grief and bereavement, Lynne Simpson has compiled a comprehensive survey of theoretical developments since Freud's 'Mourning and Melancholia' (1917). Many of the concepts and theories she analyses in her chapter form the basis for subsequent chapters on grief and mourning in the volume. With reference to Ariès's *The Hour of our Death* (1981) and Geoffrey Gorer's much-cited 'Pornography of Death' (1955) amongst others, Simpson discusses the notion of the disappearance of death with the beginning of Modernism. However, she also draws on more recent studies which reflect more recent developments in the study of grief which contest this view and show a perhaps healthier and more involved method of dealing with death than the institutionalisation described by Jenkins.

Moving from the personal and private aspects of dying and mourning into the realm of the public commemoration of loss, the section closes with an essay by Wolfgang Marx on the requiem. Taking into account the changes in the old belief systems and the waning of religious faith, Marx examines the continued presence of the requiem in twentieth-century memorial compositions by comparing three war requiems: the collaborative *Requiem of Reconciliation*, Benjamin Britten's *War Requiem* and Bertolt Brecht/ Kurt Weill's *Berliner Requiem*. He argues that many requiem compositions have now become a vehicle of political or social critique, addressing not the death of a lost individual relative or friend but rather the death of thousands or even millions in war. The focus thus lies no longer primarily on the deceased but rather on the people or institutions responsible for their deaths. Marx investigates different techniques of applying the traditional Latin text (or sometimes just movement titles derived from it) to this entirely secularised task.

Maria-José Blanco opens the next section, 'Death and Literature', with her investigation of writing as a therapeutic tool for coping with bereavement. She looks at four professional writers who all took up pen and paper and wrote down their personal experiences after the death of a loved one. Blanco not only analyses these autobiographical texts but also asks why they were written and why the authors felt a need to publish them and share their mourning with their readers. Many of the theoretical reflections on bereavement which appear in Simpson's essay return in Blanco's as they served as inspiration or support to the authors as they wrote their way through their mourning process.

In the following chapter Eleanor David takes us from the intimacy of personal loss and grief into a no less intimate encounter with bereavement and mourning on a much larger scale. David's chapter explores the religious (in particular, the Catholic) tradition of institutionalised mourning by examining Italian poet Margherita Guidacci's collection *La Via Crucis dell'umanità* (1984). Just as Marx had traced the transformation of the requiem from a religious to a secular art form, David shows how an originally religious text or concept (i.e. the Way of the Cross) can be applied to a secular context. In the form of contemporary poetry, it can serve to deal with the traumas and collective suffering of the mass deaths of the world wars and other human catastrophes. Just as for Blanco's authors, for Guidacci, writing – and for her audience, reading – here become a way of dealing with grief and ultimately overcoming it.

Corina Crisu also looks at writing as a way of gaining control over death – albeit within the fictional realm of Edward Gaines's *A Lesson Before Dying* (1993). Arguing that death, and in particular violent death, has played a prominent role in the construction of black identity in North American literature, Crisu analyses the emancipation of Gaines's black hero from physical bondage to spiritual liberation.

Triggered by the proximity of his (unjustified) execution, the hero's development is facilitated by intimate conversations and by his decision to learn to write and share his thoughts and fears of death. Crisu also examines Gaines's criticism of the racist American justice system. This system is also the focus of Iuliano Fiorenzo's chapter on John Grisham's novel *The Client* (1993). Linking to the utilisation of the corpse in the construction of identity and feelings of superiority, Fiorenzo's chapter investigates the symbolic use of the dead body in the novel. While he points out that the novel's obsession with the corpse seems somewhat unmotivated, the detailed descriptions of cruel murder fit in with what Rebecca Shillabeer describes in the next chapter with reference to crime fiction of the past twenty years in general. Shillabeer examines the growth of explicit descriptions of torture and violent death in recent crime novels. While she traces the fascination with violent death back to the ancient Greeks, she also explains that there appears to have been a remarkable increase of violence since the 1990s. Shillabeer investigates the reasons why authors such as Patricia Cornwell, Tess Gerritsen or P J Tracy feel the need to describe violence in such excruciating detail and why readers are so fascinated with this. With reference to the happy endings which occur in almost all crime novels, i.e. the murderer is caught and justice prevails, she argues that fiction allows both authors and readers to take control over the quagmire of death and violence they fear might threaten them in real life as well.

The third part, 'Death and Visual Culture', opens with Ricarda Vidal's chapter on art by serial killers, which continues the themes introduced by Shillabeer and looks at our fascination with violent death and the curious popularity of the serial killer. Starting from an exhibition of artworks created by serial killers, Vidal draws on the writings of George Bataille on murder, transgression and taboo to examine the paradox of repulsion and attraction such artworks exert on the viewer. She argues that while desiring and buying such artworks, and hence admitting to a fascination with violence and death, constitutes a transgression in itself, owning them can become a way of participating in the transgression of the murder – even if only on an imaginary plain. At the same time, ownership of an object produced by a serial killer also implies taking control over the murderer's creation, the artwork and to some degree also the murder.

In his chapter, John Horne takes up a point made earlier in the book by Jenkins and others about the institutionalisation, social exclusion and clinical objectification of those who die. Horne argues that cinema can contest such isolation of death. Analysing three films, *Lightning over Water* (1980), *My Life* (1993) and *Wit* (2001), Horne argues for the significance of film as a key site for interrogating and ethically rethinking the encounter with the dying individual. However, a meaningful engagement with death can only happen if the film manages to open up an ethical space of reflection and encourages the spectator to recognise the objectifying potential implicit in their subject position and to consider their responsibility towards the dying individual.

Julia Banwell also focuses on death on screen and the position of the spectator. However, where Horne explores films which bring the slow death by terminal disease onto the screen, Banwell looks at accidental death (Ayrton Senna's fatal crash in 1994) and injury (David Beckham's metatarsal injury from 2002) in spectator sports. While Horne's cinema audience can prepare for what they will see, the encounter with the sudden violence of death or injury during a sporting event is entirely unexpected and raw. Advances in visual technologies allow sports spectators to enjoy a privileged view of events through close-ups and slow-motion replays, and YouTube has made it possible to access and repeatedly view footage of unpredictable and disturbing occurrences. Banwell focuses on the visual location of death and injury in the media, exploring the potential for reading the repeat viewing of slow-motion footage and still images of death and injury in close-up, as ritualistic. Spectating may here also be viewed as a way of taking control not just of the athlete's body and their death, but also over death more generally.

The section closes with Diana York Blaine's study of the exhibition *Mummies of the World*, which debuted at the California Science Center in Los Angeles in 2010. While York Blaine acknowledges the museum's attempt at lending meaning to the meaninglessness of death, she also criticises the exhibition for reflecting Western ideologies of racial superiority and transcendence over the body. She contends that the exhibition ultimately operated as a modern freak show rather than giving the audience the opportunity to engage meaningfully with death and their own mortality.

The fourth part of the volume looks at cemeteries and funerals, giving voice to individuals (either the authors themselves or people they interviewed) and their private experiences of death. Focusing on the Merry Cemetery of Săpânţa in Northern Romania, Marina Cap-Bun looks at how the personalised colourful wooden crosses of the cemetery, with their light-hearted epitaphs, pick up and update traditional Romanian funeral rituals. Cap-Bun shows that while the cemetery originated from the personal vision of its founder, the wood-carver Stan Ion Pătraş (1908–1977), it can also lay claim to a much wider Romanian funeral tradition which links death intimately to laughter and joy.

Bel Deering also takes us on a journey to the graveyard – albeit in the dead of night. Rather than merry epitaphs we encounter the shadows and strange lights, which are so familiar from horror films and ghost stories. Deering's chapter draws on a series of interviews she conducted with individuals on nocturnal visits to graveyards in the UK. With recourse to Foucault's concept of heterotopia, she examines the extent, nature and qualities of real or imagined supernatural forms and thus conceptualises the sense of place of the cemetery and the contingency of experience and meaning. She postulates that the manifestation of supernatural deviance in dead spaces is in part an expression of the fear of death and disease that Foucault identified, but shows that this is located within a wider suite of personal and social needs for the spooky and ghostly. Fear, after all, can be courted in order to produce feelings of excitement and pleasure, and to reinforce the sense of being alive.

Clara Saraiva and José Mapril's contribution, too, is based on interviews, albeit here the focus lies on the bereaved and on those who help them deal with their loss – both in terms of ritual and the practicalities of the funeral. The cemeteries at the centre of Cap-Bun's and Deering's research were seen as part of the community they served, i.e. final resting places for those who lived nearby or at least for their ancestors. Focusing on emigrants from Guinea Bissau and Bangladesh in Portugal, Saraiva and Mapril, in contrast, examine the journey of the dead body to its final resting place, which is often thousands of kilometres away. Death, they argue, entails an intense circulation of material goods and wealth, but also of highly symbolic significant universes which circulate along with the goods and the people: the corpse, but also the spirits and the relations with the other world that people bring with them into a diaspora situation. Based on ethnographic data, the chapter explores the work done by immigrants' associations, as well as hospitals, funerary agencies, diplomatic and border authorities and religious institutions.

The section closes with Natasha Lushetich's reflections on the increasing popularity of self-styled 'dying parties' in the Netherlands. Her chapter explores the relationship between performance efficacy and intertextuality in the dying ritual. Aided by performance theory and departing from the notion of performance as a doing, staging, attainment and judgment, she argues for a different, *ludic-concretist* model of ritual efficacy. Lushetich takes us back to the ideas discussed by Horne of death as a spectacle and develops Jenkins' idea of dying in a humane, self-determined way.

The final part of the volume is dedicated to personal reflections on death by the writer Lala Isla and the photographer Briony Campbell. Isla gives a personal and anecdotal view of the social changes that Spain and the UK have experienced in the past thirty-five years regarding attitudes towards death. Isla recollects the funeral traditions she witnessed as a child in Castile and describes the recent introduction of the 'tanatorio' in Spain, a kind of public morgue that has all but replaced the intimate rituals of mourning within the family home. She compares these developments to the changes which have occurred in the UK in funerary customs since the 1980s which are partly due to the influence of AIDS-related deaths of young men who brought a lot of sense of humour to funerals as well as a need to personalise them. Isla concludes that Spain seems to follow Britain's lead and vice versa: while Spain is taking death outside the home and increasingly dehumanising it, death in Britain becomes more personal and, in some cases, even returns to the home.

The volume closes with a photographic essay by Briony Campbell. Campbell spent the last six months of her father's life photographing and filming their relationship, before he died of cancer in August 2009. In 2010, the work, 'The Dad Project', was exhibited and published internationally, and provoked a response she had never anticipated. While presenting selected images from the project, she reflects on the way this initially very intimate piece has developed since it was first published. As Campbell asserts through her own experiences, her willingness to share her grief touches a nerve in contemporary society. Many of us have lost, or are perhaps about to lose, someone close to us, but are unsure of how to deal with death. Campbell's work offers a way to think about leave-taking, death and mourning in a gentle, consoling and ultimately optimistic way. And it also looks towards the future, a future that is not bereft but rather enriched by the experience of death.

Bibliography

Ariès, P. 1981. *The Hour of our Death*. Oxford: Penguin Books.

Dollimore, J. 1998. *Death, Desire and Loss in Western Culture*. London: Penguin.

Goldstein, J.H. (ed.). 1998. *Why We Watch: The Attractions of Violent Entertainment*. Oxford: OUP.

Grainger, H.J. 2006. *Death Redesigned: British Crematoria, History, Architecture and Landscape*. London: Spire Books.

Hockey, J., C. Komaromy and K. Woodthorpe. 2010. *The Matter of Death: Space, Place and Materiality*. Basingstoke, Hampshire: Palgrave Macmillan.

Kellehear, A. 2007. *A Social History of Dying*. Cambridge: Cambridge University Press.

⸻ (ed.). 2009. *The Study of Dying : From Autonomy to Transformation*. Cambridge: Cambridge University Press.

Maddrell, A and J.D. Sidaway. 2010. *Deathscapes: Spaces for Death, Dying, Mourning and Remembrance*. Surrey: Ashgate.

Morris, S.M. and C. Thomas. 2005. 'Placing the Dying Body: Emotional, Situational and Embodied Factors in Preferences for Place of Final Care and Death in Cancer', in J. Davidson, L. Bondi, M. Smith (eds), *Emotional Geographies*. Aldershot: Ashgate, pp. 19–32.

Piven, J.S. 2004. *Death and Delusion: A Freudian Analysis of Mortal Terror*. Greenwich, Connecticut: Information Age Publishing.

de Quetteville, H. 2012. 'Harry de Quetteville on the Southbank's Festival of Death,' *Telegraph*, 26 January 2012. Accessed 17 September 2013, www.telegraph.co.uk/culture/art/art-features/9042292/Harry-de-Quetteville-on-the-Southbanks-Festival-of-Death.html

Rotar, M. and A. Teodorescu (eds). 2011. *Dying and Death in 18th-21st Century Europe*. Newcastle upon Tyne: Cambridge Scholars.

Schmid, D. 2006. *Natural Born Celebrities: Serial Killers in American Culture*. Chicago, London: University of Chicago Press.

Walpole, K. 2011. 'The Modern Hospice Movement: A Quiet Revolution, in End of Life Care,' in Marius Rotar and Adriana Teodorescu (eds), *Dying and Death in 18th-21st Century Europe*. Newcastle upon Tyne: Cambridge Scholars, pp. 351–55.

Wellcome Trust 2012. 'Wellcome Collection Opens "Death" exhibition'. Accessed 17 September 2013, http://www.wellcome.ac.uk/News/Media-office/Press-releases/2012/WTP040736.htm

PART I

DEATH IN SOCIETY

LIFE EXTENSION, IMMORTALITY AND THE PATIENT VOICE

Catherine Jenkins

So, today there are machines to breathe for the patient, medications to sustain blood pressure, tubes to provide nutrition, equipment to perform the tasks of the heart, lungs, kidneys, and bladder. Of course, using these devices is imperative if a patient might recover. The question is their usefulness for a person who will never be cured. (Kiernan 2010: 171)

Throughout human history, people have tried to sustain youth and grasp immortality. Dating from the third century, the *Alexander Romance* tale, 'The Water of Life', tells of a healing spring. In the Middle Ages, the 'Fountain of Youth' was said to exist in the elusive territories ruled by the mythical Prester John. *The Travels of Sir John Mandeville*, published in the late 1300s, includes a tale of the author drinking from the well of youth in India. In 1513, Ponce de Leon went in search of the 'Fountain of Youth', but died eight years later. Sadly, none of these historical or mythological figures is still breathing, so it is safe to assume that none was successful in his quest to find a cure for death. But it does point to an assumption that the living tend to make about death: everybody wants to live for as long as possible. Certainly today's medical technologies can maintain essential bodily functions, and all outward appearances of life, long after the brain's neurons have stopped firing. But does this prolong life or simply extend the dying process? Is the quality of life suffering because of our fixation on the quantity of life?

What is this persistent need we have to overcome our own mortality? In 1973, cultural anthropologist Ernest Becker published his Pulitzer Prize winning book, *The Denial of Death*. As Becker states his thesis: 'the idea of death, the fear of it, haunts the human animal like nothing else; it is a mainspring of human activity – activity designed largely to avoid the fatality of death, to overcome it by denying in some way that it is the final destiny for man' (xi). We repress the knowledge of our mortality and instead we become the heroes of our *causa sui*, we hope immortality projects will provide a sense of purpose and meaning in our lives. According to Becker, even scientific advances are delusional immortality projects. Becker argued that 'a project as grand as the scientific-mythical construction of victory over human limitation is not something that can be programmed by science' (285).

Most would admit, however, that the extension of human life expectancy that has taken place over the last few hundred years is a real and positive advancement. On a recent episode of *The Joy of Stats: 200 Countries, 200 Years, 4 Minutes* (2010), medical doctor and statistician, Dr Hans Rosling found that prior to 1810, life expectancy globally was less than forty years. United Nations' statistics now register the life expectancy in almost all countries as surpassing forty years, with many developed nations, including the UK, offering a life expectancy closer to eighty years, effectively doubling what it was two centuries ago (2007: 80).

This significant increase in longevity can be attributed to many things: initially, the improvement of public sanitation, and better availability of clean water and good food. Scientific advances pushed life expectancy even further by increasing the understanding of our biological make-up, as well as giving us tools to help combat potential threats from disease. In the last half of the 1900s, medical science leapt forward in both diagnostics and treatment, with laboratory, imaging, pharmacological and surgical advances to prolong life.

The late Dr Roy Walford sought to optimise human biology by developing a calorie-restricted, high-nutrition diet. In a 1996 interview, when asked what he thought the maximum life expectancy was for a human, he responded, 'between 110 and 120,' but added, 'If you started calorie restriction early in life, I think the survival curve could be greatly extended to 140, 150, 160' (in Mitchell 1996). But Walford was only talking about optimising our given biological potential.

Medical science is now pushing even further in the areas of genetics, stem cell, cloning, and other research – all towards the goal of life extension. For instance, since 1990, molecular biologist John Tower has been exploring the aging process in fruit flies. Part of the genetic programming of most biological organisms includes a determination of life span. By increasing the amount of superoxide dismutase, a naturally occurring anti-oxidant also present in humans, Tower has found a way to override the genetic determination of death, dramatically increasing life expectancy; his fruit flies live forty per cent longer than untreated fruit flies.

While the work of doctors like Walford and Tower is impressive, as of yet, such research has only been able to extend life, not eradicate death. There are, however, those who think that such a breakthrough is inevitable, indeed immanent. Dr Jerry Lemler is the CEO of cryonics company *Alcor Life Extension Foundation*. According to Dr Lemler, 'in the next generation, or two at the latest, people will not have to die anymore' (2006). Lemler's statement underscores the assumption that, unless they are suffering from suicidal ideation due to some form of mental illness, everybody wants to live. But is this necessarily always the case? Do we all consistently suffer from what Becker called 'death anxiety' (1973: 22) or is that an assumption made by those of us who are relatively young and healthy? Is this perspective necessarily shared by the aged and ill?

Certainly there are those who continue to rail against death to their last breath. Physician and palliative care advocate, Dr Ira Byock states, 'Avoidance of death is pervasive in our society [...]. Denial of death doesn't get easier as people get sicker; sometimes it gets more entrenched' (2010). But there is another side to this coin, one which is rarely acknowledged: those individuals who move past denial into acceptance and sink peacefully into death. Patients who believe and accept that they are dying seem to lose their death anxiety and just want to get on with it. In *Dying Well: The Prospect for Growth at the End of Life* (1997), Dr Byock recounts the story of one of his patients, Maureen Riley. After test results confirmed her worsening condition, she said: 'I'm a bit disappointed that I'm still alive' (Byock 1997: 224).

Dr Diane Meier, award-winning Director of New York's Center to Advance Palliative Care, recalls her 'light-bulb moment', when she realised how far medicine had strayed from its foundational goals of healing and relieving suffering. In 1995, while on rounds, Dr Meier noticed a patient in restraints, struggling to try to remove his feeding tube. When she asked about the patient, she was told that he had a malignant lung mass that had metastasised to his brain. When first diagnosed, several months previously, the patient had refused treatment. Having witnessed the demise of his wife from cancer two years earlier, he elected not to put himself or his adult children through the same ordeal. He simply wanted to go home and die. Unfortunately, contemporary human death is rarely that simple. In this case, the patient's son called emergency services after finding the man unresponsive where he had fallen on the kitchen floor. Once the man was readmitted to hospital, the medical machine took over and he lost his right to decide his own future. Although he had made his wishes plain earlier, he was no longer in a position to reiterate his acceptance of death. Because of increased eating difficulties, medical staff inserted a feeding tube. During brief moments of consciousness, the patient removed the tube – seventeen times. Although he was no longer able to verbally refuse treatment, the patient was sending a very clear, strong message. Yet each time he pulled out the tube, medical staff reinserted it, eventually restraining both his hands and feet to prevent his interference. When Dr Meier asked the intern in charge of the patient's care why they insisted on reinserting the tube when the patient's actions made it clear that he did not want treatment, the reply was, 'Because if we don't do this, he'll die' (in Marantz Henig 2005). Perhaps, but perhaps the medical staff in this case over-estimated their power over death.

When predicting death, Dr Byock notes that 'accuracy is almost impossible' (1997: 201). Regardless, the patient's repeated desire to forego treatment, even with the understanding that it might mean death, was ignored by medical personnel intent on artificially prolonging his life against his will. This is an example of the Hippocratic notion of doing no harm becoming twisted into an urge to forcibly make the body live longer, regardless of the psycho-emotional damage wrought, and regardless of how contrary these actions might be to the patient's wishes. Dr Meier typifies this as 'well-intended but harmful intervention' (in Marantz Henig 2005).

While a tube may be inserted temporarily to aid patients recovering from illness or surgery, nasal or gastric feeding tubes are sometimes introduced into the terminally ill. A lack of interest in food is a normal biological response to long-term illness and imminent death. Elderly or ill animals often stop eating as a precursor to death, so why is it *not* medically permissible for humans to do likewise? Dr Byock calls this loss of appetite 'part of the "wisdom of the body"' (2010) and suggests that 'Dying of a progressive inability to eat is, probably, one of the most natural and physiologically gentle ways to expire. In the context of advanced illness, hunger is rarely, if ever, a source of discomfort' (2010). Rather than automatically inserting a feeding tube when a patient stops eating, he suggests that patients and their advocates ask: '"What purpose will the feeding tube serve?" If the answer is, "I won't allow mom to die of starvation," the subsequent question might be, "What would it be acceptable for her to die of?"' (2010).

Robin Marantz Henig, author of 'Will We Ever Arrive at the Good Death?', writes:

> What we're addicted to […] is the belief that we can micromanage death. We tend to think of a 'good death' as one that we can control, making decisions about how much intervention we want, how much pain relief, whether it's in the home or the hospital, who will be by our sides. We even sometimes try to make decisions about what we will die from […]. But often, our best-laid plans can go awry. Dying is awfully hard to choreograph. (2005: n.p.)

Marantz Henig recounts the story of one patient who was intent on control-ling his demise. This geriatric patient was suffering from high blood pressure, kidney failure, and Parkinson's disease. While it was unlikely that he would regain health, his multiple conditions were being managed with a dozen different medications and regular dialysis treatments. Angry at his continued decline, the patient stopped everything – the medications and the dialysis. Both the patient and his doctor assumed that he would die of kidney failure, organ shut-down being a fairly peaceful way to go. After three weeks without dialysis treatments, his kidneys retained some level of function, but because of his uncontrolled high blood pressure, he had a stroke. This led to a very different sort of demise, a much less peaceful one than the man had planned for himself. While we have gained a measure of control over our health and can manage a multiplicity of complex illnesses, death itself remains somewhat unpredictable.

Contemporary medicine allows us to control ailments that a generation or two ago would have meant certain death. We routinely perform coronary artery bypass surgery to relieve the heart. We prescribe anticoagulants and blood pressure medication to reduce the likelihood of strokes. We insert feeding tubes when patients stop eating. We introduce vaccines and antibiotics to control infections like influenza and pneumonia, which used to be called 'the old man's friend'. Dr Byock states that 'Malnutrition and infection are two of the most natural ways for people … to die' (2010), but if we are controlling these potentially lethal conditions, what is it acceptable to die from? 'In deciding that a loved one will not be allowed to die of malnourishment, a family is making a tacit decision to let the person die of something else' (Byock 1997: 180). Is it even acceptable to die? Is the patient's voice being heard amidst the incessant clamouring of expert voices? Are doctors always treating patients in good faith that their health will improve or just going through the motions because they have the tools at their disposal?

The tension between a patient who has accepted his or her mortality and the physician, or larger medical community, who perceive death as a failure to maintain life, points to a fundamental disconnect. This urge to prolong life at all costs can unfortunately translate into a well-intentioned, but potentially cruel, prolongation of the dying process, rather than a meaningful extension of life. Stephen P. Kiernan cites studies indicating that 'more than 90 percent of Americans want limits on their medical care at the end of life, no long-term feeding tubes or ventilation, for example, if they are never going to regain consciousness. Even more people want their pain managed aggressively' (2010: 172). Unfortunately, this wish directly conflicts with physicians' concerns about legal action if they neglect to do everything medically possible to prolong life, as well as concerns about having their prescribing practices examined if they are perceived as being overly generous with pain medications. Thus, the quantity of life, rather than the quality of life and its value to the patient, takes precedence.

Medical advances have caused statistical changes in causes of death over thirty years, beginning in 1976. According to an *American National Vital Statistics Report*, sudden deaths by heart attack and stroke decreased by 61 per cent and 71 per cent respectively during this time; over the same period, however, slow deaths from cancer and severe respiratory diseases increased by 22 per cent and 77 per cent respectively (in Kiernan 2010: 163). While death used to be a sudden occurrence, it now resembles a manageable health condition. A long, slow death is a process requiring careful planning, reflection, and decisions. While the extra weeks, months, or years are a blessing for tying up affairs, optimising time with loved ones, and working towards the resolution of any long-term disputes, it may also create additional burdens. The patient and/or family now need to decide on the best living arrangements, how to finance any additional care requirements, how to keep the patient as comfortable as possible, and how to optimise the remaining time. Seeing a loved one through the dying process is a rare and emotionally charged event; there is pressure to do it correctly, to make no mistakes.

The prolongation of life is due, in part, to the movement of the dying process from the family home into the hospital, what late sociologist Norbert Elias called the 'rational institutionalization of dying' (1985: 86). In the United States, between 50 and 60 per cent of people die in hospitals, even though the vast majority would prefer to die at home (Kiernan 2010: 167). A hospital death removes many choices from the patient and their family; visiting hours are limited, patients eat institutional food on a prescribed timetable, they are no longer in control of their environment, and their medical options – including the dispensing of pain medications – may be determined by others. The 1995 *Study to Understand Prognoses and Preferences for Outcomes and Risks of Treatment* (the SUPPORT project) revealed 'that 38 per cent of patients who died in hospital spent ten or more days in intensive care or on a ventilator' (in Kiernan 2010: 168). In nearly 45 per cent of these cases, death did not occur naturally, but only after life support was withdrawn (Kiernan 2010: 168). When a patient will not recover, is it appropriate, both in terms of their quality of life and hospital resource allocation, to administer critical care, rather than palliative care? While medical technology can save and prolong lives, hospitals may be using the wrong tools in caring for the dying. The long slow death requires attentive personnel, rather than dehumanising technological resources.

The desire to avoid painful reminders of our own mortality, however, may create a tendency to shun the dying. We would rather not deal with the care of our loved ones during their dying process, and so sometimes they are consigned to hospitals. In such institutions, Elias observes:

> The dying person receives the most advanced, scientifically based medical treatment available. But contacts with the people to whom he or she is attached, and whose presence can be of utmost comfort to a person taking leave of life, are frequently thought to inconvenience the rational treatment of the patient and the routine of the personnel. (1985: 86)

This scenario can be especially true in emergency or critical care units, in which the patient may become unrecognisable, and barely visible through a curtain of tubes, wires, and machines. While the utmost care may be taken of their biological organism, this separation of the patient from his or her family can be devastating to both the patient and those left behind. Our rejection of the *ars moriendi* affects the dying most of all, as they risk being stranded in a high-tech environment with limited human contact, where their psycho-emotional or spiritual needs may not be met due to isolation, and in which their act of dying, their failure to live, may be seen as a betrayal.

Questions of who decides upon treatment, and when it is appropriate to withdraw treatment, open up a tricky ethical quagmire. Hospital ethics boards do their utmost to support patient autonomy by insisting that the patient, or their proxy, gives informed consent; patients must be advised of their medical options in a manner they understand, they cannot be coerced by either medical staff or family members, and they must be mentally competent to make their decision. While this sounds appropriate, it is an ideal that medical practice has difficulty living up to. Patients are frequently surprised by outcomes; many people have selective hearing when their welfare is at stake, and simply do not register potential adverse effects even when informed of them. Upon hearing statistics derived from evidence-based medical databases, patients may feel coerced into accepting or rejecting certain treatment options, without fully considering the impact on them as individuals. Mental competence, especially when one is very ill or dying, may become erratic; even if a proxy has been named, the patient may or may not be willing to relinquish personal control.

Byock declares that: 'Ultimate responsibility for end-of-life care must remain with the dying person and the family' (1997: 250). The problem is that the majority of people prefer not to think about their personal mortality and so they do not write living wills, advanced directives, or have a legally appointed proxy; as a consequence, medical personnel tend to take heroic measures. Making a mistake to prolong a life against an individual's wishes is less likely to draw anger or legal action from surviving family members, than making an irrevocable mistake by assuming an individual's preference for a natural death.

Unfortunately, this intrusion of technology into the act of dying harms the potential for a powerful positive resolution at the end of life. The incursion of medical devices sends a strong message to patients and their families that they are being treated, that they will be cured, that they will continue to live – even when this denial of death is a lie. Their doctor and medical staff are valiantly fighting off death, but prolonging life artificially creates unrealistic expectations of practitioners' abilities, and also makes it more difficult for patients and their families to accept that, ultimately, this is a losing battle. The medical denial of death potentially robs patients and their families of some of the most profound moments available to us as humans. Byock likens the emotions of dying to those of birth and points to the possibility for 'joy within the process of letting go' (1997: 234).

Whether with anger or acquiescence, people are still dying. And while Becker cried out against 'Manipulative, utopian science', declaring that 'It means an end to the distinctively human – or even, we must say, the distinctively organismic' (1973: 283–84), his voice seems to have been quelled by ensuing decades of medical advancement intent on reprogramming our animal nature. By refusing to accept our mortality, we stress the culture of humanity over the nature of our existence, supporting what biologist Donna Haraway dubbed the cyborg: an 'implosion of the natural and the artificial, nature and culture, subject and object, machine and organic body' (1997: 14). We strive to create a utopia without pain or suffering, where we, and those we love, will be immortal, in which the natural biological movement towards death is removed by a cultural imperative towards immortality. By doing so, we reject not only our biology, but also the emotional quickening and maturation that can only happen through grief.

Scientific advances continue to propel humanity towards more rational ways of being, further from our emotional, animal state. The completion of the Human Genome Project (HGP) in 2003, and the subsequent movement towards functional genomics, reinforce what N. Katherine Hayles calls 'bodiless information' (1999: 22), supporting the Cartesian mind-body split. Decartes's *cogito ergo sum* declared consciousness as the seat of identity; however, the HGP seems to declare the flattened, disembodied data of the biological organism as the locus of human identity. Can we declare that we have overcome death by virtue of the fact that we can code an individual's DNA? This solution hardly seems to fulfil the promise of the Fountain of Youth.

In spite of early predictions, the HGP has not become the panacea for all our ills. In fact, thus far, it has had a limited impact on human longevity. It has, however, provided a starting place for countless new projects, as well as prompting debate about what it means to be human. The HGP, and other biomedical developments, alter and underscore the complexity of our relationship with nature. As critical theorist Sherryl Vint asserts, 'The body occupies the luminal space between self and not-self, between nature and culture' (2007: 16). Since the inception of tools and language, humans have been able to change their environment, to manipulate life. The HGP adds little to this alteration, except in consideration of degree: the HGP allows for manipulation on the molecular rather than the macro level. The HGP also produced an enormous volume of information in a relatively short time, startling to those used to the slower pace of most human advancements.

Does our knowledge of the Human Genome, or our forays into stem cell, cloning, and other advanced biomedical research, spell the end of death, and the end of humanity as we know it, or has it simply introduced an alternative mind-set to the continuum of being human? Sociologist Nikolas Rose asserts:

> as with our present, our future will emerge from the intersection of a number of contingent pathways that, as they intertwine, might create something new. This, I suspect, will be no radical transformation, no shift into a world 'after nature' or a 'posthuman future.' Perhaps it will not even constitute an 'event.' But I think, in a manner of small ways, most of which will soon be routinized and taken for granted, things will not be quite the same again. (2007: 5)

Humans have always moved through time, sometimes advancing in positive ways, at other times verging on self-destruction. When scientists today predict the possibility of doubling our life span, or even enabling our immortality, we may scoff. But if a peasant in 1810 had been told that his descendants would routinely live to be twice his age, he probably would have reacted with similar disbelief.

Bibliography

Becker, E. 1973. *The Denial of Death*. New York: Macmillan.

Byock, I. 1997. *Dying Well: The Prospect for Growth at the End of Life*. New York: Riverhead Books.

———. *Dying Well*. Accessed on 13 February 2011, http://www.dyingwell.org/

———. 2010. 'From Rationing to "Rational" with End-of-Life' on *Fora TV*, 24 March 2010. Accessed on 13 February 2011, http://www.youtube.com/watch?v=I_5LK_1Ucdc

Elias, N. 1985. *The Loneliness of the Dying*. Oxford and New York: Basil Blackwell.

Haraway, D. 1997. *Modest_Witness@Second_Millennium: FemaleMan_Meets_ OncoMouse*. Oxford and New York: Routledge.

Hayles, N. K. 1999. *How We Became Posthuman: Virtual Bodies in Cybernetics, Literature, and Informatics*. Chicago, IL: University of Chicago Press.

Kiernan, S.P. 2010. 'The Transformation of Death in America', in N. Bauer-Maglin and D. Perry (eds), *Final Acts: Death, Dying, and the Choices We Make*. New Brunswick, NJ and London: Rutgers University Press, pp. 163–82.

Lemler, J. 2006. Interview from 'Medical Strategies: Flight From Death Deleted Scene'. Accessed on 8 February 2011, http://www.youtube.com/watch?v=2g9q2wFvB80

Marantz Henig, R. 2005. 'Will We Ever Arrive at the Good Death?', *The New York Times Magazine*, 7 August 2005. Accessed on 6 March 2010, http://www.nytimes.com/2005/08/07/magazine/07DYINGL.html?_r=1&pagewanted=all#

Mitchell, T. 1996. 'Secrets of Long Life: Dr Roy Walford's Plan To Live To 150', *Life, Extension Magazine* June. Accessed on 13 February 2011, http://www.walford.com/lifextin.htm

Rose, N.S. 2007. *The Politics of Life Itself: Biomedicine, Power, and Subjectivity in the Twenty-first Century*. Princeton: Princeton University Press.

Rosling, H. 2010. *The Joy of Stats: 200 Countries, 200 Years, 4 Minutes*, Wingspan Productions for BBC. Accessed on 4 January 2011, http://www.gapminder.org/

Tower, J. *Tower Lab*. Accessed on 13 February 2011, http://towerlab.usc.edu

United Nations. 2007. 'Table A. 17 Life Expectancy at Birth, Both Sexes Combined, by Country for Selected Periods', *World Population Prospects: The 2006 Revision*. Accessed on 13 February 2011, http://www.un.org/esa/population/publications/wpp2006/WPP2006_Highlights_rev.pdf

Vint, S. 2007. *Bodies of Tomorrow: Technology, Subjectivity, Science Fiction*. Toronto: University of Toronto Press.

2

BEYOND 'MOURNING AND MELANCHOLIA'

Lynne M. Simpson

Despite the weighted balance afforded mourning in the title, Freud's seminal
essay 'Mourning and Melancholia' primarily examines melancholia as a pathology rather than as a *de facto* state of mourning (1995b: 243–44). Freud's metatext
informs further accounts in two fundamental ways: first, grief is identified as
much as a metaphor as it is as a literal condition; and second, and more importantly, mourning is initially characterised as normative, albeit troublesome and
mysterious. This chapter traces the evolution of mourning from Freud to contemporary theorists and speculates about the problematics in the definition and
treatment of grief in the twenty-first century.[1]

It is no accident that Freud wrote 'On Transience' and 'Mourning and
Melancholia' near the start of the Great War. In 'Thoughts for the Times on
War and Death', written in 1915, Freud acknowledges that a war played out on
no less than the world's stage strips from us our habitual and comforting illusion:
'Death will no longer be denied; we are forced to believe in it' (1995d: 291).
He then asks a simple but compelling question: 'Would it not be better to give
death the place in reality and in our thoughts which it is due?' (1995d: 299).
Freud concludes: 'To tolerate life remains, after all, the first duty of all living
beings. Illusion becomes valueless if it makes this harder for us' (1995d: 299).
Freud reiterates this important point in his famous and influential formulation
of the 'work' of mourning itself: 'Reality-testing has shown that the loved object
no longer exists, and it proceeds to demand that all libido shall be withdrawn
from attachments to that object' (1995b: 244). This necessary withdrawal, Freud
assures us, remains 'extraordinarily painful' (1995b: 245).

The psychoanalytic community's exploration of the mechanics of this libidinal
withdrawal has come to privilege the role of introjection, a concept utilised
by Freud in his analysis of the melancholic, who seeks to incorporate the lost

object into himself (1995b: 249), rather than the mourner. Introjection may be defined as the fantasy in which 'the subject transposes objects and their inherent qualities from the "outside" to the "inside" of himself' (Laplanche and Pontalis 1974: 229). Reuben Fine argues that all psychoanalytic theory since the Second World War has stressed the central role of the introject, or internalised object: 'All human relations are now seen to revolve about the vicissitudes and the fates of this "immortal" object' (1979: 434). But even as early as 1924, Karl Abraham observes, 'In the normal process of mourning, too, the person reacts to a real object loss by effecting a temporary introjection of the loved person' (1927: 435). For Abraham introjection serves 'to preserve the person's relations to the dead object, or – what comes to the same thing – to compensate for his loss' (1927: 438). Nicholas Abraham and Maria Torok retain Freud's dichotomy between mourning and melancholia but redefine it: mourning now requires the process of introjection whereas melancholia relies instead on the fantasy of incorporation, the introduction orally of whole or part of an object into the body. Abraham and Torok's construction of incorporation is a kind of substitute for mourning or a denial of object loss itself: 'The magical "cure" through incorporation dispenses with the painful task of readjustment [to the lost object]. To absorb what has been lost in the form of food, real or imagined, when the psyche is plunged into mourning, is to *reject mourning* and its consequences' (1980: 4). Hans Loewald envisions the introject strengthening the superego, or conscience: 'elements of the lost object, through the mourning process, become introjected in the form of ego-ideal elements and inner demands and punishments' (1980: 271). Vamik Volkan, best known for his 're-grief' therapy, in 1972 coined the term 'linking object or linking phenomena' to describe the externalisation of the introject. He too affirms the centrality and tenacity of the introject: 'The representations of the dead live on in our memories and feeling states until we ourselves die' (1981: 34). As Goethe observed, we all die twice: once when we ourselves die and the second time when those who have loved us and remember us die in turn.

For Freud, to remember is to mourn, and such mourning involves 'profoundly painful dejection, cessation of interest in the outside world, loss of the capacity to love, and inhibitions of all activity' (1995b: 244). If Freud effectively defined grief for the twentieth century, then Geoffrey Gorer helped to legitimise it. The British anthropologist emerged amidst the general repression of the 1950s much like Freud was necessarily birthed by the Victorians. Gorer published in 1955 the breakthrough essay provocatively called 'The Pornography of Death', in which he finds that death had replaced sex as a taboo. He concludes that in the twentieth century 'there seems to have been an unremarked shift in prudery; whereas copulation has become more and more "mentionable," particularly in the Anglo-Saxon societies, death has become more and more "unmentionable" *as a natural process*' (1965b: 195). *Death, Grief, and Mourning*, published a decade later in 1965, expands his original assertion that 'natural death and physical decomposition have become too horrible to contemplate or to discuss' (1965b: 196–97). Gorer interrogates the 'fantasies' or sensationalising of violent death, one of the dominant preoccupations of the latter half of the last century. He astutely remarks upon the objectification of the body concomitant to pornography as well as death: 'This somebody else is not a person; it is either a set of genitals, with or without secondary sexual characteristics, or a body, perhaps capable of suffering pain as well as death' (1965b: 198). Both types of pornography function as 'substitute gratifications' (1965b: 198). Gorer concludes, 'Mourning is treated as if it were a weakness, a self-indulgence, a reprehensible bad habit instead of a psychological necessity' (1965a: 131). The pornography of death, then, can only be allayed by allowing those who grieve to mourn (1965b: 199).

In the late 1950s death and mourning became part of the curriculum. Classes were offered at college and university level, and this new subject was given a suitably Greek and therefore collegial name: 'thanatology'. Edwin Shneidman's *Death: Current Perspectives* (1994) was intended for curricular use, as its author was a Professor of Thanatology at the University of California at the Los Angeles School of Medicine. The book enjoyed four editions, the final one published in 1994; it helped to usher in the decade of development in thanatology from 1958 to 1967. In 1968 Shneidman founded the American Association of Suicidology and the foundational journal for suicide studies, *Suicide and Life Threatening Behavior*. His prolific and groundbreaking work in the field culminated in *A Commonsense Book of Death: Reflections at Ninety of a Lifelong Thanatologist* (2008), published the year before his death. Herman Feifel, another pioneer of thanatology, published *The Meaning of Death* (1959), considered a landmark for its frank exploration of death. *The Encyclopedia of Death and Dying* calls Feifel's book 'the single most important influence in galvanizing what has since become the multidisciplinary field of thanatology' (2011). Elisabeth Kübler-Ross's work (1969), it must be remembered, did not grow out of psychiatry, but day-to-day interaction with terminal cancer patients and their families. The work of Kübler-Ross and others served, in part, as a textbook intended to aid those dealing with death as part of their professional lives. In medicine, death is unavoidable, but loss of life was traditionally defined as a failure on the part of the doctor and medical staff, representing the limits of medicine and science. Death was anatomised only in terms of reviewing the (failed) course of treatment. For the medical community, the open acknowledgement of death and its ramifications was empowering. Norman Brown asks in his classic book of 1959, *Life Against Death*, 'How can Death be unified with Life? If we want to cure, we had better follow Freud and study Death' (1959: 98). Along with lava lamps, mood rings and black-light posters, thanatology has faded; however, it did represent the first popular and wide-ranging study (in the sense of controlled observations) of those grieving.

In the late 1950s, at roughly the same time, John Bowlby in England and George Pollock in the United States were writing their still seminal studies of grief and mourning. Both emphasise Freud's definition of the 'work' of mourning as a necessary ego-adaptive process. Bowlby pioneers 'attachment theory' by exploring 'behaviour that results in a person attaining or retaining proximity to some other differentiated and preferred individual' (1980: 39), culminating in three volumes entitled *Attachment and Loss*. Bowlby conceptualises four phases of Freud's 'work' of mourning: numbness, yearning and searching, disorganisation and despair, and reorganisation (1980: 85). George Pollock calls attention to Freud's reference to the 'work of recollection' (noted in *Studies on Hysteria*) preceding his fuller account of the 'work of mourning' (1989: 9). Pollock's own 'mourning-liberation' process is 'an ego adaptive process which includes the reaction to the loss of an object, as well as the readjustment to an external environment wherein this object no longer exists in reality' (1989: 8). The 1989 two-volume conclusion of Pollock's study, *The Mourning-Liberation Process*, also amplifies Freud's idea of grief 'work': the mourning process includes shock, grief, pain, reaction to separation and recognition of loss (1989: 26).

It is Kübler-Ross, however, who is most often credited for popularising an understanding of grief in terms of 'stage theory' – again, a variation of Freud's initial conception of mourning as 'work'. Kübler-Ross's stages of grief originally applied to patients suffering from a terminal illness in terms of auto-mourning, but she then applied those phases to others suffering from a real or symbolic loss. Kübler-Ross's now famous five stages of grief include denial, anger, bargaining, depression and finally acceptance. Therese Rando's *Treatment of Complicated Mourning* (1993) outlines three phases: avoidance, confrontation and accommodation. In 1999 Catherine Sanders describes an 'Integrative Theory of Bereavement' characterised by the following five phases: shock, awareness of loss, conservation-withdrawal, healing and renewal (36). *The Handbook of Bereavement Research*, published in 2001, is thorough in amassing 'a research-oriented review of the current state of scientific knowledge in the field of bereavement' (Stroebe et al. 2001: 5). In it Margaret Stroebe et al. write, 'Basic to much of this [bereavement] research has been the search for *processes* underlying the manifestations of grief' (2001: 4). They note, 'Grief work has been one of the most important concepts within the scientific discipline of bereavement, as well as among lay communities in Western culture' (2001: 757).

Currently, researchers and clinicians seem divided on the usefulness of phase theories of mourning. Janice Genevro, a psychologist who was commissioned by the Washington non-profit organisation, the Center for Advancing Health, to do a report on the quality of grief services in 2003, cautions: 'Stage theories of grief have become embedded in curricula, textbooks, popular entertainment and media because they offer predictability and a sense of manageability of the powerful emotions associated with bereavement and loss' (cited in Konigsberg

2011: 11–12). George Bonanno asserts that 'there do not appear to be specific stages that everyone must go through' (2009: 6). Stroebe et al. recognise that 'Stages or phases of grief are no longer viewed to follow a fixed and prescriptive course' (2001: 746). They find the term 'grief work' no longer useful, preferring instead 'the adaptive coping process' (2001: 757). J. William Worden is a leading figure among contemporary American grief counsellors, as well as a pioneer in the hospice movement. His authoritative *Grief Counseling and Grief Therapy: A Handbook for the Mental Health Practitioner* (2009) has been through four editions since its publication in 1984. Worden seeks to rescue his 'tasks' of mourning from passé 'stage theories' of mourning. Still, these distinctions seem to be largely semantic. Less rigidity in interpreting stages, or Freud's 'work' of mourning, may, in fact, be all that is really needed.

The burden of 'work' in struggling against the pleasure principle would lead Freud to his formulations regarding the *todestrieb* or death drive, which remain among the most controversial of his conclusions. While science may have disproved Freud's theory that biological processes lead to decay as stasis, these findings do not occlude the intrapsychic insight of his conclusions. 'Mourning and Melancholia' raises the unique question of the *todestrieb* in the ego as a specific possibility in the course of mourning. Marsha Abrams argues that Freud's conception of melancholia is fundamentally 'an exploration of desire's encounter with limitation and the point at which that encounter instigates the passing over of nonpathology into pathology, the dominance of the death instinct over the life force' (1993: 70). I would argue that this is also the case with mourning. The risk of suicide during bereavement is pervasive, and studies affirm this risk, which may arise from depression, the trauma associated with mourning or even yearning for or projective-identification with the deceased.

'Grief and mourning are powerful and stressful emotional states which can touch off unconscious psychological reactions that actually jeopardize the individual's life', Erich Lindemann concludes (1944: 322). In 1972 Colin Murray Parkes conducted a study of twenty-two London widows for thirteen months following the death of their spouses. He, too, notes an increased morbidity rate:

> Three-quarters of the increased death rate during the first six months of bereavement was attributable to heart disease, in particular to coronary thrombosis and arteriosclerotic heart disease. The origin of the term 'broken heart' goes back to biblical times. 'Bind up the broken hearted,' says Isaiah, and the idea seems to have persisted ever since that grief can somehow damage the heart. Only in this century has 'grief' not been a medically attributable cause of death. (1987: 335–36)

Charles Reynolds et al. note with concern that conjugal bereavement remains a significant risk factor for suicide in later life, particularly for men (1999: 202).

Beverley Raphael claims that increased mortality occurs in a 'small but signifi-cant' number of mourners even among a general population; however, she esti-mates that as many as one in three bereavements result in a 'morbid outcome or pathological patterns of grief' (1984: 62, 64).

Clearly, suicide epitomises the most acute failure of the ego-adaptive process of mourning in which the ego is entirely depleted and fails to adjust to life without the lost object. Surely mourning cannot be considered 'normative' given its crippling and sometimes fatal symptomatology? Bernard Schoenberg et al. preface their book on the psychosocial aspects of grief by arguing that 'bereavement is fertile ground for the development of illness, both emotional and physical' (1975: xii). Raphael too notes an increase in general ill health associated with mourning (1984: 61). Sanders argues, 'Grief is so impossibly painful, so akin to panic, that ways must be invented to defend against the emotional onslaught of suffering' (1999: 3). As a powerful 'stressor, bereavement increases risk of illness', conclude M. Katherine Shear et al. (2011: 112). An exercise in etymology is instructive. The word bereavement comes from Old English: *bereafian* literally meant 'to rob away', to deprive and leave desolate. Loss necessarily proves a narcissistic trauma. In 'On Transience', an uncharacteristically perplexed Freud announces: 'Mourning over the loss of something we have loved or admired seems so natural to the layman that he regards it as self-evident. But to the psychologists mourning is a great riddle, one of those phenomena which cannot be explained' (1995c: 306). While it is melancholia rather than mourning that Freud calls pathological, he admits that 'mourning involves grave departures from the normal attitude to life' (1995b: 243). Subsequent appraisals of grief treat it like an illness rather than a normative psychological state because it is so often acute and disruptive.

Early influential theorists like Melanie Klein believe that 'the mourner is in fact ill, but because this state of mind is common and seems so natural to us, we do not call mourning an illness' (1940: 136–37). Helene Deutsch (1937) is the first theorist to note at length that an apparent absence of grief can be a serious impediment to the successful resolution of mourning. Rando credits Deutsch with identifying 'the first type of complicated [or pathological] mourning not conceptualized as a specific variant of manic-depressive conditions' (1993: 86). Deutsch argues that grief can threaten the integrity of the ego; therefore, the 'most extreme expression' of a subsequent defence mechanism is 'the omission of affect' (1937: 14) or the apparent absence of grief. By the end of the twentieth century, researchers and clinicians 'are cautious about pathological interpretations of the absence of distress' or grief, thanks, in part, to Deutsch's pioneering analysis (Prigerson and Jacobs 2001: 746).

During the Second World War, Otto Fenichel's brief but cogent interest in loss was subsumed into his larger book-length study *The Psychoanalytic Theory of Neurosis* (1945); his taxonomy imbeds grief in pathology. Fenichel cites ambivalence towards the lost object as the primary factor in the development of pathological mourning.[2] He notes, however, that ambivalence toward the deceased and subsequent feelings of guilt are common in normal mourning as well – another break from Freud's early theorisation that guilt is a function primarily of melancholia. 'Uncomplicated mourning', for Fenichel, is 'characterized by an ambivalent introjection of the lost object [...] and the participation of guilt feelings throughout the process' (1945: 395). Fenichel was also the first to adopt Freud's conception of mourning as 'work': mourning proceeds by 'two acts, the first being the establishment of an introjection, the second the loosening of the binding to the introjected object' (1945: 394). The 'work' of mourning, then, requires the 'regression from love to incorporation, from object relationship to identification' (1945: 394). Perhaps his unwitting contribution is to challenge Freud's conception of mourning as normative given that, for Fenichel, the resolution of mourning necessitates psychological regression.

Charles Anderson's 1949 paper 'Aspects of Pathological Grief and Mourning' has been called 'the first quasi-empirical study' of pathological mourning (Rando 1993: 993). He begins by noting the overwhelming number of bereaved he treated after the Second World War, those – as he movingly calls them – 'so full of loss' (1949: 48). Anderson astutely observes, 'The post-war scene is studded with innumerable Hamlets unable to live in peace without those they have lost, nor yet able to live in peace with the memories and images they carry within' (1949: 48).

Lindemann, former chief of Psychiatry at Massachusetts General Hospital, pioneered theories of 'acute' grief, or the grief immediately experienced after a loss, based on his crisis intervention for the thirteen survivors of the infamous Cocoanut Grove Fire in a Boston nightclub in 1942, in which more than 490 people died. Lindemann begins his article with the following statement: 'At first glance, acute grief would not seem to be a medical or psychiatric disorder in the strict sense of the word but rather a *normal* reaction to a distressing situation' (1944: 141, emphasis mine). Nevertheless, the article then outlines the severe 'psychological and somatic symptomatology' (141) of grief as an illness. Lindemann describes somatic distress, preoccupation with the image of the deceased, guilt, hostility and the loss of patterns of conduct as part of grief (142), suggesting how multi-faceted and destructive so-called normal mourning can be. In a study conducted forty-five years later, Luis Vargas et al. reaffirm Lindemann's analysis: 'In fact, Lindemann offered a better representation of the possible multidimensionality of grief reactions than many more recent, empirically oriented investigators' (1989: 1484). They conclude that 'certain features [depressive symptoms, preservation of the lost object, suicidal ideation and anger at the deceased] which have been associated with pathological grief may well be present in many, if not most, of the general population during bereavement' (1488). Worden, a psychologist at Massachusetts General since

1969, also praises Lindemann's findings: 'What is of particular interest to me is that the bereaved we see today at Massachusetts General Hospital exhibit behaviors very similar to those described by Lindemann more than 60 years ago' (2009: 18).

George Engel's oft-cited essay posits the simple question 'Is Grief a Disease?' in its title. He assures us from a medical standpoint that grief is by definition pathological: 'grief is "natural" or "normal" in the same sense that a wound or a burn are the natural or normal responses to physical trauma. The designation "pathological" refers to the changed state and not to the fact of the response' (1961: 19). Most of the critical work cataloguing somatic distress in addition to psychological disruptions in response to grief occurred subsequently to his publication, further confirming Engel's supposition. While Engel acknowledges a separate category of 'complicated' mourning, he insists that its existence does not refute 'the fact that the experience of uncomplicated grief also represents a manifest and gross departure from the dynamic state considered representative of health and well-being' (1961: 20). In 2005 Richard Glass, as deputy editor of the authoritative *Journal of the American Medical Association*, published an editorial called 'Is Grief a Disease? Sometimes'. The clever title may suggest, ironically, just how little progress the medical community has made in its collective attempts to taxonomise grief.

Complicating the issue further is the fact that there is little consensus among researchers and clinicians with regard to the exact definition or diagnosis of mourning itself let alone pathological mourning. Raphael's *The Anatomy of Bereavement*, published in 1984, seeks, as its title makes clear, to anatomise different types of grief. Clinician Catherine Sander's *Grief: The Mourning After* appeared first in 1989 and then in an updated edition a decade later; the work is intended for clinical use. She cautions, 'What may appear to be a distorted reaction on the surface [to loss] may, in fact, be a very normal response' (1999: 10). In their survey of contemporary theorisations of bereavement, Beth Rodgers and Kathleen Cowles acknowledge, 'The literature related to grief is extensive, yet there is considerable evidence within that body of literature that the concept of grief is vague and somewhat ambiguous' (1991: 443). They warn, 'The lack of a consensus concerning the parameters of "normal" grief seriously jeopardises attempts to discuss aberrations from the expected responses and seems to invite the "medicalization" of grief by contributing to diagnosis and intervention based on individual concepts' (1991: 455).

Today there are over twenty highly-individualised diagnostic tools for the definition of pathological mourning. At the start of this century, 'bereavement' was classified as code V.62.82 under 'Other Conditions That May Be a Focus of Clinical Attention' (2004: 740) in the *Diagnostic and Statistical Manual of Mental Disorders* (*DSM-4*), the standard reference guide of the American Psychiatric Association. Even the punctuation of the *DSM-4* underscores the persistent challenge in the definition of mourning: 'The duration and expression of "normal" bereavement vary considerably among different cultural groups' (2004: 740–41). So-called normal grief must be qualified with quotation marks.

Stroebe et al. summarised the potential benefits of including pathological grief in the *DSM-5*: 'It would standardize clinical assessment, treatment planning, and qualifying for third-party [insurance] payment for services' (2001: 760). However, they acknowledged that 'Distinctions between normal and pathological grief are difficult to make' (2001: 6). Prigerson and Jacob (2001) also lobbied for the inclusion of what they term 'traumatic' grief in the fifth edition of the *DSM*. Prigerson and Jacob's consideration of taxonomy underscores the severity of grief and, as they assert, the need to 'identify and help those who might be at greatest risk for substantial, chronic physical and mental morbidity as a result of being traumatized by a significant loss' (2001: 621).

Still, Parkes, who has been a major contributor to our understanding of grief since the mid-1960s, finds that there is little meaningful distinction between pathological and so-called normal mourning: 'Although these atypical forms differ in intensity and duration from the more usual reactions to bereavement, certain aspects of which may be exaggerated or distorted, they do not differ in kind. There are no symptoms that are peculiar to pathological grief' (1987: 134). There is, in my opinion, no clear line between 'normative' and 'pathological' grief. We do well to remember that today those who seek relief from grief often are met with a combination of therapeutic and psychopharmacological interventions, similar to those treatments utilised for psychological 'illnesses' like clinical depression or post traumatic stress disorder.

Perhaps the latest taxonomy has become the identification of those individuals considered to be at 'high risk'. Lorraine Siggins was the first to provide what she calls 'a critical survey' of the literature on mourning after Freud in 1966, and from it she concludes, 'Both normal and pathological mourning are distinguished from a third phenomenon, clinically recognisable psychiatric illness precipitated by bereavement' (1966: 23). It is this 'third phenomenon' that researchers are currently examining. For example, Rando discusses seven risk factors:

> sudden, unexpected death (especially when traumatic, violent, mutilating, or random); death from an overly lengthy illness; loss of a child; the mourner's percep-tions of the death as preventable; [...] a premorbid relationship with the deceased that was markedly angry or ambivalent, or markedly dependent; prior or concur-rent mourner liabilities – specifically, unaccommodated losses and/or stresses and mental health problems; and the mourner's perceived lack of social support. (1993: 5–6)

Sanders lists the following as risk factors: attachment to and relationship with the deceased, the situation surrounding the death, the premorbid personality of the bereaved, social support systems (or lack thereof) and any concurrent crises in the life of the bereaved (1999: 10–11). Beverley Raphael, Christine Minkov and Matthew Dobson counsel preventative interventions for those defined as being at high risk for outcomes like chronic grief, depression or post traumatic stress disorder (2001). Stroebe et al. seem to agree, finding in their conclusions that 'There is consensus among the researchers represented in this volume [*Handbook*] that methods of counselling and therapy are only needed and effective for a minority of high-risk bereaved people' (2001: 761). Assessing risk, then, has replaced attempts to define, diagnose or even treat grief.

At least in the United States, grief counsellors currently find themselves in an oddly embattled state. Bonanno even effaces the issue of grief altogether: 'Most people get over their losses. Many cope exceptionally well' (2009: 83). He then continues, 'Sometimes the quality of life is considerably better after a loved one's death' (83). In such cases there is little point in denying death, still less in mourning a welcome loss. I will allow that this just might be an unfortunate conclusion of Bonanno's. Certainly, his 2009 book, *The Other Side of Sadness*, while controversial, seems sincere and genuinely well-intended. Trained as a clinical psychologist, he stumbled into bereavement studies by way of random employment after graduate school in the early 1990s (2009: 4). To his credit, he has persevered all of these years and relies on his two decades of study. By and large he focuses on the remarkable resilience of human beings in surviving loss, a commendable and comforting conclusion. Regrettably, though, this message of resilience hearkens back to the 'stiff upper lip' silence of the grief-phobic culture of the early twentieth century.

Much more disturbing is journalist Ruth Davis Konigsberg's 2011 *The Truth About Grief: The Myth of Its Five Stages and the New Science of Loss*, which draws in precariously piecemeal fashion from the copious but often conflicting research available. Konigsberg is also highly critical of Joan Didion's popular *The Year of Magical Thinking* but seems to mistake it for a manual or guide about grief rather than what it is: a powerfully moving memoir and a testament to suffering nobly borne. Poor Kübler-Ross fairs even worse. Konigsberg mounts what appears to be at least as much a personal attack as a critique of her 'stage theory'. Konigsberg gossips about uncovering her alleged 'abrasive relationship with her medical colleagues' (2011: 98) and her decidedly '[u]n-academic turn into life after death' (2011: 99) as if denouncing Kübler-Ross will render her findings suspect. Most troubling of all might be Konigsberg's callous dismissal both of Didion's suffering or even the death of Kübler-Ross herself, about which she writes: 'In 2004, after proclaiming for years that she was ready to expire, Kübler-Ross dies at her home in Scottsdale at the age of seventy-eight' (2011: 103). The glib tone Konigsberg maintains throughout her book strikes me as very much at odds with its subject matter.

Konigsberg also complains, 'Using personal experience or anecdote instead of research to guide treatment has been a big problem with applied thanatology all along' (2011: 122). If so, this 'big problem' has its origins in the methodology of Freud. Freud uses case studies filled with detailed observation and remains a detached, careful observer; however, the move away from Freud in psychiatry has been toward 'hard science' approaches. Generally speaking, psychoanalysis is now taught more often in English than psychology departments. The subject position of both researchers and clinicians studying grief has been fascinating to observe. Careful writers at least consider the ramifications of personal loss and its effect on their professional investigation. For example, Pollock's detailed and scientific study of mourning, conducted for over thirty years, begins, he tells us, with the 'sudden, unexpected, and untimely death' (1989: v) of his mother. His pursuit of clinical precision is not necessarily at odds with his own personal investment in the subject. However, he distances himself from the subject through decidedly Freudian semantics; Pollock writes, as Freud tends to, in the third person: 'the author had occasion to experience and observe more closely the changing aspects of the mourning process in himself' (1989: 13). Pollock shifts to the third person (read authority) and then uses passive construction for further detachment. Nevertheless, his own subjectivity can be felt throughout in the emphasis on final 'liberation'. Gorer, whose father was lost when the *Lusitania* sank in 1915, begins with a thirty-three page 'Autobiographical Introduction', which strikes me as fearless. His concern with what he calls the pornography or exploitative aspects of grief make sense, given the shock, horror and relentlessly public nature of his own traumatic loss. More recently, Bonanno contextualises the loss of his father with his own research in grief, making for a compelling dialogue throughout his book. But some current researchers remain far more reticent – and even leery of – their own personal engagement with grief and mourning. Rando's purpose was to offer a 'comprehensive clinical resource' (1993: 3) on the topic of 'complicated' mourning, and her 664-page tome does just that. But in her acknowledgements, she admits to having survived a gruelling three-year period of significant losses; she worries that 'it is difficult to discern how much of these personal experiences informed the writing of many aspects of this book' (1993: xiii). Konigsberg also reports losing 'people dear to her', yet she clings to what she calls her 'journalistic' detachment (2011: 16). Like Pollock, I too lost my mother. Her death in 1988 from breast cancer was the impetus for my doctoral dissertation and my continuing interest in bereavement research. We are all mourners in life; loss is unavoidable. Therefore, Worden recommends to all grief counsellors, the implied readers of his handbook, that they look at their own history of losses closely before proceeding with psychotherapeutic interventions (2009: 254).

In chapter five Konigsberg takes on Worden (implicitly) and the grief counselling 'industry', questioning its efficacy. While there may be a charlatan or two, and those predators who would seek to profit from the misery of others, social workers and counsellors on average do not earn much money, to say nothing of the countless volunteers who work at churches, schools, hospices and in other venues throughout the community to try to improve the quality of life of those struggling with loss. In her afterword Konigsberg simply echoes Bonanno, whom she applauds at length in her book, by assuring us that most people 'are resilient enough to get through loss' (2011: 198). But she adds that most people reach an 'acceptable level of adjustment on their own' (198). Perhaps this final claim remains her most problematic assumption: that we should all grieve alone. Arnold Stein, echoing Freud's concern, observes the following: 'The modern era is characterized by a collective "denial" of death, by unacknowledged evasion, silence, and suppression' (1986: 261). Stein then laments, 'Death becomes invisible and private, "medicalized" in hospitals, for which the most vivid example is the solitary death protracted by the determination and skills of technology' (261). For Konigsberg, grief too must be unacknowledged, silent, repressed and above all, borne alone.

Konigsberg claims to seek a 'means of escape from our habitual ways of thinking about grief' (2011: 197), as well as a 'better appreciation of just how relative grief can be' (198). Perhaps she should read *Hamlet* carefully, as Freud did. Hamlet insists to his mother – and to us – that grief is nothing if not 'particular' rather than relative. In their survey of bereavement research, Rodgers and Cowles confirm the distinctiveness of mourning: 'One of the most pronounced findings concerning the concept of grief was its highly individualized nature' (1991: 448). Bonanno concurs: 'One of the most consistent findings is that bereavement is not a one dimensional experience' (2009: 6). And perhaps that is why we ultimately find so little consensus with regard to mourning among researchers and clinicians. That said, their contributions matter; the desire to alleviate human suffering is a worthy goal. Raphael compellingly summarises the role of all grief research and therapy: we must learn to bear 'the pain of loss that must inevitably be faced', maintain a 'passionate involvement in humanity and human relationships' and 'comfort and console others with compassion' (1984: 405).

Grief remains particular; it is also relentless. Shear et al. review the current bereavement research and note that the intensity of acute grief typically abates after six months. They continue, 'This does not imply that grief is completed or resolved, but rather that it has become better integrated, and no longer stands in the way of ongoing life' (2011: 104). Among the conclusions Stroebe et al. arrive at is the following:

> In general, expectations are no longer that it takes a calendar year, nor that one returns to a baseline state of well-being. Rather, contemporary understanding is that most people adapt over time, usually taking a year or two, but even then that they are different after their loss. Most bereaved persons get used to their loss, but they do not get over it. It is now well-recognized that some aspects of grief may

never end, even among those who appear to adapt and get on with their lives. (2001: 751)

Worden prefers the term 'adaptation' rather than 'recovery' or 'resolution'.

Freud maintains in his theoretical writing that mourning does indeed end after its 'work' is completed, typically after one or two years.[3] However, in private he may have held a different view. In 1920 Freud suffered the unexpected loss of his beloved daughter Sophie Halberstadt to a virulent outbreak of influenza. He wrote to friend and confidant Sandor Ferenczi that 'way deep down I sense the feeling of a deep narcissistic injury I shall not get over' (cited in Gay 1988: 393). In 1929 Freud wrote to Ludwig Binswanger to comfort him on the sixth anniversary of the death of his own daughter:

> Although we know that after such a loss the acute state of mourning will subside, we also know we shall remain inconsolable and will never find a substitute. No matter what may fill the gap, even if it be filled completely, it nevertheless remains something else. And actually, this is how it should be; it is the only way of perpetuating that love which we do not want to relinquish. (1960: 386)

For Freud love prevails, making mourning interminable.

In conclusion, to a non-clinician like myself, significant overlap remains in the study of grief but alarmingly little accord. At the end of the twentieth century, in their exhaustive research of bereavement, Stroebe et al. observe, 'It is interesting to note that our contributors differ considerably regarding the type and scope of the theoretical frameworks that they now consider necessary in the bereavement field' (2001: 742). And they caution that 'our descriptions of grief have far outstripped our ability to explain it' (2001: 746). When the American Psychiatric Association released the DSM-5 in May of 2013 at its annual meeting, it represented the culmination of a decade of revision and taxonomy of mental illness. On their website they acknowledged the 'strong voice' of professionals 'from the mental health and medical communities, patients and their families, and members of the public' who had provided input over the years (APA DSM-5 Development). Seemingly, this voice reiterated Stroebe et al. Without consensus, perhaps the scientific community sensibly maintained grief in the hinterland of the DSM, its final section, tellingly under the auspices of 'Conditions for Further Study'.[4] Had pathological grief been legitimized as a mental disorder, its inclusion would certainly have been seen by critics as further evidence of unnecessary medicalization and bureaucracy. On the other hand, its confirmation as a disease would likely have ensured third-party payment by insurance companies in the United States for those who seek treatment. Most disconcerting for me is the unnerving recent trend, at least in America, towards rejecting grief therapy entirely. The field of bereavement studies must remain receptive to further advances in science and medicine. Who knows, then, exactly where the field will emerge in the twenty-first century, but suffice it to say that Freud will continue to cast a long shadow.

Notes

1. Following Freud (at least in English translation), I have, like the psychoanalytic community itself, used the terms 'mourning' and 'grief' interchangeably. There are, however, any number of researchers and clinicians who, over the last century and beyond, have tried to delineate these terms by offering various helpful definitions at the start of their analysis. I will discuss the move to define, taxonomise and even anatomise mourning later in this chapter.

2. In *Totem and Taboo* Freud does discuss ambivalence in relation to mourning: 'In almost every case where there is an intense emotional attachment to a particular person we find that behind the tender love there is a concealed hostility in the unconscious. This is the classical example, the prototype, of the ambivalence of human emotions' (1995e: 60). He goes on to explain that we project hostility onto the dead themselves as a defence mechanism, thereby creating a taboo upon the dead (1995e: 60–63).

3. For example, in 'Mourning and Melancholia' Freud writes, 'We rely on its [mourning] being overcome after a certain lapse of time' (1995b: 244) and that 'in mourning time is needed for the command of reality-testing to be carried out in detail, and that when this work has been accomplished the ego will have succeeded in freeing its libido from the lost object' (252). In 'On Transience' he theorises, 'Mourning, as we know, however painful it may be, comes to a spontaneous end. When it has renounced everything that has been lost, then it has consumed itself, and our libido is once more free (in so far as we are young and active) to replace the lost objects by fresh ones equally or still more precious' (1995c: 307).

4. The following is the 'Bereavement Exclusion' from the *DSM-5* ('Highlights'):

> In DSM-IV, there was an exclusion criterion for a major depressive episode that was applied to depressive symptoms lasting less than 2 months following the death of a loved one (i.e., the bereavement exclusion). This exclusion is omitted in DSM-5 for several reasons. The first is to remove the implication that bereavement typically lasts only 2 months when both physicians and grief counselors recognize that the duration is more commonly 1–2 years. Second, bereavement is recognized as a severe psychosocial stressor that can precipitate a major depressive episode in a vulnerable individual, generally beginning soon after the loss. When major depressive disorder occurs in the context of bereavement, it adds an additional risk for suffering, feelings of worthlessness, suicidal ideation, poorer somatic health, worse interpersonal and work functioning, and an increased risk for persistent complex bereavement disorder, which is now described with explicit criteria in Conditions for Further Study in DSM-5 Section III. Third, bereavement-related major depression is most likely to occur in individuals with past personal and family histories of major depressive episodes. It is genetically influenced and is associated with similar personality characteristics, patterns of comorbidity, and risks of chronicity and/or recurrence as non–bereavement-related major depressive episodes. Finally, the depressive symptoms associated with bereavement-related depression respond to the same psychosocial and medication treatments as non–bereavement-related depression. In the criteria for major depressive disorder, a detailed footnote has replaced the more simplistic DSM-IV exclusion to aid clinicians in making the critical distinction between the symptoms characteristic of bereavement and those of a major depressive episode. Thus, although most people experiencing the loss of a loved one experience bereavement without developing a

major depressive episode, evidence does not support the separation of loss of a loved one from other stressors in terms of its likelihood of precipitating a major depressive episode or the relative likelihood that the symptoms will remit spontaneously.

Bibliography

Abraham, K. 1927. 'A Short Study of the Development of the Libido, Viewed in Light of Mental Disorders', in D. Bryan and A. Strachey (eds), *Selected Papers*. New York: Basic Books, pp. 418–501.
Abraham, N. and M. Torok. 1980. 'Introjection – Incorporation: Mourning or Melancholia', in S. Lebovici and D. Widlöcher (eds), *Psychoanalysis in France*. New York: International Universities, pp. 3–16.
Abrams, M.L. 1993. 'Coping with Loss in the Human Sciences: A Reading at the Intersection of Psychoanalysis and Hermeneutics', *diacritics* 23(1): 67–82.
American Psychiatric Association DSM-5 Development. Accessed on 28 February 2014, http://www.dsm5.org/Pages/Default.aspx
Anderson, C. 1949. 'Aspects of Pathological Grief and Mourning', *International Journal of Psycho-Analysis* 30: 48–55.
Bonanno, G.A. 2009. *The Other Side of Sadness: What the New Science of Bereavement Tells Us About Life After Loss*. New York: Basic Books.
Bowlby, J. 1980. *Loss: Sadness and Depression*. New York: Basic Books.
Breuer, J. and S. Freud. 1995. *Studies on Hysteria*. vol. 2, in J. Strachey (ed. and trans.), 24 vols. London: Hogarth, pp. 3–305.
Brown, N.O. 1959. *Life Against Death*. New York: Random House.
Deutsch, H. 1937. 'Absence of Grief', *Psychoanalytic Quarterly* 6: 12–22.
Diagnostic and Statistical Manual of Mental Disorders, 4th ed-Text Revision. 2004. Arlington, Virginia: American Psychiatric Association.
Diagnostic and Statistical Manual of Mental Disorders, 5th ed-Text Revision. 2013. Arlington, Virginia: American Psychiatric Association.
Encyclopedia of Death and Dying. 2011. Accessed on 17 September 2011, http://www.deathreference.com/Nu-Pu/Psychology.html
Engel, G. 1961. 'Is Grief a Disease? A Challenge for Medical Research', *Psychosomatic Medicine* 23(1): 18–22.
Feifel, H. 1959. *The Meaning of Death*. New York: McGraw-Hill.
Fenichel, O. 1945. *The Psychoanalytic Theory of Neurosis*. New York: Norton.
Fine, R. 1979. *A History of Psychoanalysis*. New York: Columbia University Press.
Freud, E.L. (ed.). 1960. *Letters of Sigmund Freud*, trans. T. and J. Stern. New York: Basic.
Freud, S. 1995a. 'Five Lectures on Psychoanalysis', vol. 11 in J. Strachey (ed. and trans.), *The Standard Edition of the Complete Psychological Works of Sigmund Freud (SE)*, 24 vols. London: Hogarth, pp. 9–55.
⸺. 1995b. 'Mourning and Melancholia', *SE* vol. 14, pp. 237–60.
⸺. 1995c. 'On Transience', *SE* vol. 14, pp. 303–307.
⸺. 1995d. 'Thoughts for the Times on War and Death', *SE* vol. 14, pp. 275–300.
⸺. 1995e. 'Totem and Taboo' (1912–1913), *SE* vol. 13, pp. 1–161.
Gay, P. 1988. *Freud: A Life for Our Time*. New York: Norton.
Glass, R. 2005. 'Is Grief a Disease? Sometimes.', *Journal of the American Medical Association* 293(21): 2658–60.
Gorer, G. 1965a. *Death, Grief, and Mourning*. Garden City, New York: Doubleday.

_____. 1965b. 'The Pornography of Death', app. 4 in *Death, Grief, and Mourning*. Garden City, New York: Doubleday, pp. 192–99.

Highlights of Changes from DSM-IV-TR to DSM-5: 'Bereavement Exclusion'. American Psychiatric Association. Accessed on 26 February 2014 http://www.dsm5.org/Documents/changes%20from% 20dsm-iv-tr%20to%20dsm-5.pdf

Klein, M. 1940. 'Mourning and Its Relation to Manic-Depressive Stages', *International Journal of Psycho-Aanalysis* 21: 125–53.

Konigsberg, R.D. 2011. *The Truth About Grief: The Myth of Its Five Stages and the New Science of Loss*. New York: Simon and Schuster.

Kübler-Ross, E. 1969. *On Death and Dying*. New York: Macmillan.

Laplanche, J. and J.B. Pontalis. 1974. *The Language of Psychoanalysis*, trans. D. Nicholson-Smith New York: Norton.

Lindemann, E. 1944. 'Symptomatology and Management of Acute Grief', *American Journal of Psychiatry* 101: 141–48.

Loewald, H.W. 1980. 'Internalization, Separation, Mourning, and the Superego', in *Papers on Psychanalysis*. New Haven, Connecticut: Yale University Press, pp. 257–76.

Parkes, C.M. 1987. *Bereavement: Studies of Grief in Adult Life*, 2nd edn. New York: International Universities Press.

Pollock, G.H. 1989. *The Mourning-Liberation Process*, vol. 1. Madison, Wisconsin: International Universities Press.

Prigerson, H.G. and S.C. Jacobs. 2001. 'Traumatic Grief as a Distinct Disorder: A Rationale, Consensus Criteria, and a Preliminary Empirical Test', in M.S. Strobe, et al. (eds), *Handbook of Bereavement Research: Consequences, Coping, and Care*. Washington: American Psychological Association, pp. 613–46.

Rando, T. 1991. *How To Go On Living When Someone You Love Dies*. New York: Bantam Books.

_____. 1993. *Treatment of Complicated Mourning*. Champaign, Illinois: Research Press.

Raphael, B. 1984. *The Anatomy of Bereavement*. London: Hutchinson.

Raphael, B., C. Minkov and M. Dobson. 2001. 'Psychotherapeutic and Pharmacological Intervention for Bereaved Persons', in M.S. Stroebe, et al. (eds), *Handbook of Bereavement Research: Consequences, Coping, and Care*. Washington: American Psychological Association, pp. 587–612.

Reynolds, C.F., et al. 1999. 'Treatment of Bereavement-Related Major Depressive Episodes in Later Life: A Controlled Study of Acute and Continuation Treatment with Nortriptyline and Interpersonal Psychotherapy', *American Journal of Psychiatry* 156(2): 202–208.

Rodgers, B.L. and K.V. Cowles. 1991. 'The Concept of Grief: An Analysis of Classical and Contemporary Thought', *Death Studies* 15(5): 443–59.

Sanders, C.M. 1999. *Grief: The Mourning After*. New York: John Wiley and Sons.

Schoenberg, B., et al. (eds). 1975. *Bereavement: Its Psychosocial Aspects*. New York: Columbia University Press.

Shear, M.K., et al. 2011. 'Complicated Grief and Related Bereavement Issues for the *DSM-5*', *Depression and Anxiety* 28: 103–17.

Siggons, L. 1966. 'Mourning: A Critical Survey of the Literature', *International Journal of Psycho-Analysis* 47: 14–25.

Schneidman, E.S. 1994. *Death: Current Perspectives*. 4th edn. New York: McGraw-Hill.

Schneidman, E.S. 2008. *A Commonsense Book of Death: Reflections at Ninety of a Lifelong Thanatologist*. Lanham, Maryland: Rowman and Littlefield.

Stein, A. 1986. *The House of Death: Messages from the English Renaissance*. Baltimore, Maryland: Johns Hopkins University Press.

Stroebe, M.S., et al. (eds). 2001. *Handbook of Bereavement Research: Consequences, Coping, and Care.* Washington: American Psychological Association.

Vargas, L.A., F. Loya and J. Hodde-Vargas. 1989. 'Exploring the Multidimensional Aspects of Grief Reactions', *American Journal of Psychiatry* 146(11): 1484–89.

Volkan, V. 1981. *Linking Objects and Linking Phenomena.* New York: International Universities Press.

Worden, J.W. 2009. *Grief Counseling.* New York: Springer.

3

War and Requiem Compositions in the Twentieth Century

Wolfgang Marx

'but slew his son, and half the seed of Europe, one by one'

(Chase 2003: 445)

The requiem is one of the oldest genres of art music; for more than 500 years composers used it as a vehicle to express grief, sorrow and consolation as well as anger and fury in the face of death. Over the course of the last century, many requiem settings can be identified as belonging to the sub-genre of 'war requiem' – indeed, it sometimes appears as if the requiem – and the 'war requiem' in particular – is regarded as almost an ideal type of art music concerned with war.[1] But why is this? And what is a 'war requiem' in the first place? Over the following pages, the war requiem shall be introduced as a sub-genre of twentieth-century music, with a special focus on the following hypotheses:

- unlike other requiems, a war requiem typically addresses not the death of an individual but the death of many;
- a war requiem fulfils two main functions:
  – unifying audiences (and performers) in commemoration, thus acting as a symbol of reconciliation;
  – critiquing the conditions or people that can be held responsible for wars and thus for unnecessary deaths;
- this means that a secular war requiem does not necessarily address death as a biological inevitability (as most earlier requiem settings would have done) but regards the deaths of millions in the wars of the twentieth century as premature, unnecessary and avoidable at the time they occurred. Most war requiems should in fact better be called anti-war requiems.[2]

After an introduction to the history and structure of the requiem, three examples will be discussed: a collaborative 'Requiem of Reconciliation' setting the traditional Latin text only, Britten's *War Requiem* which juxtaposes the liturgical text with modern poetry, and finally Brecht/Weill's *Berliner Requiem* which is based on non-liturgical text only. The first example is the most recent composition while the final one is the oldest, yet this is coincidence – it would be easy to find examples of all three categories in the more recent past as well as in the inter-war years.

Requiem and War Requiem

Dedicated masses for the dead as part of the Catholic liturgy have been held for more than a thousand years; since 998 a mass in memory of the deceased has been read on every second of November (All Souls' Day).[3] The texts were then sung in Gregorian chant. Since the late fifteenth century, more complex, multi-part requiem settings were composed and the requiem emerged as a musical genre. In 1570, in the aftermath of the Council of Trent, the liturgical texts to be used in each requiem mass were standardised. A requiem setting often does not contain all of them, yet, in such a case, the sections not composed would still be sung in the mass in Gregorian chant.

The main function of the early requiem mass was intercession on behalf of the deceased; it was believed that the prayers of the living could help to shorten a soul's time in purgatory. During the Enlightenment, and particularly after the French Revolution, this function changed. Art music became the domain of the middle classes; the concert hall rather than the palace or the church was now the main venue of musical life. Most requiem compositions were now written with a performance in the concert hall in mind. Fauré's requiem is the best-known exception among other famous, still regularly performed nineteenth-century masses of the dead;[4] his setting displays another function that can be found particularly in post-1800 requiems – the consolation of the living. At a time when secularisation was becoming more and more widespread, the function of intercession on behalf of the dead faded into the background while that of helping the grieving relatives and friends to cope with the loss of a loved one came to the fore.

Finally, the twentieth century brought another expansion of the functions of the 'secularized' requiem. As with the fine arts, many no longer expected art music to be primarily beautiful and to please the senses but above all to truthfully reflect on and react to the times. Aestheticians like Benedetto Croce claimed that true beauty lies in being truthful in representing the object of an artwork, and if what is being portrayed truthfully is not beautiful then art itself cannot be beautiful either (Croce 1953). While his approach supposes a conscious decision on the part of the artist, other, more left-leaning writers like Theodor W. Adorno postulated that art cannot but reflect the state of the society that produces it, even if the artist does not consciously try to engage with this thought (Adorno 2006). As a result of these approaches, many artists and composers tried to make political or social statements in their work, attempting not only to entertain but also to educate the recipients of their works. Political suppression, ideological indoctrination or social inequality were among the topics addressed by some artists in a much more open way than had been previously thought possible. The two World Wars, genocides and other acts of violence triggered some of the most powerful artworks of the twentieth century.

To understand the role a requiem can play in this context, it is helpful to take into account an argument outlined by Philip Tagg. He states that we have to ask the following three questions in order to understand the nature of funeral music: Who is responsible for organising the funeral/event? Whose relationship to the deceased is ritualised? Which emotions are ritualised? (1993: n.p.).

In the case of a funeral mass in a church, the family is responsible for organising the event; their emotions and those of others close to the deceased are at the centre of attention. In this case, consolation may well be the main function of the music (Fauré's requiem being probably the best-known case in point). However, a requiem written for a concert performance (be it in a concert hall or a church) is rarely commissioned by family members while the audience also contains at most a tiny minority of people who were close to whoever may be commemorated by the composition. There may be a dedication to a particular deceased, but his/her body is not present and he or she may have died a long time ago. While the loss of a relative or friend often triggers a composer's engagement with the genre, the outcome in the vast majority of cases transcends an expression of personal loss, addressing instead more general issues.

A 'Requiem of Reconciliation'

On 16 August 1995, the *Requiem der Versöhnung* (*Requiem of Reconciliation*) was premiered in the German city of Stuttgart. It was a collaborative composition intended to commemorate the fiftieth anniversary of the end of the Second World War (which had ended in Europe in May 1945 and in the Far East in August of that year). The driving force behind this project was Helmuth Rilling, the musical director of the International Bach Academy Stuttgart, who had asked composers representing countries that had fought each other fifty years earlier to write sections of this requiem. Eventually the following composers contributed to this mass of the dead:

Luciano Berio (Italy), *Prologue*
Friedrich Cerha (Austria), *Introitus and Kyrie*

Paul-Heinz Dittrich (Germany), *Dies Irae*
Marek Kopelent (Czech Republic), *Judex ergo*
John Harbison (USA), *Juste judex*
Arne Nordheim (Norway), *Confutatis*
Bernard Rands (UK/USA), *Interludium*
Marc-André Dalbavie (France), *Offertorium*
Judith Weir (UK), *Sanctus*
Krzysztof Penderecki (Poland), *Agnus Dei*
Wolfgang Rihm (Germany), *Communio I*
Alfred Schnittke/Gennadi Rozhdestvensky[5] (Russia), *Communio II*
Joji Yuasa (Japan), *Responsorium*
György Kurtág (Hungary), *Epilogue*

The work is framed by two non-liturgical texts: Luciano Berio's *Prologue* after a poem by Paul Celan, and György Kurtág's *Epilogue* which is based on an inscription on a tombstone in Cornwall. Wolfgang Riehm's *Communio I* is an instrumental piece while Bernard Rands' *Interludium* sets the single word 'Deus!' The remaining ten movements use the liturgical requiem text.

The first performance in August 1995 reflected the international 'creative team' behind the composition; the Israel Philharmonic Orchestra was not only joined by Rilling's own choir (the Gächinger Kantorei) but also by a chamber choir from Krakow. A German conductor leading a Polish and a German choir together with an Israeli orchestra clearly reinforced the intended symbolic gesture.

Collaborative requiem settings are rather uncommon, yet there is one precedent: when Gioacchino Rossini died in 1868, Giuseppe Verdi brought together thirteen of Italy's foremost composers of the time to write a collaborative requiem mass that was to be premiered on the first anniversary of Rossini's death. The work was completed, yet remained unperformed due to financial and logistical problems – until 1988, when it was again Helmuth Rilling who organised its premiere in Stuttgart.[6] It is safe to assume that it was this experience that inspired the commissioning of the *Requiem of Reconciliation*. Even the number of participants is similar (thirteen in Verdi's case, fourteen in Rilling's).[7] Exactly like the Requiem for Rossini (and subsequently Verdi's own *Missa da Requiem*), the *Requiem of Reconciliation* includes a setting of the responsory 'Libera me', but not the antiphon 'In Paradisum' (texts that are included in some but by no means all requiem settings).

From an aesthetic point of view, the *Requiem of Reconciliation* was not much of a revelation, mainly because the composers of neighbouring sections did not harmonise their styles or even the forces they brought to bear – a full orchestral movement with a separately placed percussion group could be followed by a very intimate, almost a-cappella section; tonal passages found themselves close to atonal ones; the selection and number of soloists as well as the size and composition of the orchestra fluctuated wildly from movement to movement. However, this is not the principal issue here. Why – beyond the inspiration provided by Verdi's Rossini project – did Rilling decide that a requiem was the most suitable musical genre for this occasion? The reviews of the first performance discussed this question controversially.

Harry Draschke in *Die Welt*, for example, ascribes both an artistic and a political dimension to the work and concedes that it is more successful in the latter function than as a work of art. He also refers to the reservations that several of the composers had expressed regarding the project's artistic coherence, yet states that they were ultimately swayed by the opportunity of contributing to a symbolic gesture. Draschke quotes Marc-André Dalbavie as saying 'I felt that – seeing what is happening in the world – I had to do something. That's why I am participating, as a citizen rather than an artist' (Draschke 1995).[8] Luciano Berio is quoted as follows: 'Participating in this kind of requiem is somewhat awkward for me [...]. Of course, I agree with this project's topic and would participate if it were possible to approach it from a secular or pan-religious point of view. Yet music history does not allow for it. Can you accomplish a miracle?' (in Draschke 1995).[9] In the end, Berio's solution was to write the prologue on a secular text (a poem by Paul Celan). The composer also acknowledged the lack of artistic coherence in the piece by stating 'Individual pieces have come together and will part company again' (Draschke 1995).

In an introduction to Marek Kopelent's section of the work, Alwen Bledsoe writes: 'the requiem provides a venue for the living to remember and honor the dead. As such, *Requiem of Reconciliation* calls for an international and collective remembrance of all the victims of the Second World War. The composers [...] came together to provide the international community with the memorial' (Bledsoe 2011: 439). Remembrance and the provision of a memorial is the only function ascribed by Bledsoe to this requiem. There is no mentioning of consolation or even intercession in her (or indeed Draschke's) text.

While Draschke and Bledsoe appear to accept that the political message not only outweighs the artistic merit but has a right to do so, Eckard Roelcke in *Die Zeit* has a more critical view, as reflected by a number of questions he asks early on: 'What does a funeral mass of reconciliation mean? Who is meant to be reconciled with whom? The survivors/living with the dead? The survivors from different countries with each other? Or the victims with the perpetrators? Or the descendants of the victims with the descendants of the perpetrators?' (Roelcke 1995). Roelcke goes on to critique the work's lack of aesthetic unity, which he clearly rates as a higher good compared to the political message. Finally, Roelcke hints that this is in part a vanity project of Helmuth Rilling's who – while ensuring maximum media coverage (the premiere was televised live in several European countries) – spent far less time working towards aesthetic coherence in planning and execution (Roelcke judges that, as a conductor, Rilling did not prepare carefully enough the simultaneous premieres of fourteen different pieces of contemporary music).

It is obvious that this requiem does not fulfil the function of providing consolation for survivors of the war. It is not dedicated to a particular victim but rather – as Draschke and Bledsoe point out – is meant to act as a musical memorial to victims of war in general. To answer Roelcke's questions, quoted above, it is therefore most likely that its function is to reconcile the descendants of the victims with the descendants of the perpetrators.[10] Roelcke also appears to be right in rating aesthetic coherence higher than the political message as there have been very few performances of this work since 1995. The fact that several non-Catholic and even non-Christian composers participated confirms that the requiem genre has become something like an international symbol of death and commemoration to be used freely outside its original sacred and liturgical context.

The *Requiem of Reconciliation* does not try to be more than a symbolic gesture of reconciliation; it does not critique or accuse anyone of being responsible for the death of millions. Our next example is clearer in this respect.

Benjamin Britten's *War Requiem*

Benjamin Britten's *War Requiem* is arguably the best known of all war requiems and possibly the one that gave this subgenre its name. It shares with the *Requiem of Reconciliation* the Second World War as a point of reference; where the former commemorates a half-century of the end of hostilities, the latter was commissioned to celebrate the consecration of the new cathedral in Coventry after the destruction of its predecessor during German bombing raids in November 1940. According to Mervyn Cooke, Britten took the opportunity 'to create a unique pacifist statement fully in keeping with the composer's lifelong hatred of the violence and destruction of warfare' (Cooke 1996: 1).

Like Rilling in 1995, Britten, wishing the first performance to symbolise a spirit of reconciliation, brought together performers from countries which had fought each other during the war. He approached the German baritone Dietrich Fischer-Dieskau and the Russian soprano Galina Vishnevskaya (the wife of his friend, the cellist Mstislav Rostropovich) while the third solo part was to be sung by the English tenor Peter Pears. In the event, the Soviet authorities refused Vishnevskaya permission to participate in the *War Requiem*'s first performance on 30 May 1962; she was replaced by the British soprano Heather Harper (Vishnevskaya was to feature subsequently in the first recording of the composition).

The *War Requiem* is dedicated to Roger Burnley, Piers Dunkerley, David Hill and Michael Halliday who all fought in the Second World War and were friends of Britten. Only Dunkerley survived the war, yet in 1959 he committed suicide – at a time when Britten was already negotiating the commission that was to become the *War Requiem* (Reed 1996: 21). Apart from his pacifist interests, mentioned above, this loss of a friend might have reinforced his conviction to use his new work to make a strong anti-war statement.

In his *War Requiem* Britten follows broadly the 'usual' choice of liturgical texts for a concert-hall requiem: 'Requiem aeternam' and 'Kyrie' are united in the opening movement, followed by the 'Dies irae' sequence and the offertory 'Domine Jesu Christe'. 'Sanctus' and 'Agnus Dei' come next, but the 'Lux aeterna', which usually forms the end of the requiem mass proper, is missing. Instead, the responsory 'Libera me' and the antiphon 'In Paradisum' conclude the piece.

What makes this composition special is that Britten does not just set the Latin text but juxtaposes it with nine poems by one of the most famous British war poets, Wilfred Owen (1893–1918), who died in action just a week before the armistice in November 1918. Owen's poems are presented by the tenor and baritone soloists and a chamber orchestra while the Latin text is sung by either the soprano soloist, the choir and the full orchestra or a boys' choir accompanied by an organ positive. Thus the sound world of the poems is clearly separated from that of the liturgical texts.

In the case of the *Requiem of Reconciliation*, its status as a war requiem derived mainly from the story of its genesis and the occasion of its premiere; there is little in the composition itself that would allow us to determine its specific purpose. Britten's *War Requiem* is quite different in that respect; a closer look at its first movement will reveal how the liturgical texts and Owen's poems enter into a dialogue that results in a clear positioning of the piece.

The movement begins with bells calling for the first entry of the voices that sing the opening 'Requiem aeternam' lines in a declamatory style. The psalm verse 'Te decet hymnus in Zion' is then presented by the boys in a more melodious line, like the full choir before in an alternating two-part texture. When the tenor enters with Owen's *Anthem for Doomed Youth*, it is as if he is responding to the earlier serene and emotionally rather distant presentation of the Latin text (despite the tension provided by the prominent tritone interval discussed below). The lines 'What passing-bells for those who die as cattle?', or 'No mockeries for them from prayers or bells' (Chase 2003: 442), appear to comment directly on the bells we heard at the beginning (which – together with the distinctive sound of the boys' choir – of course indicate a sacred environment that also involves the prayers mentioned in the second line). 'Not in the hands of boys, but in their eyes shall shine the holy glimmers of good-byes' (Chase 2003: 442) harks musically back to the boys' choir – the boys we just heard singing and who Owen came to regard as destined to die in the trenches. 'Nor any voice of mourning [for them] save the choirs, the shrill, demented choirs of wailing shells'

(Chase 2003: 442) is another line that the listener can immediately apply to what just preceded this section as it was all presented by choirs. The tenor line is much more lively, emotionally charged and energetic than the stately choral presentation of the liturgical passages surrounding it; it shows real concern rather than offering standardised consolation presented in a more declamatory fashion.

The poem is followed by the 'Kyrie', presented in a style similar to the opening of the movement and again introduced by the bells. They continue to offer nothing more than what Mervyn Cooke called 'stereotyped religious sentiments' (1996: 55) that are contrasted with much more individual, full-blooded outcries against the slaughter in the trenches and more generally the horrors of war. The pseudo-medieval style of the boys' choir sounds even more archaic than the full choir and the soprano soloist, representing 'the impassive calm of a liturgy that points beyond death' (Evans 1979: 451). This, according to Cooke, 'lends further remoteness and inaccessibility to the messages of prayer and salvation they attempt to convey' (1996: 52–53).

A special musical effect used by Britten throughout the *War Requiem* is the prominent display of the interval of the tritone. This interval – called 'diabolus in musica' ('devil in music') in the Middle Ages – is extremely dissonant; its use was for many centuries avoided bar in exceptional cases. Britten makes it the central musical feature of the opening movement: not only do the opening bell and voice entries alternate melodically on the notes C and F sharp (forming the tritone), it also plays a central role in the boys' and the tenor's section. However, perhaps the most poignant moment can be found at the end of the 'Kyrie' section when the first two out of three phrases finish on the dissonant C-F sharp interval, yet the final 'Kyrie' suddenly and unexpectedly leaps to a consonant F major chord – a 'happy end' so sudden, hollow and unconvincing that it undermines the status of the liturgical text even further.

The questioning of the liturgical text continues in the subsequent movements; one of the most effective examples is probably the use of Owen's *The Parable of the Old Man and the Young* in response to God's promise to Abraham and his seed to support him forever and let his descendants grow in number and power. The parable is Owen's take on the sacrifice of Isaac; when the angel appears and points towards the ram that is to replace his son, Owen continues: 'But the old man would not do so, but slew his son, and half the seed of Europe, one by one' (Chase 2003: 445).

The juxtaposition of Owen's poetry and the 'traditional' requiem text (together with their ingenious musical treatment) results in Britten's *War Requiem* displaying a much clearer anti-war message than the *Requiem of Reconciliation*. Here it is the work itself that – regardless of the time, place and occasion of its performance – takes a stance that cannot be misread. Both compositions address the here and now rather than the afterlife, yet where Rilling's brain child advocates the unification of former enemies by way of mourning their lost ones together, Britten's work has two other functions. On the one hand it focuses on highlighting the hollowness of the consolation religion has to offer (as Cooke put it, 'the bleak portrayal of man's inhumanity offered by the Owen poems seriously undermines the stylized religious phrases of condolence and consolation voiced by the words of the *Missa pro defunctis*' [Cooke 1996: 52–53]) while secondly pointing out the horrors of war and the uselessness of the sacrifices made in its name.

The *Berliner Requiem*

In 1928, radio was still a relatively new medium. As part of an attempt to broaden their appeal, German radio stations had begun to commission new compositions for special occasions. In this context, Kurt Weill and Bertolt Brecht received a commission to collaborate on a piece provisionally described as 'Gedenktafeln, Grabinschriften, Totenlieder' ('Commemorative tablets, Epitaphs, Funeral songs') whose intended function – ten years after the end of the First World War – was to represent 'the feelings of the widest levels of the population' (Huynh 2007: 13). Brecht and Weill – then two emerging, politically left-leaning artists – had just begun their fruitful collaboration that (alongside the *Berliner Requiem*) was to result in works like *Die Dreigroschenoper* (*The Three-Penny Opera*) or *Aufstieg und Fall der Stadt Mahagonny* (*Rise and Fall of the City of Mahagonny*). They now created a number of seemingly unrelated songs and choruses that did not focus on the glory of victory and dying for the fatherland, but rather, more realistically, on what death really means to those suffering it.

The work is scored for tenor, baritone, male choir,[11] wind band, guitar, banjo and percussion. It opens with the 'Großer Dankchoral'('Grand hymn of Thanksgiving'), modelled in style and rhyme scheme on Joachim Neander's Lutheran chorale 'Lobe den Herren, den mächtigen König der Ehren' ('Praise be to God, the almighty King of Glory'). Yet, what is praised here is not the Lord and his reign but the night as our day is gone. It praises the bad memory of heaven which does not know us as individuals so that nobody is even aware of our existence, then the grass and the animals that live and die exactly like us, and finally coldness, darkness and ruin, in the face of which we realise that we do not matter and are expendable. This text does indeed address the concerns of the larger section of the population – the masses of workers and lower-ranking middle classes – who provide the 'cannon fodder' in a war, who, in the view of Brecht and Weill, do not benefit from its outcome and are regarded as on a par with plants and animals, as expendable to the ruling classes. Weill's music parodies the stylistic features of a chorale: the voices often move in archaic-sounding parallel motion while the melodic line has little rhythmic movement and is underpinned by block chords of wind instruments – these, however, provide apparently 'false', or at least extremely unusual, harmonies to indicate that this is not the homely world of the Lutheran chorale.

The chorale does not mention soldiers, yet it can certainly be applied to their fate. The following 'Ballade from ertrunkenen Mädchen' ('Ballad of the drowned girl'), however, cannot directly be linked to the fighting in war. It describes the process of a drowned girl's body gradually decomposing in the water as seaweed and algae attach themselves to the corpse, fish nibble on it until eventually even god gradually forgets her. Again, death does not lead to commemoration, transfiguration or a better afterlife. Instead, the focus is on the decomposition of the corpse, and on being forgotten even by god. There is nothing praiseworthy or memorable about this kind of death.

The third movement, entitled 'Marterl (Grabschrift)' ('Wayside Cross/ Epitaph'), is again dedicated to a woman: it is the imaginary epitaph for a woman who died after losing her virginity to a large number of men – it is unclear whether as a result of prostitution or rape, but it is clear that she had no choice. The music here has jazz inflections which clash in an ironic/parodistic way with the harmonically 'straight' 'Ruhe sanft!' ('Rest in peace!') calls by the male choir at the end – those who caused her demise now wish her a happy afterlife.

The following two movements are the first and second 'Bericht über den unbekannten Soldaten' ('Account concerning the unknown soldier'). The first of these is musically the most elaborate part of the *Berliner Requiem*, with polyphonic choral sections, arioso solo passages and dramatic orchestral effects, while the second one, in contrast, displays a quieter, recitative-like structure. Both highlight the fact that the unknown soldier was killed by people just like him. The second 'Bericht' states that the soldier will not face the Last Judgment as he is dead, just like the tombstone above him. Religion and afterlife clearly play no part in Brecht and Weill's thinking.

The final movement is entitled 'Zu Potsdam unter den Eichen' ('At Potsdam under the oak trees'); in modern performances it is sometimes left out or replaced by a shortened repeat of the chorale. This section parodies a march, quoting in the instrumental postlude briefly the Prussian hymn 'Üb immer Treu und Redlichkeit' ('Always practice loyalty and honesty').[12] It again addresses an unknown soldier whose final destination is inevitably the grave.

Esteban Buch has called the *Berliner Requiem* 'a modernist critique of official memory of the First World War' (Buch 2002: 34). Instead of trying to justify the sacrifices made particularly by the lower classes and to glorify the deaths in the trenches, the work focuses on the horrors of dying and decomposing and ultimately on the question of who benefits from the massive loss of life – the ruling classes. This helps to explain why Brecht and Weill applied the term requiem to a composition that clearly has no religious component and does not refer to the liturgical Latin text. To them, war was only one of many ways in which the rich conducted the class struggle, suppressing and exploiting the poor; their intention was to make the working classes aware of this, to make them realise that their real enemies are not the poor of another country (whom they would have fought in the war) but the rich of their own nation (or all nations).[13] The fate of poor women forced to prostitute themselves or of leaders of communist revolutions is thus related to that of the masses of unknown soldiers who will not profit even if they win the war. Brecht and Weill did not believe in an afterlife, but regarded non-natural death to a large degree as imposed on the poor by the rich. They cannot argue against the existence of death, but they clearly oppose the deaths described in Brecht's poems. Ultimately, poet and composer aimed at changing society and wanted to contribute to this by making their listeners aware of the conditions underlying its current structure.

Conclusion

In the twentieth century, the requiem has become an international and inter-cultural metaphor of musical engagement with the topic of death. The term is used in relation to compositions not only by and for Catholics but also Christians of other denominations, members of other religions or atheists (the composers of the *Requiem of Reconciliation* represent all of these groups while the *Berliner Requiem* was written by outspoken atheists). Compositions entitled 'requiem' can nowadays use the traditional Latin text entirely or in part, use other texts (entirely or in part), or be purely instrumental – but they always aesthetically refer back and react to the great canonical requiem compositions known the world over.

The three compositions discussed in this chapter are all requiems dedicated to the commemoration of war, yet fulfil this function in different ways: while the *Requiem of Reconciliation* does not go beyond pure commemoration, Britten's *War Requiem* highlights the true nature and the futility of war, simultaneously questioning the validity of the Latin liturgy in a modern context. Finally, in their *Berliner Requiem* Brecht and Weill place war in the general context of class struggle. All of these compositions address the living rather than the dead; instead of focusing on consolation, they all want to get a message across to their audiences. Through its very existence, the *Requiem of Reconciliation* attests to the fact that former enemies can work together; it also unifies its audiences across national divides in commemoration. The latter is also a goal of the *War Requiem* which, in addition, tries to convey a strong general anti-war message to its listeners. The *Berliner Requiem* is not interested in commemoration at all but presents its anti-war stance in the context of a general anti-capitalist message. At least Britten and Brecht/Weill regard death in war as an unnecessary death that – unlike its biological counterpart – could be prevented; all of us are called upon to contribute our share to make this happen.

Maybe art cannot change the world on its own, but we can benefit from artists' attempts to not only entertain their audiences but also to contribute towards making this world a better place, even if only in a small way. Looking at the war requiems of the twentieth century, one cannot help but notice that many of the more elaborate and successful ones are those that adopt a strong anti-war stance such as György Ligeti's *Requiem* (1965), Bernd Alois Zimmermann's *Requiem for a Young Poet* (1969) or Hans Werner Henze's instrumental *Requiem* (1993). All of these use the genre as a vehicle of social and political critique, raising awareness of wrongs in our world rather than worrying about the afterlife. It is probably this potential for secular application and critique that has kept the requiem as a musical genre alive over the last century (unlike, for example, the mass which has virtually ceased to exist as a genre of art music). War requiems continue to be written and performed, in an attempt to make a small contribution towards preventing another Abraham in the future from yet again slaying 'his son, and half the seed of Europe [and the world], one by one'.

Notes

1. In an article published in *The Independent* on 11 November 2011, in which Jessica Duchen contemplates the lack of music engaging with war in recent times, she uses the term 'war requiem' in a general way to refer to music dealing with war.

2. However, not all art music about war is anti-war music, as for example Tchaikovsky's *Overture 1812* or the settings of Heine's *The Two Grenadiers* show.

3. See Nohl 1996. See also Robertson 1967.

4. There were, of course, still many requiems written for liturgical use, but they were comparatively small-scale, brief works of a simpler texture. Their artistic merit clearly played second fiddle to their functionality. None of them is regularly performed today.

5. Alfred Schnittke was commissioned to write *Communio II*, but he was unable to finish the movement in time due to illness; it was completed by Gennadi Rozhdestvensky.

6. Verdi himself had contributed the 'Libera me'; a few years later he would use this setting as the starting point of his own *Missa da Requiem*.

7. The number excludes Rozhdestvensky who came in at a late stage to complete Schnittke's movement.

8. All translations of the German texts are mine.

9. Berio was not entirely correct here; there is a long history of non-religious (or even anti-religious) requiem settings in the twentieth century, not least including the ones discussed in this chapter. In fact, I would argue that the vast majority of requiem settings since the time of the First World War fall into this category.

10. Several of the composers (as well as Rilling himself) were children or young adults during the war, yet neither the programme notes nor the reviews or the subsequent CD booklet hint at their experiences being in any way relevant to them during the composition process.

11. Originally the three parts of the male choir were to be sung by three male soloists only; the practice of performing them with a larger choir (with several voices per part) emerged later. See Grosch 1996.

12. This hymn is regularly played by a well-known carillon at the Garnisonskirche (garrison church) in Potsdam, thus creating a link to the city named in the title.

13. At this point there may be a link to Wilfred Owen's Abram (as he calls him) who slays his own son despite having an alternative sacrifice at hand. Owen does not explicitly critique the ruling classes and certainly does not advocate a communist revolution, yet passages like this one allow for an interpretation of his texts as a critique of the classes responsible for the war that murder their 'children' actively and needlessly.

Bibliography

Adorno, T.W. 2006. *Philosophy of New Music*, transl. R. Hullot-Kentor. Minnesota: University of Minnesota Press (first published in German in 1949).

Bledsoe, A. n.y. 'Marek Kopelent'. Accessed on 3 May 2012, http://www.requiemsurvey.org/compos ers.php?id=439.

Buch, E. 2002. 'Ein deutsches Requiem: Between Borges and Furtwängler', *Journal of Latin-American Studies* 11(1): 29–38.

Chase, R. 2003. *Dies Irae: A Guide to Requiem Music*. Lanham, Oxford: The Scarecrow Press.

Cooke, M. 1996. *Britten: War Requiem. Cambridge Music Handbook*, Cambridge et al.: Cambridge University Press.

Croce, B. 1953. *Aesthetic as Science of Expression and General Linguistic*, transl. Douglas Ainslee. London: Vision Press (first published in English in 1909; first published in Italian in 1902). Accessed on 3 May 2012, http://www.naturalthinker.net/trl/texts/Croce,%20Benedetto/Croce,% 20Benedetto%20-%20Aesthetic%20as%20Science%20of%20Expression%20and%20General% 20Linguistic.pdf.

Draschke, H. 1995. 'Im Gedenken an die Toten, als ein Gespräch mit Gott', *Die Welt* 17 August 1995. Accessed on 3 May 2012, http://www.welt.de/print-welt/article661276/Im_Gedenken_an_ die_Toten_als_ein_Gespraech_mit_Gott.html.

Duchen, J. 2011. 'Requiem for an Art Form: Why Modern Composers are Fighting a Losing Battle', *The Independent* 11 November 2011. Accessed on 3 May 2012, http://www.independent.co.uk/ arts-entertainment/classical/features/requiem-for-an-art-form-why-modern-composers-are-fight ing-a-losing-battle-6260041.html.

Evans, P. 1979. *The Music of Benjamin Britten*. Minneapolis: University of Minnesota Press.

Grosch, N. 1996. 'Notiz zum "Berliner Requiem" von Kurt Weill. Aspekte seiner Entstehung und Aufführung', *Sonderdrucke der Albrecht-Ludwigs-Universität Freiburg* 55 (71): 66–67. Accessed on 3 May 2012, http://www.freidok.uni-freiburg.de/volltexte/1260/pdf/BerlinerRequiem.pdf.

Huynh, P. 2007. 'Kurt Weill, Asphalt Music', Booklet of the CD Weill, Berliner Requiem, musique d'abord, harmonia mundi 1951422, 2007.

Nohl, P.-G. 1996. *Lateinische Kirchenmusiktexte. Geschichte – Übersetzung – Kommentar*. Kassel et al.: Bärenreiter.

Reed, P. 1996. 'The War Requiem in Progress', in Mervyn Cooke (ed.), *Britten: War Requiem*. Cambridge: Cambridge University Press, pp. 20–48.

Robertson, A. 1967. *Requiem: Music of Mourning and Consolation*. London: Cassell.

Roelcke, E. 1995. 'Flatterzunge, schweres Blech', *Die Zeit* 35. Accessed on 3 May 2012, http://mobil. zeit.de/1995/35/Flatterzunge_schweres_Blech.

Tagg, P. 1993. '"Universal" Music and the Case of Death', *Critical Quarterly* 35(2): 54–85.

PART II

DEATH IN LITERATURE

4

UNDERSTANDING DEATH/ WRITING BEREAVEMENT
The Writer's Experience

Maria-José Blanco

When professional writers go through difficult times, many hold onto what is most natural to them: writing. In this chapter I am going look at writers who, after the death of a loved one, took up pen and paper to narrate their loss. As Mark Lawson observes: 'In most professions, bereavement leads to time off work, bureaucratically expressed as "compassionate leave". It seems to me that those in artistic jobs, though, tend to work on through – in an effort to work out – their loss' (2010). And as Jeffrey Berman states: 'For the writer [...] the way to deal with loss is through writing' (2010: 202).

In recent decades we have seen the publication of a growing number of memoirs in which writers describe the loss of a loved one:[1] Isabel Allende's *Paula* (1994); Sandra M. Gilbert's *Wrongful Death* (1995); John Bayley's *Elegy for Iris* (1999); Soledad Puértolas' *Con mi madre* (2001); Donald Hall's *The Best Day the Worst Day* (2005); Joan Didion's *The Year of Magical Thinking* (2005) and *Blue Nights* (2011); Calvin Trillin's *About Alice* (2006); Joyce Carol Oates's *A Widow's Story* (2011); Barbara Want's *Why not me?* (2010); Meghan O'Rourke's *The Long Goodbye* (2011); Eitan Fishbane's *Shadows in Winter* (2011), and so on. In these works, the writers recount the last days and moments that they lived with partners, children or parents. In some cases, such as that of Joan Didion, the need to make sense of what happened is what motivates the writing. Allende, in contrast, started taking notes during her daughter Paula's illness to help her cope with the hours she spent sitting next to her while she was in a coma. Didion also wrote during her daughter's illness, first in the book about her husband's death, *The Year of Magical Thinking* and then in *Blue Nights*, which she wrote after her daughter's death. Louise DeSalvo explains how: '[Some] writers describe how they have consciously used the writing of their artistic works to help them heal from the thorny experiences of their lives, especially from [...] loss' (DeSalvo 1999: 4).

These writers may be seen to have used their writing as a way of surviving the death of a loved one. As Berman explains about his own writing:

> Like the fabled Scherazade of the Thousand and One Nights, who must keep on telling stories to remain alive, I find myself writing books about death, partly to work through my grief, partly to commemorate and honor my wife's memory, partly to remain securely attached to her, partly to understand my changing relationship to her, and partly to help others – my students and my readers – understand and cope with their own losses. (Berman 2010: 1)[2]

This type of 'writing therapy' has now been well studied with books such as Louise DeSalvo's *Writing as a Way of Healing* (1999), Gillie Bolton's *The Therapeutic Potential of Creative Writing* (1999), Celia Hunt's *Therapeutic Dimensions of Autobiography in Creative Writing* (2000), Lepore and Smith's *The Writing Cure: How Expressive Writing Promotes Health and Emotional Well-Being* (2002), James W. Pennebaker's *Writing to Heal: A Guided Journal for Recovering from Trauma and Emotional Upheaval* (2004), and so on.

Nowadays some aspects of death and bereavement are finding a more prominent position in society. The taboo that surrounded death and which Gorer wrote about in his 1955 seminal essay 'Pornography of Death' (Gorer 1987)[3] is slowly being modified – at least in art, literature and academia, if not in everyday life. Illnesses such as AIDS or cancer have obliged contemporary western society to see death in a different light. Memoirs, diaries and letters are also going through a renaissance. Politicians, writers, journalists, actors, singers, sport personalities, cooks, all publish their stories, and some of these books have become bestsellers.[4]

Writing as therapy helps to 'cure', or at least to manage grief. In this chapter I look at four writers from four different countries (Ireland, the USA, Chile and Spain) who use this type of writing to articulate their pain: C.S. Lewis (1898–1963), Joan Didion (1934–), Isabel Allende (1942–) and Soledad Puértolas (1947–). They all had very different experiences but each felt the need to express them on paper. Their books have become bestsellers and, in the case of Lewis, Didion and Allende, have been re-edited and translated into other languages. Lewis and Didion both lost spouses, but while Lewis' wife was ill with cancer for a long time, Didion's husband died suddenly of a heart attack. Allende lost her daughter after she fell ill and sank into a coma and Puértolas lost her mother also after spending some time in hospital; both losses were expected but that did not make them less painful. I will look at the way in which the writers inscribe their memories, telling one of the most difficult stories they ever had to tell. I will refer to books on writing as therapy such as DeSalvo's *Writing as a Way of Healing* (1999) and Bolton's *The Therapeutic Potential of Creative Writing* (1999) to make sense of that need before I analyse the writers' work.

Writing as Therapy

The therapeutic benefits of the 'talking cure' developed by Freud are well known, but the 'writing cure' is still in its infancy as a relatively new way of therapy.[5] As Bolton explains:

> The natural way of dealing with an upheaval is to talk about it extensively over a long period. [...]. Expressing thoughts and feelings about a massive upheaval enables people to learn more about the event and their own reactions to it, and the way in which it is represented in the memory. Once it has been put into words, it should be easier to organise and assimilate. If it doesn't happen, longstanding personality processes are affected, a trauma is cognitively prolonged and, because the person cannot talk to friends and relatives about the distressing subject, they can become socially isolated. (Bolton 1999: 199)

Writing allows the writer to go back to what has been written, to reread and rewrite, making it easier to 'organise and assimilate' his or her thoughts. Further, as Pennebaker states: 'writing permits subjects to engage their traumas to a degree and at a rate at which they feel comfortable' (in Bolton 2008: 200). As we will see with the works studied in this chapter: 'Writing, *done at the right stage*, which makes sense and accurately conjures up a past situation, will offer its writer the most release and relief because it will have expressed and communicated their feelings effectively' (Bolton 2008: 200, my emphasis).

The four authors whose work I analyse here started writing about their loss for different reasons, but in the course of their work they all ended up writing about themselves. In analysing their loss the authors analyse themselves. As Bolton explains about therapeutic writing: '[It] is a process of exploring; an expression of different aspects of myself and an encouragement of these disparate voices within me to communicate with each other, and with other people. This can lead to greater understanding and greater respect for the diverse aspects of myself' (Bolton 2008: 197).

In *Writing as a Way of Healing*, Louise DeSalvo gives a number of reasons as to why the writer needs to write her/his loss. Amongst others, she gives the example of Kenzaburō Ōe and his memoir *A Healing Family*: 'By seeing his experience transformed into art, Ōe achieved, if only for a time, acceptance' (DeSalvo 1999: 65). Furthermore, by writing about those who are no longer with us the author is able to give them a 'posthumous life' in writing (57). Also, the detailed account of the events and feelings surrounding the death give the writer space to think and reflect about it in a more detached way: 'as we write we become observers [...]. We regard our lives with a certain detachment and distance when we view it as a subject to describe and interpret' (73).

It is easy to see and understand the need of the writers to write about their loss but the fact that they publish and sell their stories is more difficult to grasp. Is it because they want to use their own experience to help other people cope with their own losses? Bolton suggests that it could be seen as a 'way of sharing a journey of pain with other sufferers' (2008: 13). As Lawson states: 'the genre provides answers to audiences as well as authors' (2010). The cover of the paperback edition of Didion's *The Year of Magical Thinking* contains the catchphrase: 'Will speak to and maybe comfort anyone who has lost for ever the one they loved'. What we do see for example is how authors like Didion or Berman read C.S. Lewis' *A Grief Observed* and other works to understand their own loss and maybe this need to read other writers' experiences is what makes them see the need to publish their own. Nouwen believes we receive consolation and hope from reading authors 'who, while offering no answers to life's questions, have the courage to articulate the situation of their lives in all honesty and directness. [...] Similarly, we receive consolation and hope from writing that enters deeply into our suffering, that articulates the situation of our lives with honesty and directness, that connects our situation to that of other people' (in DeSalvo 54).

C.S. Lewis – A *Grief Observed*

Published in 1961, a year after the death of his wife Joy Gresham ('H.', in the book) who died of cancer of the bones, C.S. Lewis' book is a reflection on and an analysis of grief. When he thinks of grief he feels it as 'fear', 'pain', 'laziness', 'suspense', 'waiting'. He states at the beginning of the book: 'No one ever told me that grief felt so like fear' (Lewis 1966: 5). 'And no one ever told me about the laziness of grief' (7). The analysis of his feelings continues and develops throughout the book: 'And grief still feels like fear. Perhaps, more strictly, like suspense. Or like waiting; just hanging about waiting for something to happen' (29). As Stephenson explains: 'Grief can be described as an overwhelming and acute sense of loss and despair. The entire personality is helplessly engulfed in strong, sometimes frightening, feelings' (1985: 121).

In his book Lewis writes about his feelings after his wife's death as well as his religious doubts. He is an practising Christian, yet he asks: 'Where is God?' (7) and questions the existence of another life, of life after death. He knows he is writing more about himself and his feelings than about his wife. His writing is about living with grief, about feeling the absence and writing it all down: 'Part of every misery is, so to speak, the misery's shadow or reflection: the fact that you don't merely suffer but have to keep on thinking about the fact that you suffer. I not only live each endless day in grief, but live each day thinking about living each day in grief. Do these notes merely aggravate that side of it?' (10–11).

He, like many other writers, reads his notes and reflects on them: 'For the first time I have looked back and read these notes. They appal me' (16). Reading those notes also makes him recapitulate some of his thoughts, being able to transform them or make them more clear: 'I wrote that last night. It was a yell rather than a thought. Let me try it over again' (27).

Towards the end of the book he starts to feel better: 'Something quite unexpected has happened. It came this morning early. For various reasons, not in themselves at all mysterious, my heart was lighter than it had been for many weeks. For one thing, I suppose I am recovering physically from a good deal of mere exhaustion' (38–39). This recovery leads him to understand the need to think less about H.'s loss: 'the less I mourn her the nearer I seem to her' (48). And to be able to have her more present obliges him to see bereavement from another perspective and to understand it better: 'bereavement is a universal and integral part of our experience of love. It follows marriage as normally as marriage follows courtship or as autumn follows summer' (43). The need to end writing also follows naturally: 'This is the fourth – and the last – empty MS. book I can find in the house […]. I will not start buying books for the purpose' (50). And as with many other narratives on bereavement, he goes back again to the beginning, closing the circle once the pain has lessened and the therapeutic benefits have been felt: 'In so far as this record was a defence against total collapse, a safety-valve, it has done some good' (50).

Joan Didion – *The Year of Magical Thinking*

Joan Didion needed to go back to the moment her husband John Gregory Dunne died to be able to understand how it had happened and to stop blaming herself for his death. As Lynne Simpson argues in this volume (p. 28), 'feelings of guilt are common in normal mourning'.

In January 2004, a few days after John's death, Didion wrote on her computer:

'Life changes fast.
Life changes in the instant.
You sit down to dinner and life as you know it ends.
The question of self-pity.' (2011: 3)

After these words it took many months for Didion to return to her writing. As she states, she turned on her computer in May 2004 but did not write anything, and it was not until October of that year that she sat down to start work on her book (6). Didion explains her need to write: 'I had to write my way out of it. Because I couldn't figure out what was going on' (in Brockes 2005). Thus, she needed to narrate the events that happened when her husband suddenly died of a heart attack: 'Nine months and five days ago, at approximately nine o'clock on the evening of December 30, 2003, my husband, John Gregory Dunne, *appeared to (or did) experience*, at the table he and I had just sat down to dinner in the living room apartment in New York, a sudden massive coronary event that caused his death' (6–7, my emphasis). The detailed account of the moment of his death, and her doubts about the exact time when it happened, will continue throughout the narrative, interweaving with her memories of the years lived with her husband her happiness and her regrets, as well as the moments spent with her daughter in hospital or recovering at home.[6]

> This is my attempt to make sense of the period that followed, weeks and then months that cut loose any fixed idea I had ever had about death, about illness, about probability and luck, about good fortune and bad, about marriage and children and memory, about grief, about the ways in which people do and do not deal with the fact that life ends, about the shallowness of sanity, about life itself. (7)

And that is exactly what she does, even though any sense that comes out of this will derive mainly from her own experience, her own way of dealing with death and illness: 'During the past months I have spent a great deal of time trying to keep track of, and, when that failed, to reconstruct, the exact sequence of events that preceded and followed what happened that night' (63). As Lawson explains: 'The genre of grief memoir is by definition questioning: trying to come to terms with what happened and whether anything else might have been done' (Lawson 2010).

Through the reconstruction of the events she is trying to make sense of the death. Didion's repetitive and almost obsessive description of her husband's heart attack is reminiscent of the endless playback of televised sports injuries or deaths which Julia Banwell describes in chapter 11 of this volume. As Banwell argues, the need of the spectator to look at the images over and over again 'may be seen as a mechanism for coping with trauma' (p. 147). Didion dissects the moment of her husband's death and explains in detail every movement in order to try to deal and cope with her trauma. As Berman suggests, she 'replays her loved one's death again and again, as if by doing so she can reverse it, undo it. When her magical thinking fails to bring him back to life, she does the next best thing: she writes a book about her confusion following unexpected loss, transforming his corporeal absence into linguistic presence' (2010: 206).

While Lewis's account is an inward reflection of his feelings, Didion's narrative relies on other texts for an understanding of her loss. She looks for answers in other writer's experiences: 'Given that grief remained the most general of afflictions its literature seemed remarkably spare. There was the journal C.S. Lewis kept after the death of his wife, A Grief Observed. There was the occasional passage in one or another novel [...]. There were certain poems, in fact many poems' (44–45).[7] She turns to psychological and medical books on bereavement to find answers. As Berman explains: 'Believing, with Freud, that knowledge is power, Didion researches the subject of mourning and bereavement as if it were a doctoral dissertation, complete with full bibliographical citations' (Berman 2010: 206). Freud's 'Mourning and Melancholia'; Melanie Klein's 'Mourning and Its Relation to Manic-Depressive States'; 'Bereavement: Reactions, Consequences, and Care, compiled in 1984 by the National Academy of Sciences' Institute of Medicine'; 'Emily Post's book of etiquette, Chapter XXIV, "Funerals"'; Geoffrey Gorer's Death Grief and Mourning or Philippe Aries' Western Attitudes towards Death: these are some of the works she reads. Chapters 3 and 4 are dedicated to her readings. But she doesn't restrict herself to 'theoretical' books, but also goes to literature to find comfort and understanding: 'Didion derives comfort and knowledge not from the psychotherapists, whose jargon-filled language offends her, but from literary writers' (Berman 2010: 209). Didion explains: 'In time of trouble, I had been trained since childhood, read, learn, work it up, go to literature'. C.S. Lewis' A Grief Observed; Thomas Mann's The Magic Mountain; Matthew Arnold's 'The Forsaken Merman'; W.H. Auden's 'Funeral Blues': these all help her to understand and cope better with her loss.

The narrative of the death of her husband ends a year and a day later when she writes: 'This day a year ago was December 31, 2003. John did not see this day a year ago' (225). She fears forgetting him, his image: 'I did not want to finish the year because I know that as the days pass, as January becomes February and February becomes summer, certain things will happen. My image of John at the instant of his death will become less immediate, less raw. It will become something that happened in another year' (225). These feelings contrast with Lewis' need to stop writing to have the image of his wife more clearly in his head. And while Lewis feels the need to finish writing his diary, Didion fears the end of the writing: 'I realize as I write that I do not want to finish this account' (224), even though she has answered the main question of her quest: 'At the time I began writing these pages, in October 2004, I still did not understand how or why or when John died. I had been there. I had watched while the EMS team tried to bring him back. I still did not know how or why or when. In early December 2004, almost a year after he died, I finally received the autopsy report and emergency room records' (199). The autopsy shows that John must have been dead by the time the ambulance arrived and that she could not have done anything to prevent his death.

The suddenness of her husband's death made Didion's grief even more difficult to come to terms with: 'The death happened so fast, without warning or preparation, without an opportunity to say goodbye, without time to process it, that Didion still finds herself in a state of shock, disbelief, and denial while completing the book' (Berman 2010: 157). Throughout the narrative, though, she is able to analyse the stages of her grief: 'Until now I had been able only to grieve, not mourn. Grief was passive. Grief happened. Mourning, the act of dealing with grief, required attention. Until now there had been every urgent reason to obliterate any attention that might otherwise have been paid, banish the thought, bring fresh adrenaline to bear on the crisis of the day' (143). Or as Emma Brockes puts it: 'after a period of derangement Didion turned to face her grief' (Brockes 2005). And even though she does not want to finish writing as 'it maintained a connection with him' (in Brockes 2005), at the end of her book she understands the need to let her husband go: 'I know why we try to keep the dead alive: we try to keep them alive in order to keep them with us. I also know that if we are to live ourselves there comes a point at which we must relinquish the dead, let them go, keep them dead' (225–26).

Isabel Allende *Paula*

In her book, *Paula*, Isabel Allende writes that it was her agent who gave her a notebook in which to write while she was looking after her daughter Paula (1963–1992) who fell into a porphyria-induced coma in December 1991: 'Then write a letter to Paula. It will help her know what happened while she was asleep' (Allende 1996b: 75), her agent told her. She started writing in Madrid, where her daughter was living at the time she fell ill and finished in her home town in California where she took Paula for the last months of her life. In *Paula*, Allende goes back to her first novel, *The House of the Spirits* (1982), where she started writing a letter to her grandfather after his death. *Paula* opens with a letter to her daughter: 'Eleven years ago I wrote a letter to my grandfather to say goodbye to him in death. On this January 8[8] 1992, I am writing to you, Paula, to bring you back to life' (1996b: 9–10). As in that letter, her writing will retrace her life and family history. As Linda Maier explains: 'The pretext of chronicling her daughter's decline affords Allende the opportunity to record her own life story while also tracing the author's passage through the stages of grief' (Maier 2003: 237).

Throughout the book she cycles between hope and despair: 'When you wake up we will have months, maybe years, to piece together the broken fragments of your past [...]. What good are all these words if you can't hear me? Or these pages you may never read? My life is created as I narrate, and my memory grows stronger with writing; what I do not put in words on a page will be erased by time' (1996b: 8). And later on she writes: 'I plunge into these pages in an irrational attempt to overcome my terror. I think that perhaps if I give form to this devastation I shall be able to help you, and myself, and that the meticulous exercise of writing can be our salvation' (1996b: 9).

Often she seems to be talking directly to her daughter: 'I imagine that you prefer to hear about the happiest part of your childhood, the days when Granny was still alive, and your parents loved each other, and Chile was your country, but this notebook is coming to the seventies, when things began to change' (1996b: 163). The second part of the book is mainly written in the first-person as Allende comes to terms with the fact that her daughter will never recover.

In May 1992, Allende decided to take Paula to her home in California. There she writes: 'I am not longer writing, so when my daughter wakes up she will not feel so lost, because she is not going to wake up. These pages Paula will never read....' (1996b: 205). And even though she knows her daughter is never going to read the letter that she started writing for her, Allende continued writing because she understood that she needed to write in order to survive: 'I had a choice... Was I going to commit suicide? Sue the hospital? Or was I going to write a book that would heal me?' (in Maier 2003: 237). From the moment she travelled to California with her daughter, Allende began to prepare for her death. As Stephenson explains: 'As modern medicine becomes more exact, it is becoming more commonplace for people to know of impending death. Since death can be anticipated, grief ensues before the death has occurred' (Stephenson 1985: 158); this is what he calls 'anticipatory grief' and it is what we will see in Isabel Allende's narrative.

Lewis does not write of the moment of death. However Allende, like Didion with her husband, was with her daughter when she died and in the epilogue to the book she describes the last hours of Paula's life: 'Near dawn on Sunday, December 6, after a miraculous night in which the veils that conceal reality were parted, Paula died. It was at four in the morning. Her life ended without struggle, anxiety, or pain [...]. She died in my arms' (325). In the following pages she explains in detail how her daughter died, who was with her (including the spirits of those who have died in the family) and her feelings about her daughter leaving this life: 'Godspeed, Paula, woman. Welcome, Paula, spirit' (330), are the last words written in the book. By writing this book, as DeSalvo comments, Allende is '"say[ing] good-bye" in writing' (1999: 36). She is ready for Paula's death and as Stephenson explains, 'One of the emotions present at the end of anticipatory grief, the time of death, is feeling of relief' (1985: 163). As Maier indicates, 'the writing process converted the author's grief into a celebration of life' (2003: 237).

The narration ends with Paula's death. Allende does not really write about bereavement, if we understand this as something that follows death, perhaps because during her daughter's illness Allende had already undergone the first stages of bereavement. In contrast to the other authors studied in this chapter, Allende's writing started before the death, giving her account a slower pace; she is reflecting with her daughter about their lives. Even though in the second part she is anticipating death, the first part is full of hope for the future. The second part helps Allende cope with what is coming and this can be seen in the way she writes about the moment of death.

Soledad Puértolas Con mi madre

In her book Con mi madre [With my Mother], Soledad Puértolas describes her feelings after her mother's demise. Like Didion and Allende, she recalls her life before her mother's death. She explains from the beginning the need to write: 'My mother died on 26 January 1999. Since that day, so as not to feel overwhelmed with pain, I have been writing about her, about what her life and death have meant for me.'[9] She goes on to explain what she wants from her writing: 'I am looking for truth and comfort, I am trying to live with my mother's absence' (Puertolas 2001: 9). For Puértolas, the writing represents a way of holding onto something, rather than a quest for answers as it is for Didion. Even though, like Lewis, she is articulating her loss and how she deals with it, Puértolas is addressing this loss through remembering her life with her mother, rather than reflecting on grief, as Lewis does. Puértolas reflects on death: 'I was taught that we don't know how to die, that we treat the sick like uncomfortable characters, infantilised, confined, marginalised' (38), and is aware of the benefits that her writing and the publication of the book can offer: 'To offer [the book], to her and all the people who would like to read it, to make public my evocations and reflections, will help us both' (11). Puértolas, like Didion and in particular like Allende, writes about the time spent in hospital, about the people they meet there, about the solidarity and the suffering of other people around them (31–34). She looked after her mother until the end but was not there at the time of her death: 'She wanted it that way, I have told myself during the last few months, she chose to die when I was not with her' (46).

In adulthood, a mother's death is a much more natural and expected event; we are somewhat prepared for it, while we don't expect our children to predecease us or our partners to die when we are still relatively young. Nevertheless, a parent's death can still be traumatic and can expose to us our unpreparedness. Parents have been our support throughout our lives: 'My mother's death had been announced, but it took me by surprise' (132). As Sanders explains: 'Sudden unexpected death has been found to cause a greater degree of shock in the bereaved than does grief in which there is long preparatory period. Yet, even when death had been mentally rehearsed over and over, even when death had been anticipated, some degree of shock and disbelief is still present' (1999: 49).

With her writing, Puértolas is trying to keep her mother alive: 'In life death writes those words [the end]. But writing can erase these words "the end"' (29). Her life has to go on and her writing will help her to go on with that life:

'My mother had died. Life has not stopped. Tears don't stop life. [...] I have not stopped writing' (47). As we have seen with the other works studied here, what begins as writing of a loss ends up being the writing of Puértolas's own autobiography. By remembering her mother, she remembers her own life.

In the first instance, Puértolas tried to escape through fiction writing and realised that the only way to be able to write fiction again was to reorganise her life before going on:

> I remember again the summer of 1999. [...] I could not leave my house, I could not go away from Madrid, the city where my mother had died. I was writing feverishly [...] morning, evening and night. I was writing about a woman who had just lost her mother, a woman who, immersed in the most absolute desolation, was desperately looking for a way to survive. Mid autumn I abandoned the novel. I wrote many articles and finally I started writing about my mother. I have written these pages sitting on my living-room sofa [...] surrounded by photographs of my mother and my children. (139)

Puértolas writes about moments she spent with her mother, about her mother's phone calls full of fear and loneliness of the last days of her life, about her mother's religious beliefs, about her openness and friendliness. She concludes her writing in December 2000 by recollecting the letters her mother wrote to her over the years and looking at one of her mother's photographs in which her image is that of one who is still moving. Just as Roland Barthes suggested in 'Camera Lucida', photographs serve to recall loved ones back to life.

In Puértolas's text we find not so much the conclusion that is present in some of the other narratives; rather we encounter an extending of her life with her mother. As she explains, her title, *With my Mother*, shows that her mother is still with her even after her death: 'Now that she is not there, I continue living with her' (76).

Conclusion

All of the writers analysed here used their writing not only as a means of healing but also as an instrument to help them to understand themselves better. Writing about their loved ones brings memories of their past together and those memories restore them to their present, to who they are now. The narratives studied here were all published about eighteen months after the death of the loved one. Apart from Allende, the authors started writing them a few months after the relevant death and the writing process did not take very long. They needed time before they started writing but once they had started, the need to write those memories made it easier to put down.

Catherine Sanders recognises five phases of bereavement: 1, 'Shock – The Impact of Grief'; 2, 'Awareness of Loss'; 3, 'Conservation – Withdrawal'; 4, 'Healing – The Turning Point'; and 5, 'Renewal' (1999: 49–113). John S. Stephenson identifies three periods: 1, 'Reaction'; 2, 'Disorganization and Reorganization'; and 3, 'Reorientation and Recovery' (1985: 131–41). In the works studied, we can see how writing begins after the first shock or reaction, as the awareness of loss instigates the writing, while Sanders' conservation/ withdrawal, or the disorganisation/reorganisation in Stephenson's schema, will drive the writing later. The writing process brings the writers to the turning point or reorientation and this will usher in the final stages of renewal or recovery.[10] As DeSalvo explains: 'Through writing, we allow ourselves to move through the most important aspects of mourning – but at a safe and symbolic distance [...]. We engage in searching for exact, concrete details and language evocative enough to communicate' (56).

We have seen how at the beginning of the writing process, in most cases, authors are looking for answers, trying to make sense of their loss. The end of the narratives brings a clear phase of recovery or being able to go on with their lives even though their memories of their loved ones will never leave them. As Maier comments on Allende's writing, 'the very act of writing serves as a creative, therapeutic release to help the author cope with personal tragedy and go through mourning to renew both her faith in life and her literary career' (Maier 2003: 237); this could be applied to the other writers studied in this chapter.

Notes

1. We find memoirs written after the death of a loved one in earlier decades but these are rarer. The following could serve as examples: C.S. Lewis, as will be discussed in this chapter, published A Grief Observed in 1961 after the death of his wife; Roland Barthes published Camera Lucida in 1980 after his mother's death; and Simone de Beauvoir published Adieux (1984) after Sartre's death.

2. It is interesting to note how many of the studies on grief started with the loss of a loved one, as Simpson points out in chapter 2 of this volume.

3. Gorer writes: 'In the twentieth century, however, there seems to have been an unremarked shift in prudery; whereas copulation has become more and more "mentionable", particularly in the Anglo-Saxon societies, death has become more and more "unmentionable" as a natural process' (1987: 171–72, emphasis in the original).

4. American politicians such as Barak Obama or Colin Powell and personalities such as Steve Jobs' biographies are amongst those on the bestsellers lists.

5. The work of James Pennebaker on writing therapy in the 1980s and 1990s is considered one of the most important studies on the writing cure.

6. Her daughter Quintana died of pancreatitis on August 2005, before Didion finished writing the book.

7. We can see the use of poetry in grieving or bereavement in Eleanor David's chapter in this volume.

8. This is the day of the year when Allende starts a new book as she explains: 'partly out of superstition, but also for reasons of discipline. I have begun all my books on January 8' (Allende 1996b: 9).

9. All translations from *Con mi madre* are mine.

10. Simpson, in chapter 2 of this volume (p. 25), points out how 'currently, researchers and clinicians seem divided on the usefulness of phase theories of mourning'.

Bibliography

Allende, I. 1996a [1994]. *Paula*. Barcelona: Plaza & Janés.

———. 1996b. *Paula*, trans. Margaret Sayers Peden. New York: Harper Perennial.

Barthes, R. 2000 [1980]. *Camera Lucida*, trans. R. Howard. London: Vintage.

Bayley, J. 1999. *Elegy for Iris*. New York: Picador.

Berman, J. 2010. *Companionship in Grief: Love and Loss in the Memoirs of C.S. Lewis, John Bayley, Donald Hall, Joan Didion and Calvin Trillin*. Amherst and Boston: University of Massachusetts Press.

Bolton, G. 1999. *The Therapeutic Potential of Creative Writing*. London: Jessica Kingsley.

Brockes, E. 2005. 'Interview: Joan Didion', *The Guardian*, 16 December 2005. Accessed on 9 July 2012, http://www.guardian.co.uk/film/2005/dec/16/biography.features

De Beauvoir, S. 1984 [1981]. *Adieux: A Farewell to Sartre*, trans. Patrick O'Brian. New York: Pantheon.

De Salvo, L. 1999. *Writing as a Way of Healing*. London: Women's Press.

Didion, Joan. 2011 [2005]. *The Year of Magical Thinking*. London: Fourth State.

———. 2011. *Blue Nights*. London: Harper Collins.

Fishbane, E. 2011. *Shadows in Winter: A Memoir of Love and Loss*. New York: Syracuse University Press.

Gilbert, S.M. 1995. *Wrongful Death*. New York and London: W.W. Norton & Company.

Gorer, G. 1987 [1965]. *Death, Grief and Mourning in Contemporary Britain*. Salem, New Hampshire: Ayer Company.

Hall, D. 2005. *The Best Day the Worst Day*. New York: Houghton Mifflin Company.

Hunt, C. 2000. *Therapeutic Dimensions of Autobiography in Creative Writing*. London: Jessica Kingsley.

Lawson, M. 2010. 'Writing a Way through Grief', *The Guardian*, 12 March 2010. Accessed on 9 July 2012, http://www.guardian.co.uk/commentisfree/2010/mar/12/bereavement-grief-books-biography-death

Lepore, S.J. and J.M. Smith. 2002. *The Writing Cure: How Expressive Writing Promotes Health and Emotional Well-Being*. Washington DC: American Psychological Association.

Lewis, C.S. 1966 [1961]. *A Grief Observed*. London: Faber and Faber.

Maier, L.S. 2003. 'Mourning Becomes "Paula": The Writing Process as Therapy for Isabel Allende', *Hispania* 86(2): 237–43.

Oates, J.C. 2011. *A Widow's Story*. Waterville, Maine: Thorndike.

O'Rourke, M. 2011. *The Long Goodbye: A Memoir of Grief*. London: Virago.

Pennebaker, J.W. 2004. *Writing to Heal: A Guided Journal for Recovering from Trauma and Emotional Upheaval*. Oakland, California: New Harbinger.

Puértolas, S. 2001. *Con mi Madre*. Barcelona: Círculo de Lectores.

Sanders, C. 1999. *Grief, The Mourning After: Dealing with Adult Bereavement*. New York: John Wiley and Sons.

Stephenson, J.S. 1985. *Death, Grief and Mourning: Individual and Social Realities*. New York: Macmillan.

Trillin, C. 2006. *About Alice*. New York: Random House.

Want, B. 2010. *Why Not Me?* London: Weidenfeld & Nicolson.

5

A Way of Sorrows for the Twentieth Century

Margherita Guidacci's *La Via Crucis dell'umanità*

Eleanor David

~~~~~~~

This chapter focuses on the Italian twentieth-century poet Margherita Guidacci (1921–1992), and the continual tension in her poetry between religious faith, loss and trauma. In particular, it considers the effect of such a tension on her poetic language, an aspect which has yet to be fully explored by critics.

My analysis centres on one of Guidacci's later poetic collections, which places a strong emphasis on the civic role of poetry in a commemorative context. *La Via Crucis dell'umanità* (1984) uses the structure of the Stations of the Cross to address contemporary suffering and death, with overt references to Hiroshima, J.F. Kennedy and Martin Luther King. Guidacci makes consistent use of Biblical motifs and lexicon throughout as a potential means of 'translating' these traumas and instances of collective suffering.[1] The textual examples drawn from this collection, which illustrate the complex interplay between religion, politics and death in Guidacci's work, are considered here within the framework of trauma theory, where the use of studies by figures such as Cathy Caruth, Jenny Edkins, Ann Kaplan and Dominick LaCapra aims to contribute to a fuller understanding of loss in Guidacci's poetry. *La Via Crucis* does not merely constitute a verbal interpretation of death; the poems are also a written commentary on the Italian priest and artist Leonardo Rosito's 1984 series of Florentine bronze bas-relief sculptures of the same name. As such, I will also give space in this chapter to a discussion of the resultant dialogue between visual and verbal codes.

I argue here that Guidacci's work makes for a particularly fascinating case study in modern commemorative poetry, as she interrogates issues of death, genocide, collective mourning and civic duty within the framework of one of the most fundamental Christian devotions. Indeed, what becomes clear in Guidacci's re-writing of the 'Via Crucis' is that these are not the traditional Stations of Christ that allude to man, but rather the Stations of Twentieth-Century Man that are reflected in Christ's journey.

Guidacci's early years were dominated by two elements in particular. The first, somewhat proleptic of her future career, is her literary precociousness. An intellectually curious and creative child, by the age of eight, Guidacci had already written a number of short stories and plays (Del Serra 2005: 8–9). The second element involves another reality linked with familial loss. In 1931, as a young child, Guidacci lost her father to cancer. The subsequent death in 1977 of her husband Luca Pinna, whom she had married in 1949, was to further darken her life and had a profound effect on her poetry, which maintains a distinctly melancholy quality throughout. Guidacci describes the conflation of beginning and ending occasioned by her father's death thus: 'I knew what it meant to wither before I knew what it meant to flourish; I had seen death before I had seen life [...] without being able to detach my gaze from the end which awaits us on this earth' (1999a: 8).[2] A palpable 'sense of an ending' (to use a term from Frank Kermode [1966]) thus pervaded not only Guidacci's poetic output, but also her biography from the outset. Furthermore, this tendency towards conclusion, death and finitude, identified by Guidacci as a central tenet of her personal and poetic perspective, was also one she associated with the work of the influential Italian twentieth-century poet Eugenio Montale, saying that 'No one quite like him has been the poet of an ending world' (Del Serra 2005: 11).[3] Guidacci's early biography, coloured by experiences of loss, also bears a striking resemblance to that of Giuseppe Ungaretti, a highly influential figure in the landscape of Italian twentieth-century poetry. Ungaretti was born to Italian parents in Egypt in 1888, and described his own early childhood as indelibly defined by the process of constant mourning occasioned by his father's death, a tragedy that occurred when the poet was just two years old (Piccioni 1979: 23).

The link established here between Guidacci and Ungaretti is by no means a casual one and extends far beyond mere similarities in their biographical circumstances. Guidacci wrote her undergraduate thesis at the University of Florence on the symbolist resonances in Ungaretti's first major collection of philosophical war poetry *L'Allegria* (1914–1919) [*The Joy*], a thesis which she successfully defended in 1943.[4] In terms of the topic at hand, both poets are united by their aim to express loss in its various forms through poetry, though an in-depth, comparative analysis of the work of the two poets is unfortunately beyond the scope of the present study. In Ungaretti's case, the treatment of loss and death in his work ranges from bereavement in the First World War and the search for a 'lost' identity in his first major collection *L'Allegria*, through the overwhelming sense of emptiness which the Roman landscapes engender in the poetic subject of *Sentimento del tempo* (1933) (*Feeling of Time*), towards his middle and late style (1939–1970), typified by a distinct intensification, and more mature development, of a melancholy subjectivity. Beyond the Ungarettian model, the influences on Guidacci's work are numerous, and into her poetry is woven a dense and complex web of intertextual references. Her readings include the Bible, Dante, Petrarch, Leopardi, Pascoli, Rilke's elegiac poems and a great number of English-speaking poets, including John Donne, Emily Dickinson and T.S. Eliot.

Guidacci's own poetry quickly gained critical acclaim: she received Italian literary prizes – the 'Premio Carducci' in 1957, and the 'Premio Il Ceppo' in 1971 for her 1970 collection *Neurosuite*. This collection recounts Guidacci's *discesa negli inferi* [descent into hell], that is to say, the time she spent in a psychiatric hospital in the late 1960s.[5] In *Neurosuite*, the poetic voice continually shifts between the personal and the collective as Guidacci, in offering her own story of psychological crisis, expresses a sense of solidarity with others who suffer from the alienating and solipsistic anxiety of depression. Following the cathartic experience of suffering recounted in *Neurosuite*, the 1980s sees a new Guidaccian poetics typified by a renewed force and a pronounced sense of civic duty, as the examples from *La Via Crucis* attest.

In 1976 Guidacci visited Colmar and saw Grünewald's 'Isenheim Altarpiece', which inspired her 1980 collection of the same name. *L'Altare di Isenheim* [*Isenheim Altarpiece*], an important collection in Guidacci's poetic trajectory of trauma, is a symphonic long poem that draws inspiration from the cycles illustrated by the altarpiece's panels, depicting in varying order the Crucifixion, Annunciation, Resurrection, the Temptation of St Anthony and others. It also includes a section entitled 'Un addio' ['A farewell'] dedicated to Guidacci's dead husband and concludes with 'Plus', a formally experimental fugal poem in free verse. The very experience of seeing the altarpiece was traumatic for Guidacci and she was plagued by anxious dreams following the event.[6] Evidence of trauma remains in the text as there is a recurring tension between an awareness of the symbolic relevance of the situations depicted on the one hand, and the shocking physicality and inescapable horror of Grünewald's images, on the other.

Guidacci places a particular emphasis on the light-darkness duality central to the Christian idiom in the later collections *Inno alla gioia* (1983) [*Hymn to Joy*] and *Il buio e lo splendore* (1989) [*Darkness and Splendour*].

Margherita Guidacci has been largely neglected by scholarship on Italian twentieth-century poetry and religious discourse. The balance has been somewhat redressed by the publication of the proceedings from a series of study days in Florence in 1999 and by a number of recent monographs and essays.[7] Translations by Ruth Feldman (1992) and Catherine O'Brien (1993) have also helped to bring her to the attention of the English-speaking world. By focusing on the tension between death and religious faith in her poetry, and by bringing her work into dialogue with contemporary trauma theory for the first time, I hope here to evoke a more general interest in Guidacci's work as a whole.

Guidacci's poetry engages with the issue of trauma in a number of significant ways. Trauma studies encompasses a wide range of disciplines, and, as in the case of Caruth (1996) and LaCapra (2001),[8] often draws heavily on the psychoanalytical model of subjectivity, that is to say, of the subject as formed around a fundamental lack. While definitions of what constitutes trauma are numerous, one of the most pervasive is that proposed by Caruth: 'In its general definition, trauma is described as the response to an unexpected or overwhelming violent event or events that are not fully grasped as they occur, but return later in repeated flashbacks, nightmares, and other repetitive phenomena' (1996: 91), elements of which will be important as we turn to a discussion of Guidacci's poetic approach to trauma.

Guidacci's *Via Crucis* aims to bear witness to some of the twentieth century's most traumatic episodes, from the death of influential individuals, to unspeakable tragedies such as the Holocaust. In so doing, Guidacci directly confronts and engages with many of the debates surrounding testimony and responses to trauma which have been recently theorised by trauma studies. Indeed it is the Second World War which becomes a fundamental reference point for trauma critics in the second half of the twentieth century. In considering the atrocities of the Holocaust and Hiroshima, two central issues surrounding the problem of 'translating trauma' have emerged with great force. Theodor Adorno's famous contention that post-1945 poetry was impossible points to the concept of the 'unrepresentable', in turn linked to what Caruth later terms the 'incomprehensibility' of the trauma experience (1996: 92). At the same time, there exists a (perhaps seemingly paradoxical) imperative to somehow bear witness and to commemorate, a tension which may be linked to what Edkins defines as the 'chasm between the duty to speak and the impossibility of speech' (2003: 177). The position of the speaking subject therefore emerges as paramount in the problem of how to bear witness, particularly as the only 'true' witnesses might be considered to be Primo Levi's '*sommersi*' ['drowned'], those who do not survive (Felman and Laub 1992: 139). The problem of adequate and just testimony and commemoration might also be thought of in terms of their rather complex relationship to memory: in addition to the obstacle of finding an appropriate linguistic means through which to translate trauma, there is often a further tension between a deliberate forgetting of the event, on the one hand, and a strong imperative to remember, on the other.

Many of the texts addressed by the above theorists tend to be narrative or cinematic in terms of genre (for example, Levi's *Se questo è un uomo* [1947] [*Is This a Man?*], Marguerite Duras' *Hiroshima mon amour* [1960] and Claude Lanzmann's film *Shoah* [1985]).[9] I argue that there is room for creating a critical space in which modern poetry, particularly that of the Italian tradition, might be considered as a rightful part of this framework, and I consider Guidacci's religious poetry a particularly stimulating case study in this field.

Traditionally, trauma critics, such as LaCapra, have associated 'keeping faith with trauma' with the problem of the 'hiddenness, death, or absence of a radically transcendent divinity' (LaCapra 2001: 23). In these terms, religious faith, and, by extension, the affirmative use of liturgical language in a non-ironic and potentially consolatory system of symbolisation, might be associated with a 'coming to terms' or a sense of triumphant mastery over the disruptive presence of trauma. I would like to suggest here that Guidacci's poetry makes for an especially interesting case in this regard. Alongside her religious faith and systematic recourse to Christian motifs and linguistic codes, the recurrent representations of trauma in her poetry, both personal and collective, attest to a more complex melancholy strand in her work.

In Guidacci's work, a number of interesting issues emerge in relation to trauma and its relationship to religious discourse: her poetry frequently involves the interplay between personal and collective trauma and the roles of the listener and witness become somewhat conflated. The language of liturgy thus becomes Guidacci's way of trying to ascribe meaning to traumatic events which often resist this kind of symbolising practice.

In her attempt to linguistically codify trauma, Guidacci retains a strong fidelity to the scale of suffering involved and to the issue of altered temporality, as we see in particular in the example of her poetic collection *L'orologio di Bologna* [*The Bologna Clock*], which is structured around the central motif of the clock stopped at 10.25 on 2 August 1980, marking the time of a terrorist attack which killed 85 and injured more than 200. In this collection time is presented as cyclical, non-linear and repetitive, symbolised in the liturgical refrains collected in the 'Echi Finali' section such as 'Alto si leva il lamento sopra le nostre vie' (1999a: 329) ['The cry is raised high above our roads']. Trauma does not, in Edkins' terms, 'fit the story we already have' (2003: xiv). This is particularly the case with the terrorist attack to which Guidacci makes reference in *L'orologio* (the 1980 Bologna bombing), as this not only threatens the individual, but the state at large, and notions of temporality and redemption become forever altered.

The persistent recurrence of responses to trauma throughout Guidacci's work also poses an interesting question concerning the nature of trauma itself. According to Freud (and later Caruth, LaCapra and others who draw on the Freudian heritage), the original traumatic event cannot be known in that moment, it exists through its very repetition: 'the trauma as experience is "in" the repetition of an early event in a later event – an early event for which one was not prepared to feel anxiety and a later event that somehow recalls the early one and triggers a traumatic response' (LaCapra 2001: 81–82) A traumatic event in the present also has the potential to therefore trigger an earlier trauma; in Caruth's terms, the 'story of trauma [may be seen] then, as the narrative of a belated experience' (1996: 7).

Guidacci's work also explores what occurs when the trauma being referenced was not experienced by a 'first-degree' witness. LaCapra draws a very clear distinction between victims, perpetrators and bystanders in his work (2001: 114–40). In her study, Kaplan gives more space to a discussion of the potential for vicarious trauma, particularly in the case of the psychoanalyst (2005: 87–100). It seems to me, however, that Felman's term 'second-degree witness' (the witness of witnesses or the witness of the testimonies) is the most suitable for the Guidaccian case (1992: 75).

In her poetry, Guidacci assumes the appointment to bear witness (both to her own traumas and those of others), one which, according to Felman, is 'an appointment to transgress the confines of that isolated stance, to speak for others and to others' (1992: 3). The reason for this self-appointment is twofold: Guidacci chooses to bear witness through poetry both out of a Christian awareness of the importance of commemorating the dead, and out of her recognition of the poet's role as citizen with a strong civic responsibility.[10] Her work looks both backwards (to a Biblical language with its potential universality), and forwards to a world where these traumas will hopefully never have to be repeated, as well as attempting to acknowledge the impact of the traumatic moment itself.

What are the reasons for Guidacci's use of Biblical language in this context? The use of the Biblical idiom might be seen as a means of transferring her frame of reference to temporal and spatial coordinates that are far removed from her twentieth-century subject matter. This means of linguistically translating trauma does not, however, function in her case as a distancing device. It is instead closely bound up with the Guidaccian philosophy of poetry and the poet's own relationship with her Christian faith. According to Guidacci, there are three constants which define her work: 'the thirst for knowledge', a 'desire to communicate' and 'the simplicity and concreteness of expression' (1984: 39–40). It is the very desire for immediacy and a sense of communicative openness expressed here (an interesting contrast to the hermetic poetic climate within which she grew up) that becomes bound up with Guidacci's sustained use of Biblical language and tropes in *La Via Crucis*. For Guidacci, there is an inextricable link between faith, the sacred and the creative impulse. She does not, however, believe in overly abstract or disconnected images, or in the use of Biblical motifs or liturgical language for mere artifice or artistic conceit. Rather, she believes in the strength of the ultimate sacrifice which Jesus our Saviour performed for our deliverance and in the clarity that Biblical language and motifs can afford. The Son of the Father is thus fully accepted by Guidacci as both human and a symbol of God's love for mankind. As Raffaele Crovi states: 'Guidacci always positioned herself counter to an unpersonified or abstract metaphysics, distant from the redemptive ways of eschatology, mysterious and hypnotic (which might be defined nowadays as *new age*: Guidacci believes in the re-consecration of History by Christ, Son of God and Son of Man' (2001: 24).

Guidacci's 1984 collection *La Via Crucis dell'umanità* further develops the traumatic trajectory that defines her work. The Stations of the Cross are liturgically linked to the stations of the Gospel narrative and, whilst there is no one fixed 'text', can be expressed visually or verbally as a mode of following Christ's journey. This devotion thus embodies the subjective-collective binomial common to Guidaccian poetics and reinforces notions of inclusion and identification. Guidacci's Stations are defined as follows:

1. *Caino e Abele* [Cain and Abel]
2. *Strage degli Innocenti* [Massacre of the Innocents]
3. *Passione e Morte di Cristo* [Passion and Death of Christ]
4. *Martiri* [Martyrs]
5. *Incas*
6. *Indios*
7. *Schiavitù* [Slavery]
8. *Deportazioni* [Deportations]
9. *Razzismo* [Racism]
10. Kolbe
11. Gandhi
12. Martin Luther King
13. J.F. Kennedy
14. Hiroshima
15. *Gesù Risorto* [Jesus Resurrected]

Guidacci's *La Via Crucis* is not merely a verbal re-coding of this Christian devotion: the collection functions as a poetic commentary on fifteen bronze panels collected under the same title and produced by the Florentine priest Leonardo Rosito in 1984. There is no doubt that Guidacci is working with the well-established tropes of the Christian tradition with this collection, but hers are not the traditional Stations of the Cross. In a re-writing of the Way of Sorrows for the twentieth century, Guidacci focuses her attention on the fate of the victims of various contemporary tragedies, those named (J.F. Kennedy, Gandhi, Martin Luther King) and those unnamed, in sections entitled 'Deportations', 'Racism' and 'Slavery'.[11]

The third station 'Passion and Death of Christ' appears to be the only one that recalls the original titles and situation of the traditional Stations of the Cross:

Mystery of suffering, mystery of salvation,
mystery of death restoring life.
O Lord, by this Thy sacrifice
let Thy infinite peace descend on us.
When men's roads intersect, they always make a cross.[12] (1999a: 371)

This station is marked by a number of syntactic parallelisms. 'Dolore' [pain] can be linked to 'salvezza' [salvation] in the first line, reinforcing the Christian notion of productive pain. The rhymes in the first two lines unite 'death' and 'pain', and 'salvation' and 'life'. This could, however, be read in terms of a chiasmic structure, thereby foregrounding the idea of universal salvation through Christ's death and simultaneously situating suffering as an inevitable part of human life. The overall balance in syntax reinforces the idea of Jesus' sacrifice as restoring the bond between man and God that was broken by transgressive behaviour in Eden. The bleak simplicity of the related bronze panel's composition reflects these central ideas; it is uncluttered with no markings in the background. The crucified Saviour assumes the central position with the centurion of Mark's Gospel on the left and a blurred mourning figure (most likely Mary Magdalene) at his feet on the right.

Moving away from the traditional Stations, Guidacci and Rosito give artistic space in this rendering of the Via Crucis to both the unnamed and certain eponymous named victims of atrocities in the twentieth-century traumatic landscape. The eighth station 'Deportations' makes clear reference to the Holocaust:

> To migrate by compulsion, driven in herds, like animals,
> to unknown sufferings; then to be received
> by some huge pit, or barely by the air,
> reduced to smoke [...]. (1999a: 373)

In this Station, Guidacci linguistically reinforces the idea that these victims were acted 'upon', as she employs a number of devices that situate agency most definitively with the 'other', the perpetrator. A number of past passive constructions ('driven'; 'received by'; 'reduced to'), serve to highlight the dehumanised (and dehumanising) context of suffering in the *Lager*. The use of the infinitive 'To migrate' rather than a conjugated form of verb also removes the gap between victim and second-degree witness in the text which results in an ambiguity in poetic subjectivity. The enjambment between 'driven / towards' syntactically reflects the idea of an unknown end where any awareness of the destination is delayed.

In Station 11, Guidacci cites Gandhi as an 'example / of such great sanctity' and the poetic text that follows carries a clear echo of the Beatitudes, notably the inheritance of the earth by the meek in Matthew 5:5:

> Perhaps one day the meek will own the earth
> otherwise than being buried in it. (1999a: 374)

In a melancholy re-writing of this Beatitude, with 'buried', Guidacci brings to light a distinct earthliness and more pronounced awareness of the imminence of death than exists in the original Biblical text. We witness a similar use of a historical figure in Station 12 in Guidacci's choice of Martin Luther King:

> For the dream he had dreamt, they killed him.
> but could not kill the dream. Even more holy
> it is made by his blood and even louder
> is now the call of his way.
> Let us walk together, to make the dream come true! (1999a: 374)

The choices made by both Guidacci and Rosito are designed to establish a clear parallel between the outspoken and leaderly characters of Martin Luther King and Jesus. Rosito's artistic interpretation of the former places him in central position on the panel with a group of followers behind him holding his left hand. The image paints Luther King as a shepherd and a leader of men, a common representation of the Messiah in Biblical language (Psalm 23: 'The Lord is my Shepherd'). In the textual interpretation, Guidacci seems to affirm this image and exploits the reader's awareness of the multiple Biblical and historical resonances of particular lexical choices. 'Dream' becomes synonymous with Martin Luther King's eponymous 1963 speech and recalls numerous Biblical oniric episodes. 'Path' brings to mind the Biblical path of the righteous, and the first person plural 'let us walk together' promotes a sense of collective identity and invites the reader's involvement in the suffering and trauma of the subject.[13] A cornerstone of Biblical rhetoric, it is also a clear reference to King's hope that children of all colours might 'walk together as sisters and brothers' ('I Have a Dream', 28 August 1963).

The final two Stations are particularly illustrative of Guidacci's use of Biblical language in this collection and show appositely the deft interweaving of devotional and historical codes. In the fourteenth Station, entitled 'Hiroshima', she establishes a parallel between Golgotha and Hiroshima:

> Have mercy, O Lord, on this convulsed earth,
> [...]
> where any hill may be a Golgotha,
> where any town may be a Hiroshima.[14] (1999a: 375)

By situating both place names at the end of the lines, and through syntactic parallelism, Guidacci is able to strengthen the comparison between the two sites of trauma, separated both geographically and temporally. The anaphoric 'any' also leaves the reader with the frightening reminder common to testimonial literature: that any recurrence of these events would be shocking and yet is hauntingly possible. Visually, there is a striking sense of darkness and confusion in Rosito's pictorial representation of this scene (reflected in Guidacci's 'convulsed earth' of this section's opening line). There is a concentration of fine lines in the carving of the bottom half of the panel depicting destruction and confusion, and a relief dark cloud of atomic destruction rises out of the panel's centre. This provides a stark contrast to the empty outline of the ever-present cross to the left of the atomic cloud which leaves the viewer with a sense of ambiguity which is latent in Guidacci's text. The polyvalent cross might be interpreted as a lone beacon of hope, or may function merely as an empty symbol in the midst of such atrocious human suffering. Furthermore, it could symbolise an awareness of Christian (or more broadly Western) guilt in bombing a non-Christian country.

The language of supplication which opens Station 14 – 'Have mercy, O Lord' – is continued in the ending of the 15th Station, 'Jesus Resurrected', where Guidacci quotes directly from the Liturgy of the Eucharist: 'Dying you destroyed death / Teach us Your resurrection' (1999a: 375), thereby highlighting one of the central tensions of her work: that between suffering and death, on the one hand, and God's grace and the possibility of transformation and transcendence, on the other. The composition of the final panel is markedly different to the others in Rosito's series. The image of Jesus' face takes up the entire panel, and there is no attempt on the part of the artist to insert any form of relational commentary; the one image of Christ with its symbolic power is left to resonate with the viewer.

Guidacci's *Via Crucis* is a striking case in modern commemorative poetry, as she interrogates issues of death, genocide, collective mourning and civic duty within the framework of one of the most fundamental Christian devotions, the Stations of the Cross. Guidacci and Rosito draw on the traditional Passion narrative, but depart from it, using some of the defining twentieth-century traumas as reference points on a Via Dolorosa which comes to symbolise modern man and the atrocities endured by both named and unnamed victims.

In conclusion, I will draw on Guidacci's own words regarding the relationship between temporality and Biblical reference, from a 1983 interview:

> This means that, beyond religious interest, I was driven by similar motives to other poets who are inspired by classical myths: that is, the imperative to have wide-ranging and well-established structures into which to put one's own content [...]. The characters and episodes from the Bible have always seemed to me to be so full of meaning across all time periods, including our own, that I have always been surprised that contemporary poetry does not make more use of them.[15] (1999b: 139)

By expressing the discontinuity of the traumatic experience through the medium of Biblical motifs and the language of liturgy, Guidacci is able to align it with a more timeless, almost mythical temporality. For the poet, this is not an escapist way of avoiding contemporary historical reality; it is quite the reverse. It allows her to produce a civic commemorative poetry which is both grounded in the trauma par excellence of the Christian tradition, that of Christ's crucifixion, and in some of the most defining traumas of the twentieth century.

Maurice Blanchot, in *The Writing of the Disaster*, said: 'Know what has happened, do not forget, and at the same time never will you know' (1986: xiii). When considering traumatic events, it seems that complete comprehension or closure is impossible. In her poetry, Guidacci assumes the role of a witness-listener, in a process that 'involves a kind of virtual experience through which one puts oneself in the other's position while recognizing the difference of that position' (LaCapra 2001: 78). Through the sustained use of religious language and tropes, Guidacci engages with the problem of how trauma may be represented through the medium of literature. In LaCapra's terms: 'Trauma brings about a dissociation of affect and representation: one disorientatingly feels what one cannot represent; one numbingly represents what one cannot feel. Working through trauma involves the effort to articulate or rearticulate affect and representation in a manner that may never transcend, but may to some viable extent counteract, a reenactment, or acting out, of that dissociation' (42).

Guidacci's poetry engages with this performative effort to articulate, whilst never simplistically claiming to transcend; rather, it acts out and engages with that dissociation, drawing out tensions between finitude and transcendence, between despair and hope. Her multi-layered portrayal of the problem of witnessing and commemorating makes a rich and undervalued contribution to the poetic landscape of twentieth-century religious poetry.

Notes

1. These collections and subsequent Italian quotations from Guidacci's poetry can be found in Guidacci (1999a). All translations from Italian into English in this chapter are my own, unless otherwise stated.

2. This statement originally appeared in an article entitled 'La morte come vita' ['Death as Life'] (*Il Popolo*, 5 January 1958).

3. As Lynne Simpson argues elsewhere in this volume, grief itself can be defined as pathological, a counter-argument for the traditional Freudian mourning-melancholia binary that has been explored by many post-Freudian theorists and commentators.

4. Guidacci's 1945 meeting with Ungaretti is documented in Del Serra (2005: 11).

5. Obvious parallels may be drawn here in the Italian poetic tradition with Amelia Rosselli's 1969 *Serie ospedaliera* and Mario Luzi's *Su fondamenti invisibili* of 1971.

6. Guidacci's full testimony of her reaction to the altarpiece can be found in Magherini (2001: 122–23). In the same passage, she refers to the visual stimulus of Grünewald's work as paradoxically both the cause of, and the cure for, this unsettling reaction, highlighting the potential therapeutic function that writing the poem might afford (123). For a detailed discussion of writing as therapy, see Maria-José Blanco's contribution in the present volume.

7. See Del Serra (2005), Pieracci Harwell (1991) and Mazzanti (1997). A selection of Guidacci's own prose writings and interviews have also been recently published (Guidacci 1999b), as well as a catalogue of a 1999 Florentine exhibition dedicated to Guidacci (Ghilardi 1999).

8. These works situate Freud's writings on hysteria and on the repetition compulsion (such as in *Beyond the Pleasure Principle* and *On Moses and Monotheism*) as some of the founding texts in the

'trauma' tradition. Other important recent studies on trauma, the problem of bearing witness, and personal and civic commemorative practices to which I refer in my argument include Edkins (2003) and Felman and Laub (1992).

9. One notable exception to this pattern is 'Poetry and Testimony: Paul Celan, or The Accidenting of Aesthetics', in Felman and Laub (1992: 25–42).

10. This civic responsibility is one which Wolfgang Marx also identifies in the composers involved in the *Requiem of Reconciliation*; see chapter 3 in this volume.

11. Guidacci's engagement with commemorative poetry has clearly transcended instances of personal loss in the poet's own life, leading her to write poetry that engages with contemporary tragedies in this collection and in *L'orologio di Bologna* in particular. A similar move from individual to collective concerns is also explored by Wolfgang Marx in his contribution on war requiems in chapter 3 of this volume.

12. The English translations of Guidacci's stations are © http://www.umilta.net/crosstations. html, unless otherwise stated.

13. Guidacci's sustained use of the first person plural in this collection might be compared to what Wolfgang Marx defines in chapter 3 of this volume as the 'unifying' function of the war requiem. According to Marx, the requiem mass acts as a 'symbol of reconciliation', bringing together audiences and performers in an act of commemoration.

14. The English translation is my own.

15. Guidacci is speaking here about Biblical references in *L'altare di Isenheim* and *L'orologio di Bologna* in particular.

Bibliography

Blanchot, M. 1986. *The Writing of the Disaster*, trans. A. Smock. Lincoln: University of Nebraska Press.

Caruth, C. 1996. *Unclaimed Experience: Trauma, Narrative and History*. Baltimore: Johns Hopkins University Press.

Crovi, R. 2001. 'Il sacro nella poesia di Margherita Guidacci', in M. Ghilardi (ed.), *Per Margherita Guidacci: Atti delle Giornate di Studio Lyceum Club, Firenze, 15-16 ottobre 1999*. Florence: Le Lettere, pp. 23–32.

Del Serra, M. 2005. *Le foglie della Sibilla: Scritti su Margherita Guidacci*. Rome: Studium.

Dickinson, E. 1979. *Poesie*, trans. M. Guidacci. Milan: Rizzoli.

Edkins, J. 2003. *Trauma and the Memory of Politics*. Cambridge: Cambridge University Press.

Felman, S. and D. Laub. 1992. *Testimony: Crises of Witnessing in Literature, Psychoanalysis and History*. London: Routledge.

Ghilardi, M. (ed.). 1999. *Margherita Guidacci. La parola e le immagini, Firenze, Lyceum 15-23 ottobre 1999, Scarperia, 30 ottobre-14 novembre 1999, mostra documentaria e catalogo*. Florence: Polistampa.

_____. 2001. 'Bibliografia degli scritti di Margherita Guidacci', in M. Ghilardi (ed). *Per Margherita Guidacci: Atti delle Giornate di Studio Lyceum Club, Firenze, 15-16 ottobre 1999*. Florence: Le Lettere, pp. 277–85.

Guidacci, M. 1958. 'La morte come vita' [Death as life], in *Il Popolo*, 5 January 1958.

_____. 1984. *Quinta Generazione* a.XII, 125-6, November-December, 39–40.

_____. 1992. *Landscape With Ruins: Selected Poetry of Margherita Guidacci*, trans. R. Feldman. Detroit: Wayne State University Press.

_____. 1993. *In the Eastern Sky: Selected Poems of Margherita Guidacci*, trans. C. O'Brien. Dublin: Dedalus.

_____. 1999a. *Le poesie*, ed. M. Del Serra. Florence: Le Lettere.

_____. 1999b. *Prose e interviste*, ed. I. Rabatti. Pistoia: C.R.T.

Kaplan, E.A. 2005. *Trauma Culture: The Politics of Terror and Loss in Media and Literature*. New Brunswick; New Jersey; London: Rutgers University Press.

Kermode, F. 1966. *The Sense of an Ending: Studies in the Theory of Fiction*. New York: OUP.

LaCapra, D. 2001. *Writing History, Writing Trauma*. Baltimore: Johns Hopkins University Press.

Magherini, G. 2001. 'Pertubante estetico e creazione artistica. Margherita Guidacci e L'altare di Isenheim', in M. Ghilardi (ed.), *Per Margherita Guidacci: Atti delle Giornate di Studio Lyceum Club, Firenze, 15-16 ottobre 1999*. Florence: Le Lettere, pp. 119–34.

Mazzanti, G. 1997. 'Tra pienezza e declino: l'esperienza poetica e religiosa di Margherita Guidacci', in G. Ladolphi et al. (eds), *Il sacro nella poesia contemporanea*. Novara: Interlinea, pp. 91–100.

Piccioni, L. 1979. *Vita di Ungaretti*. Milan: Rizzoli.

Pieracci Harwell, M. 1991. 'L'opera di Margherita Guidacci', in M. Pieracci Harwell (ed.), *Un cristiano senza chiesa e altri saggi*. Rome: Studium, pp. 151–96.

6

FROM SELF-ERASURE TO SELF-AFFIRMATION
Communally Acknowledged 'Good Death' in Ernest Gaines's *A Lesson Before Dying*

Corina Crisu

The anticipation of death and dying figured into the experiences of black folk so persistently, given how much more omnipresent death was for them than for other Americans, that lamentation and mortification both found their way into public and private representations of African America to an astonishing degree [....] Black culture's stories of death and dying were inextricably linked to the ways in which the nation experienced, perceived, and represented African America. Sometimes it was a subtext, but even then the ghostly presence of those narratives reminded us that something about America was, for black folk, disjointed. Instead of death and dying being unusual, untoward events, or despite being inevitable end-of-lifespan events, the cycles of our daily lives were so persistently interrupted by spectres of death that we worked this experience into the culture's iconography and included it as an aspect of black cultural sensibility. (Holloway 2003: 6)

Our individual fragile lives are made stronger in the process of shared meaning about life and death. (McNamara 2001: 42)

In a growing field of study on the representation of death in literature and cultural studies, critics such as Sharon Patricia Holland, Karla F.C. Holloway, Orlando Patterson and Anissa Janine Wardi pay special attention to the racial, social and psychological aspects of black death and to its complex representations in African American narratives – in works where writing takes place at the unstable boundary between the world of the living and that of the dead. These critics consider the omnipresence of death in African American culture and its intricate literary depictions in texts described as 'complicated requiems', which offer 'readings of death – as a cultural and national phenomenon or discourse' (Wardi 2003: 134; Holland 2000: 5).

'Ceremonies of proper burial' – this is how an important number of contemporary African American novels can be subtly defined, taking into account their constant preoccupation with death, from preparations and rituals surrounding death and dying to funeral practices and mourning ceremonies (Matus 1998: 2). The multiple modulations of the death leitmotif are to be found in literary masterpieces written by Ernest Gaines, Charles Johnson, Toni Morrison, Ishmael Reed, Alice Walker, John Edgar Wideman, Sherley Anne Williams and many others. These writers feel the need to rewrite a literary tradition, to fill in its silences and gaps and retell those unspeakable events and 'proceedings too terrible to relate' (Morrison 1987: 109).

Read together, these contemporary authors chart a historical map of the most significant moments in black history, attesting to a violent past 'persistently interrupted by spectres of death' – from past episodes of mass murder during the Middle Passage, to present-day unjust applications of the death penalty (Holloway 2003: 6). The authors reveal how the combination of racial injustice and violence against African Americans still influences their perception of death, how a history of oppression, segregation and violence has left its imprint on their representation of death and mourning.

As Holloway stresses, instead of being an unusual limit experience, death becomes the abnormal norm, a recurrent theme in black people's lives, making them reconsider its meaning and its temporal reference. This is why contemporary authors pay attention not only to the single moment of 'passing away', but also to the 'before' and the 'after', to the preparation for death, its impact on others and the subsequent process of coping with grief and the possibility of healing.

Dealing with Death: The Cohesiveness of the Community

As its emblematic title suggests, A Lesson Before Dying is a novel about the preparation for death, about the temporal limbo in the main character's life, when he has to wait for his death sentence and execution. The title also suggests that this is not simply a novel about one individual's way of facing death, but a novel about the community's way of 'handling' death – of understanding the profound significance of its 'lesson'. While treating in depth the racial and social implications of capital punishment, Gaines makes us aware of the meaning of death as a culturally mediated and socially constructed notion, by showing the cohesiveness of the black community, its 'shared fragility' and 'frailty in the face of death', its collective way of dealing with death and grief and of influencing individual responses (McNamara 2001: 1, 4).

Gaines chooses the period of the late 1940s: a difficult time characterised by post-war economic uncertainty and racial tensions in a segregated South where Jim Crow laws prevailed and black civil rights were still unrecognised. Documenting the violent changes of the time, Gaines describes an event that shakes a small Louisiana Cajun community: the trial of a young black man, Jefferson, who is accidentally involved in shooting a white storekeeper. Even though he is innocent, Jefferson is accused of murder and condemned to death in the electric chair several months later. During his imprisonment, Jefferson is able to reinvent himself and proves to be a glowing example of humanity for both the black and the white characters. He appears as a symbolic person whose emancipatory movement from physical bondage to spiritual liberation takes place within the circumscribed area of panoptic white power.

Gaines's choice of the 1940s – just after the Second World War and before the Civil Rights Movement – is not accidental. This troubled chapter in black history is placed into perspective and made relevant to the contemporary reader by disclosing how little has improved, how old mentalities have survived and how the chances of receiving the death penalty are still dictated by racial factors.

Drawing on a variety of African American studies, thanatology studies, as well as on philosophical and ethical views, this chapter analyses the way in which capital punishment – which acquires the special meaning of a heroic lesson – can offer the possibility of crossing social and racial lines. The chapter discusses in particular the African Americans' understanding of death and how the novel focuses not simply on an individual's view on death, but on the interaction between him and a whole community, mostly on how the community has the strength to influence his perception of death and make him stand as a hero.

By redrawing the negative image of the black male –outcast, criminal, prisoner – and his inner transformation while awaiting death, Gaines moves away from Richard Wright's Sartrean, existentialist tradition, where the individual is left alone in the face of death and where there is no prospect of transcending subjectivity.[1] Whereas Wright's Native Son (1940) is set in Chicago after the Great Migration (a cityscape where his protagonist, Bigger, becomes alienated from the others), Gaines's setting is a Southern town in the late 1940s (a rural community that helps Jefferson and gives him guidance in his final hours). While Wright places his hero in a communal void and the main theme of his novel encodes 'the inability of the individual to find satisfactory fellowship in the group', Gaines stresses the connection between his hero and the others (Ford 1970: 29).

As I will demonstrate, the indestructible relationship between Jefferson and the community represents the key issue in understanding his inner conversion and ultimately his way of approaching death and dying. As the novel subtly suggests, there are different types of death, as well as different – creative or destructive – ways of approaching it. Death becomes a many-layered notion and it does not simply take the form of *biological* death (in Jefferson's case a premature and violent death), but also that of *social* death (which is related to Jefferson's marginal status and lack of interaction with the others) and *heroic death* (which refers to Jefferson's inner transformation and symbolic 'lesson' for the others).

There is a long, thorny path from Jefferson's initial apathy to his final words: 'Tell Nannan I walked' (254). At the beginning, Jefferson experiences a form of social death, in which self-deprecating images correspond to a refusal to communicate with the others. Gradually, through the others' united efforts, channelled towards a collective project of spiritual redemption, Jefferson becomes aware of the uselessness of his anger and acknowledges that a courageous, dignified attitude is the ultimate solution. Self-erasure is replaced by self-affirmation, as expressed by the hero's final gesture of overcoming the determinism of social forces.

Significantly, Gaines does not simply restore Jefferson's dignity, humanity and sense of liberation. He also places him in the middle of a supportive community, in a religious environment, where his heroic death and redemption resonate deeply in the others' consciences. Jefferson's final words inscribed in his journal can be understood as a 'lesson' that encompasses a *peratology* – a science of crossing one's limits – in which the student/teacher roles are interchangeable.

'Hiding from Humanity': Social Death

In *Raising the Dead: Readings of Death and (Black) Subjectivity*, Sharon Patricia Holland correlates the idea of invisibility and social death with the lack of social status for African Americans. Combining Toni Morrison's *Playing in the Dark: Whiteness and the Literary Imagination* and Orlando Patterson's *Slavery and Social Death*, Holland discusses the invisibility of African Americans, their marginal(ised), peripheral existence, located in a social 'outdoors' or 'outside' (2000: 17). African Americans inhabit the metaphorical territory of the margins, where the silence and abjection of the literal dead are 'mapped onto the literal and figurative silence of the excluded and marginalized' (150). Holland's insistence on 'life in death', on 'the possibility of being among the dead in the course of living', highlights the connection between racial status, existential marginality and social death (17, 18).

In *A Lesson Before Dying*, social death does appear as the result of a lack of social status: the main character's subordinate status which is 'culturally determined by expectations coming from the opposite world, that of whiteness' (Draga 2000: 41). The writer portrays a young male character who seems to 'hide from humanity', by experiencing feelings of anger and shame – feelings triggered by the racist views of others (Nussbaum 2004: 173).

In prison, Jefferson appears as a lonely, victimised, orphaned character, a naïve young man who suffers undeservedly, an innocent protagonist wrongly accused and sentenced to die. Even if he is accidentally involved in the shooting of a white man, even if the defence calls him 'an innocent bystander', the prosecutor keeps stressing Jefferson's premeditated crime, placing his story in a stereotypical scenario where he presumably plays the role of the 'bad Nigger'. Jefferson's attempt to establish the truth is useless, his testimony does not count:

> A white man had been killed during a robbery, and though two of the robbers had been killed on the spot, one had been captured, and he, too, would have to die. Though he told them no, he had nothing to do with it, that he was on his way to the White Rabbit Bar and Lounge when Brother and Bear drove up beside him and offered him a ride. After he got into the car, they asked him if he had any money. When he told them he didn't have a solitary dime, it was then that Brother and Bear started talking credit, saying that old Gropé should not mind crediting them a pint since he knew them well, and he knew that the grinding season was coming soon, and they would be able to pay him back then (4).

Noticeably, Jefferson's friends do not commit a premeditated crime, since their only intention is to have a drink. As the white storekeeper refuses to offer them alcohol, a shooting ensues where all three are killed. Left alone at the scene of the crime, Jefferson acts unintentionally, in a state of prostrated bewilderment. His half-conscious decision to have a drink and get the money from the counter stigmatises him in the white people's eyes as a criminal, a drunkard and a robber for whom capital punishment seems to be the right decision.

Without social and moral status, Jefferson suffers another humiliation in jail: he is deprived of his manhood, his intelligence and his humanity. This blow does not come from the prosecution, but from the defence that uses the argument of racial inferiority as the very proof of Jefferson's lack of guilt. In front of a racially mixed audience, the court-appointed attorney invokes Jefferson's racial inferiority as an argument for his innocence. The zoomorphic definition that the attorney manages to imprint on Jefferson's identity – 'a cornered animal', 'a hog' – discloses the attorney's adoption of white prejudices (7).[2]

In his turn, Jefferson adopts the racist views of the others and defines himself as 'a old hog they fattening up to kill' (83), referring to the idea of self-sacrifice, of seeing himself as a scapegoat, the one singled out to carry the blame of his peers. His self-degrading image and his perception of himself as lacking human value show his internalisation of the others' racism. Hence the double aspect of Jefferson's trauma, which is deeply related not only to the imminence of his death, but also to the self-annihilating effects of racism.

In Gaines's novel there is a deep interconnection between Jefferson's social death and his negative self-image, between his refusal to interact with the others and his desire for self-effacement and invisibility. Jefferson perceives himself as already 'dead' to the others, that is, 'excluded and marginalized' – living his last days in prison, in a peripheral space, at the border between the visible and the invisible (Holland 2000: 150).[3]

Jefferson's body language betrays his broken spirit, his total powerlessness and self-withdrawal. His body becomes a visible site of trauma, his whole attitude – 'his big hands clasped together between his legs', 'his head bowed, his shoulders stooped' – revealing his inner defeat in corporeal terms (127, 137). Moreover, his apathy and impassiveness serve as a shield to hide his inner turmoil from the others. His symbolic blindness, his staring at walls, his refusal to look at the others, talk to them or share their food – all testify to his uncontrollable, utter fear of death and the impossibility of conveying its meaning to the others.

In their turn, the members of the African American community are taken aback by the daunting task of reaching out to Jefferson. It is the duty of Grant Wiggins, the teacher – the narrator of the novel – to try to find a bridge of communication with Jefferson and change his negative image of himself. Prompted by the members of the community, Grant has to assume the pedagogic role of making Jefferson aware of his moral obligation to the others:

> 'You're a human being, Jefferson', I said.
> 'I'm a old hog', he said. 'Youmans don't stay in no stall like this. I'm a old hog they fattening up to kill'.
> 'That would hurt your nannan if she heard you say that. You want me to tell her you said that?'
> 'Old hog don't care what people say'.
> 'She cares', I said. 'And I do too, Jefferson'.
> 'Y'all youmans', he said.
> 'You're a human being too, Jefferson' (83).

In addition to the reference to Jefferson's humanity, this dialogue also contains the solution employed by Gaines for the inner transformation of his protagonist. As this chapter further explores, A Lesson Before Dying reveals that only Jefferson's responsible care for the others, as well as the others' united efforts to help him in his final hours, can be channelled towards a collective project of spiritual redemption.

The Lesson: Heroic, 'Good Death'

Gaines's novel subtly presents the stages of an initiatory process, during which Jefferson's self-awareness is triggered by the knowledge of his imminent death. Madelyn Jablon cogently notices that 'the death sentence propels [...] Jefferson on the journey to self-discovery', precipitating a 'relentless self-study' during which the character becomes 'aware of how racism has defined him' (1997: 89).

By focusing on the interconnection between self-discovery and the death sentence, Gaines's view on human solidarity distances him from Wright who emphasised the character's isolation from his community and utter loneliness in the face of death. By describing the last days in Jefferson's life, Gaines ultimately aims at rewriting the former image of the lonely, rebellious African American man by creating a strong relationship between the individual and his community.

Gaines creates a constellation of symbolic characters who contribute to Jefferson's inner development and final heroism: the teacher (Grant Wiggins), Jefferson's godmother (Miss Emma), Grant's lover (Vivian), Grant's aunt (Tante Lou), the priest (Reverend Ambrose) and the children whom Grant teaches. During the weeks prior to Jefferson's execution, this small community helps him take advantage of the short interval before dying to demonstrate his courage and manly status.

The others offer Jefferson 'a communally acknowledged model of good death', of dying in 'appropriate ways' (McNamara 2001: 43). Through the others, Jefferson is beneficially influenced by traditional Southern culture, communal values and ethical principles, 'which include African-American religion, respect for elders, loyalty to family and neighbours' (Folks 1999: 259).

By highlighting the principles of the elders, Grant makes an important contribution to Jefferson's conversion. His role is reminiscent of a mediator between the *puer* and the *senex*, between Jefferson (the rebellious youth) and Miss Emma (the wise elder). Grant has to assume the role of an educator, spurred on by Miss Emma's words: 'I don't want them to kill no hog. I want a man to go to that chair, on his own two feet' (13).

Miss Emma's words allude to the famous lines written by the Harlem Renaissance poet Claude McKay: 'If we must die, let it not be like hogs/Hunted and penned in an inglorious spot' (1997: 984). McKay's insistence on death as heroic self-reconstruction is also echoed by Grant's ideas. Grant helps Jefferson regain his self-esteem and develop his personality and asks him to become a hero, in his own words, to be one who does something for the others.

Grant's demand of sacrificial heroism is essential not just for Jefferson's redemption, but also to educate those around him. In this respect, the black children need someone who can stand as a genuine model of higher conduct. Jefferson's godmother also needs his courage in order to die peacefully and in his turn Reverend Ambrose needs Jefferson's conversion as a religious example for his community. Last but not least, Grant himself acknowledges Jefferson's importance for his own self-discovery and development as a true teacher.[4]

At a deeper level, Jefferson's heroism represents a means of destabilising the white supremacy, the 'old lie that people believe in' (192). As Grant explains to Jefferson, the black people need someone who is able to embody the 'common humanity that is in us all' (192). Through Jefferson's example, the meaning of a whole history of slavery is overturned, left without a justification. By demonstrating his humanity, Jefferson proves the falsity of the white myth, as shown by Grant (his words here echoing again Wright's novel): 'I want you – yes, you – to call them liars. I want you to show them that you are as much a man – more a man than they can ever be… You – you can be bigger than anyone you have ever met' (192–93).

Gaines's novel stresses the significance of Jefferson's visibility and exemplary status as a means of undermining white rules. Above all, it conveys a strong message of racial uplift in Jefferson's final transfiguration. While at the beginning of the novel white people perceive African Americans in a degrading way, by the end some of them have gradually changed their views. Impressed by Jefferson's Christ-like, courageous death, a white man, symbolically named Paul Bonin, is 'converted' to a new understanding that transcends racial limits. Witnessing Jefferson's death, Paul tells the others about Jefferson's heroic attitude, which is symbolically ingrained in his last message: 'Tell Nannan I walked' (254).

Jefferson's Notebook: 'Humanity Masked with Blackness'

Jefferson's 'standing', his courageous way of facing death and heroic reformation are emblematically accomplished in the process of writing – which emerges as a fundamental means of reconstructing black male identity.[5]

Oscillating between *testimony* and *testament* (from the same Latin root, *testis*, 'witness'), Jefferson's journal has a double function. While helping him in a therapeutic way to control his fear and reshape his identity, his writing also has the testamentary role of transmitting to those around him his most intimate thoughts, of making them witnesses to his last moments before death.

Returning to the initial argument of this chapter, we notice that writing comes to represent a way of overcoming social death, of changing the focus from Jefferson's marginality and invisibility to his central role and visibility within his community. When Jefferson's journal is given to the others, his writing takes on the form of 'communication' that has the role of 'community-making', of creating links between him and the community, of keeping his memory alive and his lesson imprinted on the others' conscience (Sell 2004: 29).

As Jefferson's journal remains the only material token of his existence, it becomes part of a symbolic 'arc of mourning', part of the process of grieving 'that bridges the living with the dead' (Wardi 2003: 134). His journal presents Jefferson's last moments – his coming to terms with his sentence, his shift in attitude from blind anger to subdued passivity, to courageous acceptance of death.

Written in the local dialect, Jefferson's vernacular text speaks the language of his people, it strikes a chord in them, conveying meaning through very simple vocabulary. Framed by Grant's educated narrative, Jefferson's semi-literate text gives depth to the novel, presenting Jefferson's profound humanity, his unconditional love for the community and his gratitude to them. In telling us about his godmother's love, the teacher's appreciation of him and the care of those around him, Jefferson demonstrates that he is part of the community and shares their values. His heroic attitude – ingrained in his short message: 'Tell Nannan I walked' (254) – can be seen as an answer to his godmother's desire to make him stand as a hero.

Gaines thus succeeds in recreating Jefferson's image from enslaved man into someone who is able to transfigure his imprisonment and death into a liberating 'lesson'. His novel reveals the African American man as a standing hero, whose final endurance remains an exemplary 'lesson' inscribed in a 'communally acknowledged model of good death' (McNamara 2001: 43).

Notes

1. Many critics have pointed out that Wright's novel must be seen as the major intertext for Gaines's *Lesson*, taking into account the two authors' interest in similar literary matters. Both Wright and Gaines deconstruct the stereotype of the black man as a 'beast' reflected in numerous literary portrayals at the end of the nineteenth and the beginning of the twentieth centuries. While denouncing public exposure and imprisonment as ways of reinforcing white morality, both authors rethink the rebellious image of the *native son* as a means of reconstructing African American manhood.

2. Intertextually, this definition evokes a scene in Wright's *Native Son*, where Buckley, the prosecuting attorney, repeatedly calls Bigger a 'half-human black', a 'thing', a 'beast' and a 'fiend' (403).

3. Through Michel Foucault's lens, the prison can be seen as a 'heterotopia of deviation', being one of those places located 'outside all places', inhabited by 'individuals whose behaviour is deviant in relation to the required norm' ('Of Other Spaces' [1967]).

4. As Suzanne Jones specifies, Jefferson's ability to make something of himself becomes a true lesson for Grant, 'who by succeeding with Jefferson learns that he can make a difference by teaching in the rural South' (2004: 140).

5. The pen and the notebook – that were symbolically given to Jefferson by the teacher – come to represent essential instruments in redefining Jefferson's identity. Jefferson's emancipation and inner freedom are finally accomplished through literacy, which points to 'the pregeneric myth' of African American literature, 'the quest for freedom and literacy' (Stepto 1979: ix). Rewriting the 'trope of the talking book', Gaines reconsiders a long tradition stretching back to slave narratives, where the acquisition of a literate voice was the first step towards emancipation.

Bibliography

Draga, Sabina Maria Alexandru. 2000. 'Black/White Masks: Performing the Imaginary Negro in Contemporary American Culture', in Rodica Mihaila and Irina Pana (eds), *Transatlantic Connections*. Bucharest: Integral, pp. 40–48.

Folks, Jeffrey. 1999. 'Communal Responsibility in Ernest Gaines's *A Lesson Before Dying*', *Mississippi Quarterly* 52(2): 259–72.

Ford, Nick Aaron. 1970. 'The Ordeal of Richard Wright', in Donald B. Gibson (ed.), *Five Black Writers: Essays on Wright, Ellison, Baldwin, Hughes and LeRoi Jones*. New York and London: New York University Press/University of London Press, pp. 26–35.

Foucault, Michel. 1967. 'Of Other Spaces: Heterotopias', http://foucault.info/documents/heterotopia.

Gaines, Ernest J. 1993. *A Lesson Before Dying*. New York: Vintage.

Holland, Sharon Patricia. 2000. *Raising the Dead: Readings of Death and (Black) Subjectivity*. Durham, NC: Duke University Press.

Holloway, Karla F.C. 2003. *Passed On: African American Mourning Stories: A Memorial*. Durham and London: Duke University Press.

Jablon, Madelyn. 1997. *Black Metafiction: Self-Consciousness in African American Literature*. Iowa City: University of Iowa Press.

Jones, Suzanne W. 2004. *Race Mixing: Southern Fiction since the Sixties*. Baltimore and London: The Johns Hopkins University Press.

Matus, Jill. 1998. *Toni Morrison*. Manchester and New York: Manchester University Press.

McKay, Claude. 1997 [1919]. 'If We Must Die', in Henry Louis Gates, Jr. and Nellie Y. McKay (eds), *The Norton Anthology of African American Literature*. New York and London: Norton, p. 984.

McNamara, Beverley. 2001. *Fragile Lives: Death, Dying and Care*. Philadelphia: Open University Press.

Morrison, Toni. 1987. 'The Site of Memory', in William Zinsser (ed.), *Inventing the Truth: The Art and Craft of Memoir*. Boston: Houghton Mifflin, pp. 109–11.

_____. 1992. *Playing in the Dark: Whiteness and the Literary Imagination*. Cambridge, MA and London: Harvard University Press.

Nussbaum, Martha. 2004. *Hiding from Humanity: Disgust, Shame and the Law*. Princeton and Oxford: Princeton University Press.

Patterson, Orlando. 1982. *Slavery and Social Death: A Comparative Study*. Cambridge, MA and London: Harvard University Press.

Sell, Roger D. 2004. 'Decency at a Discount? English Studies, Communication, Mediation', *The European English Messenger* 13(2): 23–34.

Stepto, Robert. 1979. *From Behind the Veil: A Study of Afro-American Narrative*. Urbana: University of Illinois Press.

Wardi, Anissa Janine. 2003. *Death and the Arc of Mourning in African American Literature*. Gainesville: The University Press of Florida.

Wright, Richard. 2000. *Native Son*. London: Vintage.

7

HABEAS CORPSE
The Dead Body of Evidence in John Grisham's
The Client

Fiorenzo Iuliano

The Client, published in 1993, is one of the first novels written by John Grisham and one of his most famous. Conceived by the author as a realistic portrayal of the American judicial system, it turns out to be an updated version of the traditional 'American dream', its characters and plot working as powerful icons imbued with various symbolic meanings. The novel's emphasis on the dead body, as both a repository of collective projections and anxieties and a semiotic kernel in the narrative economy of the text, will be crucial to my reading. Grisham implicitly theorises death as the unreachable limit of the US juridical system and as the assumption that provides it with its proper meaning and function. The corpse in *The Client*, in other words, is crucial to decipher and fully grasp the essence of the American way of justice as significantly depending on symbolic elements. Among these, death is figured as a border that cannot be reached or trespassed, an actual threat that sanctions and categorises American juridical norms inasmuch as it keeps operating as an external, untouchable principle.

I will devote the first part of this chapter to an analysis of the objections that have been raised to the novel's lack of realism and historical truthfulness; in the second part I will outline a tentative symbolic structure of the novel, which can be read as a metaphorical rendering of the relationship between the actual system of justice and what I will refer to as its secret and hidden counterpart, that has to be repressed and transcended so as to allow the law to function, and is illustrated by death and by the dead bodies represented or simply evoked in the text. Grisham's novel, thus, will be configured as a quintessential text that celebrates the US as the land of justice, whose visible constitutive elements acquire their strength and profound meaning by becoming slowly detached from their unspeakable counterpart. According to this perspective, detective fiction and legal thrillers, which, as literary genres, overtly thematise law and justice, work as organising grids through which the law can ultimately display its inner dynamics, in a process completely and almost perfectly overlapping with the (explicit) narrative detour of the text.

The story narrated in *The Client* starts with the infringement of a prohibition. While hiding in the woods to escape their mother's ban and smoke a cigarette, two young brothers witness a suicide. Before taking his life, an ugly, fat man, whose car they had accidentally spotted, reveals to the elder brother, eleven-year old Mark, the site where the body of the murdered Senator Boyd Boyette has been buried. Shocked by the man's suicide, Mark's brother Ricky goes into a coma. The man committing suicide, Jerome Clifford, a famous lawyer, had been defending Barry 'The Blade' Muldanno, a *mafioso*, accused of having murdered Boyette. Muldanno had previously told Clifford that he had buried the body in concrete in Clifford's garage and, after the latter's death, Mark is the only person who knows.

The remainder of the novel is constructed as a desperate quest for the dead body of Boyd Boyette, the only evidence that could prove Muldanno's guilt. Suspected by the FBI of knowing where the body is, but too intimidated by both the police and the mafia who have threatened his family, Mark gets in touch with a lawyer, Reggie Love, who takes on his case and assists him in the course of the story, giving him the comfort of a warm family-like atmosphere (Mark's mother had been deserted by her husband and the family live in a trailer park). Mark and Reggie eventually flee together to New Orleans, where they finally find Boyette's body.

Useless Synecdoche: the Symbolic Residue of Life

Despite the success of his novels, Grisham has been criticised for the incongruities of his stories, and for using narrative devices and tricks which, though necessary to the plot development, are sometimes preposterous or illogical. *The Client*, too, has been attacked for the same reasons. The whole novel is based on the postulate of a juridical principle that is never questioned by any of the characters: that with no direct evidence of the victim's corpse nobody can be charged with murder. This is stated from the very beginning of the novel: 'Of course, there was no body, and this presented tremendous problems for the United States of America. No corpse, no pathology reports, no ballistics, no bloody photographs to wave around the courtroom and display for the jury' (Grisham 2007: 35).

As is well known to his readers, before starting his career as a writer, John Grisham was a lawyer, and would hence be familiar with American laws and codes. Yet, in the history of American legal cases, charges of murder with no 'corpse of evidence' had occurred several times, the first and best known of them being People of California v. Scott, dating back to the 1950s. After Evelyn Scott, a Californian woman, went missing in 1955, her husband was charged with murder, although no personal or physical remains were found as evidence. He was sentenced to life imprisonment, and, for the first time in the history of American court cases, the *corpus delicti* of the crime was proved by circumstantial evidence alone, with no eyewitness account, human remains, or confession whatsoever to corroborate it. As a study of the case puts it, the reason why there seemed to be no need for any direct evidence was the 'fear that such inflexible requirements would enable a murderer to escape punishment by the simple expedient of completely destroying his victim's body' (Willmarth 1960: 852). Even on the sole basis of this precedent, the novel's assumption that a corpse is needed for the alleged culprit to be charged with murder seems to make no sense.

While the People of California v. Scott case dates back to the 1950s, John Grisham was undoubtedly aware of the major developments in forensics in the early 1990s, when he wrote his novel, and when DNA tests began to be taken as part of investigations. New trends in criminal law are fostered by scientific developments; laboratory analyses are replacing the need to discover extensive material evidence, and the apparently most insignificant object found on the crime scene can prove crucial to finding the culprit, with no further need for larger bodily evidence. These developments found their way into crime fiction, becoming almost immediately familiar to a wide range of readers. As triumphantly declared in Patricia Cornwell's *Postmortem* (1990), by arguably the most famous Chief Medical Examiner of American crime fiction, Kay Scarpetta, 'now there was the DNA profiling, newly introduced and potentially significant enough to identify an assailant to the exclusion of all other human beings' (1990: 16). *The Client*, however, is characterised by a number of other visible incongruities. Not only, as I have mentioned, is the corpse not, in juridical terms, indispensable as a *corpus delicti*; Mark is also unjustly accused of obstructing the investigation. After all, as the novel points out, 'they were investigating a murder, not a suicide. There was no law against suicide' (314), and a suicide is all Mark has actually witnessed, thus raising some doubts on the usefulness of suing him for information he might actually not have.

The scientific discoveries of those years also produce a dramatic shift in the *meaning* of the corpse, as an idealised repository of different cultural and psychic projections. In his essay 'The Empire of the Living Dead', American sociologist William Bogard describes this shift as a transition between two radically different cultural and figurative understandings of the corpse. While inside what he terms 'symbolic societies' there was no substantial symbolic difference between living and dead bodies, made interchangeable by the very status of the body as 'an indeterminate figure moving between human and non-human forms' (Bogard

2008: 188), at the end of the twentieth century living bodies were clearly set apart from dead ones, the latter being deprived of any symbolic role and dismissed as mere waste. This shift, according to Bogard, stemmed from the new role of 'genetics and technologies of birth, [which] promised the power to regulate life in advance, and as a result the corpse began to lose much of its former utility' (188). Control over human life began to be exerted from its beginning rather than from its ending, as had happened in the past, thus completing and, at the same time, radically overthrowing Michel Foucault's exploration of death as a means of fully displaying the human as a perfectly intelligible paradigm. Foucault's words, thus, which identify the dead body as a scientific tool to construct the taxonomy of human life, could appropriately elucidate the role played by the human genome in the last decades of the twentieth century:

> It is from the height of death that one can see and analyse organic dependences and pathological sequences. Instead of being what it had so long been, the night in which life disappeared, in which even the disease becomes blurred, it is now endowed with that great power of elucidation that dominates and reveals both the space of the organism and the time of the disease. (Foucault 1973: 144)

The widespread use of DNA by forensic scientists which started in the early 1990s, and, more generally, the enthusiasm and the anxieties that followed crucial scientific discoveries surrounding the detailed functioning of the human body (like the Human Genome Project or the Visible Body Project), represent a crucial watershed that marks the shift from a symbolic to a utilitarian paradigm in the juridical-scientific usage of the corpse, on the one hand, and in its symbolic reconfiguration, on the other. In fact, the discovery of DNA lead to a heterogeneous array of popular visionary and fanciful myths about immortality, traced to the perennial and potentially infinite transferability and interchangeability of codes. The solid and well-defined borders of the dead body gave way to the volatile image of haphazard combinations of discrete elements. As Jacque Lynn Foltyn states, 'DNA has become an icon in contemporary popular culture as science, medicine, and the law use genetic codes to establish identity, explain individual behaviours and, by implication, many aspects of human society' (2008: 162): in this regard, Amitav Ghosh's sci-fi novel *The Calcutta Chromosome* (1995) effectively evokes the atmosphere of hectic curiosity and interest that surrounded the scientific and technological breakthroughs of the early 1990s, when the myth of immortality seemed to be a possibility thanks to the recombination of genetic codes.[1]

Bogard maintains that the corpse has been radically re-signified in the new frame of bio-political power; it has discarded its former symbolic value, to be repositioned within the unceasing flux and exchange of commodities that characterise late capitalism. In particular, he reminds us that 'the dead body becomes "standing reserve" in modern societies [...] targeted by a complex assemblage of desiring machines, technical machines, and semiotic and decoding machines that convert it into a resource for production and Capital [...] an object of probes and surveillance, interpretation, and analysis and exchange' (2008: 189). This shift could also be read as the terminal stage of transformation of the body into a bio-political data-set. The beginning of this process, according to Giorgio Agamben, dates back as early as 1679, when the writ of *habeas corpus* sanctioned the bare life of the human body as the 'new subject of politics' (Agamben 1998: 73). A decline of actual bodies within the apparatuses of knowledge would take place more than three centuries later: by the end of the twentieth century not a body but a simple code had become the synecdochic equivalent of the human as a political and juridical subject.

The corpse as the quintessential bio-political body is clearly at odds with Grisham's text, which, on the contrary, insists on a symbolic dimension of the dead body that, according to Bogard's and Foltyn's analyses, proves to be completely obsolete. If, as Foltyn remarks, 'DNA has emerged as a pop cultural icon [...] because it in some sense has replaced the soul and become a sacred entity, a way to explore immortality' (2008: 170), it necessarily follows that a different understanding of the body, as well as of the soul, was also emerging at the time. Its kernel was to be found not just in the corpse as the main emblem of death and its mysteries, but, on the contrary, in its recently acquired status of surplus, exceeding, and even useless residue of human life, and, as such, as a commodity to be reinvested in the economy of cultural representations. *The Client*, therefore, steps into this crucial phase by constructing a phantasmatic paradigm of knowledge based upon the epistemic necessity of the dead body in its entirety. If the corpse is no longer necessary to establish the responsibility for a crime, it is still essential to give coherence to a system of values and symbols.

Before the Dead, Beside(s) the Law

The mystery around which *The Client* is constructed can be solved thanks to a corpse, whose retrieval proves essential to the novel's happy ending. However, Boyette's body is not the only dead body in the novel as the story begins with a suicide, witnessed by Mark and his brother Ricky. Even more remarkably, after watching the scene, Mark's brother goes into a coma that lasts throughout the story, himself turned into, and often described as, a *de facto* corpse, 'zombielike, with pale skin and glazed eyes' (Grisham 2007: 41). And yet, as mentioned above, there is no real need for an actual body to solve a crime, which makes the novel's insistence on these details, discarded by both American jurisprudence and the popular imagination, all the more intriguing.

The finding of Boyette's corpse is something of a rite of initiation, emblematically representing Mark's passage from childhood to manhood. *The*

Client is not the first, nor the only, literary place where the finding of a corpse becomes a rite to be minutely narrated and celebrated. In Raymond Carver's short story 'So Much Water So Close to Home' (1981), a group of (male) friends find the body of a murdered girl during a fishing trip. Stephen King's novella 'The Body', published in 1982, could also (and more convincingly) be read as one of *The Client's* most interesting forerunners: in it four boys, aged twelve, set off into the woods of rural Maine to find the body of a boy their age, who has been killed accidentally.[2] Significantly, at the end of the story two of the boys are described as now fully aware of adult (and masculine) values, like bravery and camaraderie; unearthing the corpse of another young man has heightened their awareness of life as transient and unpredictable, under the constant menace of impending death. However, *The Client's* stakes seem to be higher. Rather than being an imperfect legal thriller, it aspires to sanction a definite archetype of justice, actually encoded in the inspiring principles of American law, thus conflating universal principles with the true essence of the US as a nation. Constructed as a system of metaphors, the novel foregrounds the corpse as the emblematic divide that separates the space *before* from the space *beyond* the law, focusing on a non-existent prohibition that nevertheless has to be violated, and whose final transgression marks the shift from the defective frame of human law to the universal paradigm of justice. The latter, however, is identified by Grisham with the American judicial system, which is arguably conceived, and implicitly featured, as the most perfect and universally valid.

The value of the dead body, 'imbued [...] with the tension of paradox [...] extraordinary and banal, wild and tame, useful and useless' (Foltyn 2008: 155), is thus symbolically retrieved by Grisham, who constructs the novel as a refined structure of abstract concepts, assembled as a cautionary tale leading to a predictable ending. American justice is questioned and interrogated inside a system of perfectly balanced symmetries and isotopes. The gradual empowerment of the young protagonist is paralleled by the increasing emphasis given to the dead body's symbolic role, which reaches its climax with Mark and Reggie's final discovery of Boyette's body, as they watch Muldanno and his men unsuccessfully attempting to remove it from Clifford's garage.

But exactly how does Grisham's symbolic apparatus work? As I explained earlier, the novel opens with Mark and Ricky violating a prohibition. In the course of the novel, Mark's rebellious attitude towards any kind of ban is repeatedly highlighted: not only does he smoke despite his mother's severe prohibition, he also succeeds in escaping from the juvenile lock-up where he has been placed, and stubbornly does the opposite of whatever adults order or ask him to do, refusing to answer his prosecutors when they try to persuade him to tell the truth about Clifford's death. Of course, this is a conventional way of portraying a young (male) hero, whose final triumph must be at least partially ascribed to his strength of will.[3] This is all the more relevant because the archetype of a prohibition (not) to be infringed is the basic premise of the whole narrative, and not just of the construction of Mark as the novel's positive hero: Jeremy Clifford, too, is forbidden to reveal the secret of Boyette's place of burial by his role as the defender of a criminal. *The Client's* plot depends on the infringement of a prohibition for no apparent reason: Clifford gives the secret away, violating a promise he was supposed to keep. The narrative trigger of the whole action, thus, sounds quite unconvincing: why is Clifford, before dying, so eager to reveal his secret to Mark? It is probably because of the lack of any apparent or logical explanation that Grisham insists so much on Clifford being totally drunk and high on drugs, bursting with the urge to tell Mark where Boyd Boyette has been buried.

Prohibition plays a crucial role in the novel; it represents the hindrance that can only be overcome by the symbolic power of the corpse, so as to be simultaneously discarded as a real obstacle and to be itself rendered as a symbolic tool in the economy of the text. Boyette's corpse is the unapproachable and magnetic catalyst of the novel, and this is why it is kept off scene for most of the narrative. Everyone knows that there is a corpse somewhere, and the continuous deferral of its discovery makes the plot unfold. The traditional structure of the crime thriller is thus overturned: it is not the evidence of a dead body that sets the action in motion, but rather its absence. Boyette's given name, Boyd, is an all too evident anagram of 'body'. It works like the Ur-corpse, the emblem of the body of evidence needed to solve the mystery. Moreover, as the novel points out, Boyette also embodies the perfect, exemplary politician. His portrait is provided by Grisham in a passionate resume of his life and political career, a singular and noteworthy success story: Boyette was a scrupulous man, devoted to his duties, abandoned by his former supporters and political allies, who, as Grisham writes, 'became a radical environmentalist, something unheard of among southern politicians', a man that 'embraced the crumbling ecology of his beloved state, and studied it with passion' (2007: 217–18). Boyd Boyette spent his life in the service of his country and, in particular, in preserving the Louisiana environment from the toxic dumps the Mafia wanted to create, thus incarnating an idealised loyalty and devotion to the Law and the nation. He is consequently prized as the perfect servant of the State; his body, thus, becomes an ideal icon to be either highly commended and celebrated by the good Americans or destroyed and consigned to oblivion by the enemies of the State.

The novel's insistence on something that has no real importance, like the actual presence of Boyd Boyette's corpse, symbolically redefines the space of law and justice as a space that is manifestly open, but, as such, paradoxically impossible to enter. Acting as a mute doorkeeper, Boyette's corpse functions in narrative and symbolic terms more as a cautionary and abstract hindrance than as a material obstacle. This function is not dissimilar to that of the doorkeeper's in Franz Kafka's famous story 'Before the Law' (1995), which features a peasant who wants to access the law, and is constantly forbidden by the doorkeeper. The door that grants the access to the law is open, and nevertheless the peasant is forbidden to enter, although he is unaware of the possible consequences of the ban's violation. There is no official prohibition, insomuch as the doorkeeper addresses the countryman by saying, 'If you are so drawn to it, just try to go in despite my veto' (Kafka 1995: 148); nevertheless, the countryman cannot enter the law. At the very end of his life, the doorkeeper tells him that he is finally allowed to enter, and that the door has always been kept open for him alone. Commenting on this very short and cryptic story, while discussing the sovereign ban and the state of exception, Agamben theorises the law as something that 'is *in force* but does not *signify*' (1998: 35). He argues that '[n]othing – and certainly not the refusal of the doorkeeper – prevents the man from the country from passing through the door of the Law if not the fact that this door is already open' (34): the law draws its strength not just from what it actually states or predicts, but from its pure existence, its being potentially devoid of any precise reference to real circumstances and, still, being *in force*, thus capable of arbitrarily regulating access to its own space. In *The Client*, the abstract principle of the law, discussed by Agamben in the logic of the sovereign ban, forcibly turns into a eulogy of the US juridical system. Entering the law, in *The Client*, basically amounts to retrieving the founding principles of the American nation. It is not only Grisham's conservative ideology that allows for such an interpretation (despite its great importance in his whole oeuvre),[4] but the very description of Boyd Boyette as, simultaneously, the perfect servant of the State and the perfect American hero, aware of his duties towards the nation and naturally imbued with the sound principles of 'old America'.

The tradition of American rhetoric, dating back to Puritanism and the verbal mechanism of the jeremiad, silently surfaces in the text: any critique of the present system is morally and rhetorically justified only inasmuch as it operates as a way of invoking an older, and supposedly infringed, norm. In this sense, while, on the one hand, the true spirit of the law is (more or less) convincingly embodied in the figure of Reggie Love,[5] on the other hand the crucial function of marking the imaginary divide that sanctions the *force* of the law is played by the corpse of Boyd Boyette, which, as in Kafka's allegory, cannot but proclaim the eventual opening of that which has always been accessible and never actually forbidden.

Grisham intersperses his novel with various, sometimes almost imperceptible, traces that transform *The Client* into a novel about justice in America or, rather, about America as the land where justice can be restored to its ideal and authentic nature – a means of individual redemption and social affirmation. The American way of justice, simultaneously a symbolical construction and a cultural myth, can be epistemically achieved and comprehended thanks to the dialectic opposition between a metaphysical, abstract notion of justice and its actual administration, figured as the actual fight between Mark and Reggie on the one hand, the novel's heroes, and the villains on the other, represented not only by Muldanno and his gang, but also by those who have reduced the principles of American justice to a matter of mere bureaucracy or, even worse, to the means of narcissistically pursuing their own career.

The equation of the dyad law/justice with the US is confirmed by the need to differentiate the elements of authentic American jurisprudence from external, spurious ones, as shown in the novel's double location of legal action, which takes place both in Tennessee and in Louisiana. The villains, Barry 'The Blade' Muldanno and Jeremy Clifford, are from New Orleans, and Roy Foltrigg is the district attorney for the southern district of Louisiana, running for Governor, while, on the other hand, both Reggie Love and the juvenile judge Harry Roosevelt are from Tennessee. Here Grisham deliberately makes up things, since no Southern District of Louisiana exists, the State being divided into Western, Middle and Eastern districts in the 94 US District Court system, thus confirming *The Client*'s blend of authentic and fictive elements. This 'geographical' opposition, far from being accidental, can be read as an implicit praise of what the novel presents as the most perfect, because authentically American, system (Tennessee): the alleged distinctiveness of the Louisiana legal way, which '[m]odern Louisianans pride themselves on' (Billings 1991: 63), derives from its being based not on the Anglo-Saxon common law, as all other US systems, but on the Roman and the Napoleonic code. Finally awarded by Tennessee judge Roosevelt, justice is thus promoted as a genuinely American, or at least Anglo-Saxon, product. The construction of the American myth, thus, is supported not only by the traditional rhetoric of the US as the land of opportunities, whose Constitution generically states the right to pursue one's own happiness, but as the only nation where the law and the juridical system actually grant everyone the means to enjoy this right. American exceptionalism, whose rhetorical overtones often surface in Grisham's novel, implicitly turns civil and juridical rights into privileges, only bestowed onto those who are true born Americans.

At the end of the novel, Mark and his mother are given the opportunity to start their lives over in a new place, under the Federal Witness Protection Program, thus reinforcing the idea of America as the land of opportunity, and updating the American dream according to modern paradigms. Unlike traditional success stories, focused on individual efforts as the only means to fulfil one's own potential, the novel implies that something different is now necessary to achieve the same end: it is the State, and not entrepreneurialism, that provides Mark and his family with an opportunity to start a better life. Indeed, individual struggle does not necessarily guarantee the righteousness of the objectives pursued; even Muldanno and his *mafiosi* are self-made men in their own right. Therefore, the idea of self-accomplishment shifts from the simple, undifferentiated level of individualism and individual self-affirmation to the need to find a universally shared code of norms and values to sanction and legitimise individual efforts: in the total absence of any form of welfare state, justice is the only means of granting everyone an equal opportunity for individual and social affirmation. As Rubin argues in a review of *The Client*, '[a]t the root of the tort system is the notion that the law is a great equaliser between the powerful and the weak, and ultimately a source of justice. But justice depends on an unbiased eye toward the facts and a refusal to be blinded by emotion' (2009: 60).

The Client thus reads as a symbolic drama, a modern morality with a predictable happy end and a perfectly balanced structure. American justice embodies the eternal, and eternally accessible, spirit of the law, aptly exemplifying what Agamben refers to as the 'already open' (Agamben 1998: 34). Yet, it cannot be accessed and fully enjoyed without violating a prohibition. This prohibition, symbolically foreclosing the attainment of this ideal (and/as American) spirit of the law, paradoxically shows that it has always been accessible, as in Kafka's 'Before the Law'. Justice is thus evoked and idealised as a timeless principle, but American founding values constitute the only instrument to reach and fully embody it.

Notes

1. Not to mention TV series like *CSI*, broadcast since 2000, whose popularity can be at least partially attributed to their precise rendering of the anatomy of the dead body, with scrupulous and sometimes disturbing attention to detail. This visual representation of the corpse, paradoxically, ends up in increasingly detaching the knowledge of human physiology from the naked materiality of the body as an organism, to subsequently reconstruct the body itself as an almost abstract, artificial structure.

2. I would like to thank Giannicola Metello for bringing this book to my attention.

3. As for the names and characterisation of the novel's protagonists, they are blatantly presented as the true offspring of an authentic America: the benevolent judge is called Roosevelt; and the very name of the protagonist, Mark Sway, seems to resonate with the name of Mark Twain (and Tom Sawyer), an overtone that seems all the more convincing if related to the episode of Mark and Reggie's escape. Heading to New Orleans, they cross the Mississippi, mirroring the better known trip on the Mississippi undertaken by Huckleberry Finn (who, incidentally, is the same age as Mark), and whose father, like Mark's, was an alcoholic and a violent man. Above all, of course, both Mark and Huck are trying to run away from the Law.

4. As Joel Black argues in a brief essay, 'An obvious problem with Grisham's aesthetic and legal perspective is that it is informed by a rigidly conservative ideology' (1998: 38).

5. As a study on the novel has put it, 'In Reggie Love, Grisham comes close to affirming the value of our nation's legal system. She protects Mark from its most unattractive aspects and for one dollar affords him ample protection' (Pringle 1997: 80).

Bibliography

Agamben, G. 1998. *Homo Sacer: Sovereign Power and Bare Life*, trans. D. Heller-Roazen. Stanford: Stanford University Press.

Billings, W.M. 1991. 'Origins of Criminal Law in Louisiana', *Louisiana History: The Journal of the Louisiana Historical Association* 32(1): 63–76.

Black, J. 1998. 'Grisham's Demons', *College Literature* 25(1): 35–40.

Bogard, W. 2008. 'Empire of the Living Dead', *Mortality* 13(2): 187–200.

Carver, R. 1981. 'So Much Water So Close to Home', in R. Carver, *What We Talk about When We Talk about Love*. New York: Knopf, pp. 79–88.

Cornwell, P. 1990. *Postmortem*. London: Time Warner Books.

Foltyn, J.L. 2008. 'Dead Famous and Dead Sexy: Popular Culture, Forensics, and the Rise of the Corpse', *Mortality* 13(2): 153–73.

Foucault, M. 1973. *The Birth of the Clinic: An Archaeology of Medical Perception*, trans. A.M. Sheridan. New York and London: Routledge.

Ghosh, A. 1995. *The Calcutta Chromosome*. New York: Perennial.

Grisham, J. 2007. *The Client*. London: Arrow.

Kafka, F. 1995. 'Before the Law', in F. Kafka, *The Metamorphosis, In the Penal Colony, and Other Stories*, trans. W. and E. Muir. New York: Schocken Books, pp. 148–50.

King, S. 2007. 'The Body', in S. King, *Different Seasons*. London: Hodder, pp. 383–582.

People v. Scott, 176 Cal.App.2d 458. [Crim. No. 6272. Second Dist., Div. Three. Dec. 21, 1959]. Accessed on 30 November 2011, http://law.justia.com/cases/california/calapp2d/176/458.html

Pringle, M.B. 1997. *John Grisham: A Critical Companion*. Westport and London: Greenwood Press.

Rubin, J. 2009. 'John Grisham's Law', *Commentary*, June: 56–60.

Willmarth, F. 1960. 'Criminal Law: Murder: Proof of Corpus Delicti by Circumstantial Evidence', *California Law Review* 48(5): 849–52.

8

THE FASCINATION WITH TORTURE AND DEATH IN TWENTY-FIRST-CENTURY CRIME FICTION

Rebecca Shillabeer

Although in its most basic term, crime fiction can be described as fiction that incorporates the presence of crimes, criminals and their motives, crime fiction also provides a critique of society. Immigration, social control, sexuality, scientific discovery, race, religion and gender are just some of the issues that crime fiction touches upon. Many literary novels have crime and the basics of the crime novel at their centre. The main ingredients of this genre – violence, sudden reversals, mystery, deception, moral dilemma and so on – can be found everywhere from the Greek epics to the present day (Turner 2003: 4). In order to understand the fascination with torture and death in twenty-first-century serial killer and post-mortem crime fiction[1] it is important to examine the earlier forms of literature which have so heavily influenced the genre.

The human fascination with the dissected body can be traced back to medieval times. The critic Sawday described the renaissance as a 'culture of dissection' (Sawday 1996: 50). Even in this early modern era public anatomy demonstrations were not uncommon. The public viewed the fascinating dissecting of the human body as entertainment, which is arguably what crime fiction is providing for the readers of today. The public display and performance of autopsies by Gunther von Hagen since the 1990s shows that even with the scientific developments and knowledge of the body, the public is still enthralled by the body interior. It was in 2002 that the first public autopsy was aired on television – a modern-day renaissance demonstration.

Criminal narratives were extremely popular in the late eighteenth and early ninetieth centuries. It is believed that the narratives of this era hugely influenced the patterns and themes of the later fully-fledged genre of crime fiction (Worthington 2005: 1). It was at this time in history that *Broadsides* and the *Newgate Calendar* were popular. The *Broadsides* were cheap single sheets of paper upon which news stories, public speeches, notices and even songs were written. This was before the introduction of newspapers and the public used this street literature as a way of hearing about the latest crimes and scandal. The narratives were based on real crimes that had occurred in society at the time. The *Broadsides* were produced to entertain their audience and included as much violent crime and violent punishment as possible. Heather Worthington argues that these were produced for didactic reasons, circulated to the working classes as a lesson against corrupt living (2005: 33). This may have been an incentive, but it cannot be ignored that they were produced for profit – and murder sells. These criminal narratives were produced cheaply and their readership was not limited by sex, age or class. All members of society attended public executions and this was often where the *Broadsides* would be distributed.

The *Broadsides* did not shy away from graphic descriptions of murder, incest, rape, bigamy, robbery and infanticide. There was even a pornographic element to the narratives with graphic illustrations of sexual violence. The narratives aimed to shock and titillate the readership. Although the *Broadsides* were based on real crimes, it is argued that much of the detail was embellished in order to please the readership. The same wood block illustrations were often used repeatedly for different murderous tales, bearing little relevance to the narrative. There was an obsession with the dismembering of female victims and the female body was often sexualised. An example of this is the murder of Ann Pullin by George King: the *Broadside* depicts the decapitated victim and the severed head lying at the centre of the illustration. It is clear that these early examples of crime narratives show that the public preoccupation with violence, and in particular the dissected female form, is not a modern phenomenon. Already in the eighteenth and nineteenth centuries the literature was awash with pathology and intrigue.

In *The Rise of the Detective in Nineteenth-Century Popular Fiction* Heather Worthington analyses the content of a number of *Broadsides*, including the *Life, Trial, Confession and Execution of James Greenacre*. This *Broadside* is of particular interest for this study because it shows many similarities to the post-mortem crime novels of the modern day. Unlike some *Broadsides* of the era, the narrative did not use illustrations to excite the reader. Instead it is the examination of the victim that is most thrilling: 'the head had been severed from the body while the person was yet alive; that this was proved by the retraction [...] of the muscles [...] where they were separated by the knife, and further, by the blood vessels being empty, the body was drained of blood' (quoted in Worthington 2005: 16).

This style of dissecting the body is very common in twenty-first-century literature. The scientific description of the mutilated human body in Cornwell's post-mortem novel *Scarpetta* (2008), which sparked moral outrage, can be compared with post-mortem descriptions in *Broadsides* such as the *Life, Trial,*

Confession and Execution of James Greenacre. The idea of using the violated body to provide answers and catch the perpetrator is a common trait in contemporary crime fiction.

Throughout history people have not only been fascinated by the torn body but have also been intrigued by the minds of serial killers. Jack the Ripper, who committed the atrocious murders of prostitutes in London in 1888, became an infamous figure and has continued to captivate the public's imagination to this day. A search for Jack the Ripper on the internet uncovers 248 books, 24 DVDs, 15 links to popular music, a video game and an action figure (Jarvis 2007: 326). He featured heavily in the *Broadsides* of the nineteenth century and his popularity is still apparent today with the author Patricia Cornwell spending six million dollars financing an investigation into the Ripper case. In her book *Portrait of a Killer: Jack the Ripper – Case Closed* (2003) she put her knowledge of forensic science to the test, aiming to solve the world's most famous unsolved serial killer case. The critic Chris Greer stated in *Crime and Media: A Reader* that serial killer memorabilia now constitutes a global market (Greer 2010: 33). Violent crime is marketed as a spectacle to be consumed. Whether it is through reading fiction or real-life accounts, or through buying murderabilia, or, as Vidal explores in Chapter 9 of the present volume, serial killer art, it is clear that there is a mainstream obsession with the serial killer (Jarvis 2007: 326). Even though some argue that the obsession with murderabilia is a fairly recent phenomenon (Schmid 2004: 5), it is clear that, throughout history, murder and torture have captured the public's imagination. In *Serial Killers: Death and Life in America's Wound Culture* Mark Seltzer describes the society of today as a 'wound culture' consisting of a 'public fascination with torn and opened bodies and torn and opened persons, a collective gathering around shock, trauma and the wound' and serial killers are the 'superstars of our wound culture' (Seltzer 1998: 22). I would argue that this has always been the case. However, the interesting question is: why are people so interested in reading fiction that incorporates death and scenes of torture?

According to Nielsen Bookscan, in 2010 crime, thriller and adventure adult fiction books had a UK turnover of £145 million and this figure has continued to rise with crime fiction accounting for thirty per cent of all fiction sold in the UK. The most widely published style of crime fiction today is that of post-mortem and serial killer fiction. As already established, these themes have been present in literature throughout the ages. However, gratuitous violence seems to be so much on the rise that one could even speak of escalation. Number one bestsellers like *Book of the Dead* (2007) by Patricia Cornwell and *Hard Girls* (2009) by Martina Cole are just two examples of narratives that incorporate graphic scenes of torture, decomposing bodies and nude mutilated corpses; descriptions such as these are the norm in serial killer and post-mortem crime novels: 'The bastard had set about his business, slicing, burning and raping her while she choked in agony' (Cole 2010: 30).

James Patterson's bestseller *Kiss the Girls* (1996) features two male serial killers who keep beautiful young women in a basement and sexually abuse, torture and kill them. In one never-to-be-forgotten scene, a girl is tied up and a live snake fed into her anus by her captor. It has been argued that this breed of gruesome and explicit crime fiction began with Patricia Cornwell's first Kay Scarpetta thriller *Postmortem* (1990) (Flood 2008). Many subsequent authors have been heavily influenced by Cornwell's style, labelled by critic Jessica Mann as 'torture porn' for the way the literature evokes a physical reaction in the reader (fear, sexual arousal, tears) which is not unlike pornography (Allen 2007: 89). In response to this, P.J. Tracy expressed the opinion that 'the violence that has always existed has become more visible and more tolerated – glorified to a certain degree – and perhaps even statistically more prevalent' (in Shillabeer 2010: 47).[2] Author Tess Gerritsen describes current crime fiction as 'highly charged with graphic violence,' and referred to some recent novels as going 'over the top with scenes of torture' (in Shillabeer 2010: 51). Ironically the pioneer of the 'torture-porn' style, Patricia Cornwell, stated in an interview for *The Guardian* that she finds the crime fiction now being published 'too realistic in many ways, transitioning into something rather frightening' (Flood 2008). Supporting this viewpoint, Mann has criticised the increasing number of novels published within the genre of serial killer and post-mortem crime fiction. She has described these novels, which include graphic descriptions of the mutilated human body, as misogynistic, representing a hatred for women and sadistic with regard to the ways in which characters and readers gain sexual gratification from inflicting pain or emotional abuse on others. If violence within literature is escalating, what could be influencing this trend?

A parallel can be drawn between the rise in popularity of serial killer and post-mortem fiction to the increase in consumption and commodification in society (Greer 2010: 35). Jarvis compares violence within novels such as Cole's *Hard Girls* to the violence involved in consumerist society, where sweatshops and the slaughter of animals are becoming the norm to feed consumer greed (Jarvis 2007: 326). The violence and dissection of the body within twenty-first-century crime fiction novels can be viewed as part of this consumer culture, where women are continuously inspected, dissected and analysed: 'Images of the deconstructed body are everywhere in the infantile fantasies of consumer culture: perfect legs, perfect breasts, perfect hair, perfect teeth, bodies endlessly dismembered in a ceaseless strafing of advertising imagery' (Jarvis 2007: 326).

Advertisements for brands such as Pretty Polly,[3] Dior and Seksy, which focus on one part of the human body, for example legs, mouth and arms, can be compared to the book covers of crime novels by Tess Gerritsen,[4] Chelsea Cain and Patricia Cornwell. These dissections of the female body have been described as 'fragmentary fetishes' (Jarvis 2007: 326), with advertisements and book covers sexualising parts of the female body in order to sell products. Another similarity that can be drawn between these advertisements and twenty-first-century crime fiction is that the subject or victim is almost always a woman. Advertising reflects the ongoing public interest in not just the body, but the female body. The idea of the forensic pathologist dissecting the body is not viewed as grotesque by the modern reader because it bears resemblance to the visual dissection of the female body in the advertising that bombards consumers on a daily basis; the 'Serial killer is unmasked as a gothic double of the serial consumer,' writes Jarvis (2007: 326). Further, building on consumerist arguments, the psychological profiles of serial killers typically diagnose the cause of the subject's compulsive behaviour as a profound sense of incompletion. This translates to the collection of victims in order to fulfil a desire and need for the serial killer, much like consumer greed. 'Consuming means purchasing, eating and destroying' (Annesley 1998: 211) and in the same way a serial killer takes possession of his victim and destroys. The well known fictional serial killer Hannibal Lecter could be seen as a literal representation of the killer consumer as he is a cannibal and literally consumes the human body. Another example comes from the fictional serial killer Patrick Bateman from *American Psycho* (1991), who consumes in all possible ways: buying, eating and destroying (Allue 1991: 71–90).

Another influence on the genre of modern crime fiction has been television and film. Crime drama series are very popular with the BBC, such as the pathology drama *Silent Witness* which attracted around three million viewers in 2010 and the US drama *CSI: Miami* which attracted two million viewers in 2010 in the UK alone. Like crime fiction, television crime dramas are focusing more and more on forensic pathology. It has therefore been argued that television and film have directly altered the literary genre of crime fiction. Being able to see crime scenes and dead bodies on the television may have 'blunted our disgust reaction' (Shillabeer 2010: 40) and it is obvious that 'art in all mediums influence each other' (Shillabeer 2010: 49). Lynda La Plante's novels were adapted for the drama series *Prime Suspect* which pushed at the genre boundaries 'through its frank and unflinching look at the dead, tortured and decaying bodies of its murder victims' (Allen 2007: 79). *Prime Suspect* was first broadcast in the 1990s and since then there has been an influx of similar forensic dramas: 'Penetrating skin, arteries and organs to take the audience on a spectacular visual ride through the corporeal – the boundaries are not merely of the genre, or of television, but of the body itself, have been dissolved' (Allen 2007: 80).

Critics have pointed out the sexual connotations of the 'CSI shot' which penetrates the body and have even described this drama as 'stylistically pornographic' (Greer 2010: 326). Crime fiction and drama aim to create a response in the viewer/reader and represent the 'excesses' of the human body. Tess Gerritsen has expressed the opinion that due to the media representation of crime and violence the public has 'developed a far stronger stomach' for descriptions of gore, violence and torture (Shillabeer 2010: 52). Undoubtedly these visual representations of crime will have played a part in how the genre of crime fiction has changed. The public's appetite for violence is growing. Authors feel the need to come up with 'ever more ghastly scenarios as the readership becomes more desensitised' (McKay 2008: 141). This demand for increasing gore is exemplified by the first five *Saw* movies based around torture and violence grossing $699 million. The Internet Movie Database (imbd.com) lists over 1000 films featuring serial killers worldwide and most of the contributions to this genre have been made since 1990. There is clearly an increasing demand for film and television that incorporates 'torture porn' and 'graphic gore'. Modern scientific discoveries and forensic developments have altered the processes of examining the human body. Advances in forensic science and the coverage of pathology in the media have meant that 'readers are much more savvy' (Shillabeer 2010: 44) and authors need to be accurate and precise with their descriptions of the body and crime scenes.

It is important when examining this genre to look at the consumers who buy these novels. An article in *The Telegraph* by Amy Willis stated that 'Women account for more than 60% of the readership with females over 55 the most avid readers'. According to the critic Julie Bindel:

> Over half of all novels in the genre (crime fiction) are written by women, and their books are most popular with a female audience – which is useful for the authors since women read considerably more books than men. Last year a survey in Woman and Home Magazine bolstered the notion that women nowadays prefer blood and guts to hearts and flowers. (Bindel 2007)

If the main target market for the serial killer and post-mortem novels is women, understanding the driving force behind their decision to read such fiction is very important. Although it is clear that fiction of this kind is written by men and women, it seems that women are vilified for doing so. No one questions men in the same way 'How does it feel, as a man, to be writing such extreme violence against women?' But as soon as women decide they want to explore the same territory, gender becomes an issue (McDermid 2009). The author Val McDermid has spoken openly in the press on this claim, criticising the way in which women are being blamed for the public's interest and lust for reading such fiction. It has been suggested that the increase in gratuitous violence written by women can be attributed to the need of female authors to assert themselves. Cooper (2008) has argued that female authors write at least one novel containing very graphic violence in order to establish their credibility and prove they are not 'girly'. It is therefore a possibility that women writers are exploiting their femininity, producing extremely violent stories in order to subvert the assumption that ladies are all round softer creatures (Brooks 2007). P.J. Tracy has responded strongly to this accusation: 'Everybody with a penis automatically thinks that those who don't have one want one! Maybe there are women writers who are motivated by some post-feminist hangover, and want to show that they can be as hardcore as their male counterparts. Or maybe they're just feeding into the commercialism of an ever-evolving genre' (in Shillabeer 2010: 49).

Likewise Karin Slaughter responded to these claims, stating that she has no 'ulterior motive' when writing a novel and is just 'seeking to understand through the craft of writing why people do the horrible things that they do'. She does not feel that she has 'something to prove', or that she is 'swinging around some imaginary dick' (in Shillabeer 2010: 44). According to Tess Gerritsen, female crime writers produce these novels because: 'It is dramatic and it's riveting and we want our stories to have high stakes and to capture the reader's attention. We're not trying to prove that we're as rough as guys; we're just writing the stories we want to tell' (in Shillabeer 2010: 52).

The duo P.J. Tracy have made the point that fiction reflects reality, as women and children are primarily the victims of violent crime; serial killers are psycho-sexually motivated and male, with very few exceptions – so there is an 'inherent misogyny attached to the genre just because it's the reality of the pathology' (in Shillabeer 2010: 48). As established it is female bodies that adorn book covers and women are predominantly the victims within the narrative. According to the UK Office of National Statistics, in 2006 eighty per cent of offenders in the UK were men and ninety-seven per cent of offenders found guilty of, or cautioned for, sexual offences were also male. Women are the most common victims of sexual offences with 12,165 recorded rapes of women in 2009 and 19,740 sexual assaults. Roughly between eighty-eight and ninety-five per cent of serial killers are male. The suggestion is that by trying to be realistic, authors may automatically be incorporating misogynistic themes within their narrative; however this does not automatically equate to a hatred for women. Jarvis supports this claim; stating that 'According to the binary logic of patriarchy, the killer/victim dyad produces a polarization of gender norms: the killer embodies an uber-masculinity while the victim who is dominated, opened and entered, personifies a hyper-femininity (irrespective of biology)' (Jarvis 2007: 326).

This is further supported by Bindel who suggests that women write about sexual abuse, murder and violence because women are 'overwhelmingly the victims of sexually motivated brutality and homicide' (2007). A second strand of the argument questioning the proliferation of female crime fiction authors and readers is that women are drawn to read and write crime fiction because they can identify with the violence as a threat. This genre of fiction is appealing because it mimics women's own sense of susceptibility as females to violence, be it rape or other physical violence. The emotion within the female crime fiction is 'elicited from a deeper understanding of how violence, and the threat of violence, resonates for women' (Shillabeer 2010: 42).

As female authors are able to empathise with crimes which have predominately female victims, the narrative can develop into something all the more frightening: 'Good female writers provide us with the opportunity to feel the awful affects of such abuse and empathise with the victims' (Bindel 2007). When asked to respond to the claim that women write about violence because they have been brought up with a fear of violence, Jessica Mann agreed that 'girls grow up cautious' but stated that 'this is true of boys too' and in reality it is boys 'who are more at risk of encountering violence' (Mann 2009). The UK Office for National Statistics provides some interesting insights into how men and women feel about the threat of violence. Although the British Crime Survey in 2007/08 showed young men, aged sixteen to twenty-four, were most at risk of being a victim of violent crime, women were more than twice as likely as men to be worried about violent crime: twenty-one per cent of women compared with eight per cent of men. Women aged sixteen to twenty-four expressed the highest level of worry at twenty-eight per cent. Women were also more likely than men to say that fear of crime had an impact on their quality of life; two-fifths of women and one-third of men reported that fear of crime had a moderate or high impact on their quality of life. This supports the idea that women grow up with a heightened awareness of the threat of violent crime and are therefore able to give a better insight into these fears in their work. It is clear that in some cases writers feel they are interpreting society's ills and providing a 'safe haven' in which the horrors are mitigated at the end. In fiction at least, women feel confident that justice will be served. This can serve to explain why sixty per cent of the readers of this genre of fiction are women (Willis 2009).

The media further exacerbates a fear of crime by focusing primarily on violent crime, especially sex crimes. This has the effect of creating a moral panic in society, where the representation of 'stranger danger' and impending doom in the media is more apparent than ever before (Carrabine et al. 2002: 112). Slaughter is in agreement that we are more informed about crime and violence as a society (in Shillabeer 2010: 41). As a result, women are being made to feel afraid of society around them. Val McDermid stated that 'as a result of 24-hour news, we are more aware than ever before of the atrocities that are happening to women all over the world, and, to make sense of what is going on, we turn to art and fiction (Turner 2003: 4). Perhaps women are drawn to write – and read – about extreme violence because they have a greater ability to escalate incidents that are experienced daily in the imagination. As Brooks (2007) has suggested, perhaps there is something about containing these fantasies between the covers of a book that allows them to face up to their own worst fears. All too often a writer's desire to depict responsibly the real horror, pain and distress caused by violence is misinterpreted as gratuitous titillation.

In her critical work *Talking about Detective Fiction*, P.D. James states that the crime novels, in particular those of detective fiction, offer reassurance to the reader. Fiction 'confirms our hope that, despite some evidence to the contrary, we live in a beneficent and moral universe in which problems can be solved by rational means and peace and order restored from communal or personal disruption and chaos' (James 2009: 140). A majority of post-mortem and serial killer novels in this genre offer the reader a resolution. In Cornwell's *Scarpetta* the murderer is shot and killed, in Cole's *Hard Girls* the serial killer is arrested and in Slaughter's *Fractured* (2008) the killer commits suicide. In most novels of this genre the reader can feel a sense of satisfaction that the killer has got their comeuppance. Unlike in real life, 'in the crime novel the senseless acts of existence are given explanation. In crime novels, death never happens without a reason and the causes of death never go unpunished' (Turner 2003: 4). Although the novels express consumer greed, violence, fear and perversion, they are ultimately offering reassurance to the reader. They are cathartic, serving as a cheap therapy for the viewer or the reader (Taylor 1998: 39) and in many ways crime fiction is able to offer moral closure for the reader (Greer 2010: 362).

It is clear that there are multiple reasons and motivations for people to read, and more importantly, enjoy, crime fiction in the twenty-first century. Consumerism, gothic and horror literary genres, media representation of crime, the desensitisation of the readership and the increasing number of crime television dramas can all be held responsible for changes in the genre. As has already been established, for many reasons it has been the consumer that is driving this trend and the majority of the consumers are women. This chapter has argued that contrary to the argument of misogyny, the overwhelming reason women choose to read crime fiction novels is because they are being offered a vent for their own frustrations and are in search of an understanding regarding their position in society.

Kierkegaard's nineteenth-century dictum that 'revulsion and fear are combined with attraction and desire' (1957: xii) is particularly relevant to the crime fiction of the twenty-first century. Although the 'graphic gore' may repulse the reader, it also enthrals. While there are many reasons why a reader might be attracted to the genre, the 'undeniable fact' is that certain kinds of 'fear are pleasurable' (Johnson 2002: 4:1). Many theories support the idea that it is an inherent human instinct to feel both fear and excitement from what some would label as 'sadism'. Since the *Broadsides* of the eighteenth century this dichotomy of pleasure and pain, combined with the empowerment of fiction in the realm of the imagination which I have described above, has been the driving force behind the sales of crime fiction.

Notes

1. Post-mortem crime fiction can be described as fiction that not only incorporates crime but includes detailed autopsy scenes. The victim's damaged body is used to provide clues that will inevitably lead the protagonist to the murder.

2. Bestselling authors Tess Gerritsen, Karin Slaughter and P.J. Tracy were interviewed in 2010 for the MA dissertation *Female Crime Writers are Pivotal to the Popularity of Graphic Gore in the Twenty-First Century*.

3. Since the 1960s the brand *Pretty Polly* has used the dissected female form in their advertising of women's tights. Their 1990s billboard campaign simply depicted a pair of woman's legs in black stiletto heels. This idea of just showing the legs and no other part of the body is a common feature in their product marketing.

4. Tess Gerritsen's novels are renowned for their use of the naked female form on the cover. A great example is the UK paperback edition of her novel *Vanish* (2010) which depicts the torso of a naked woman lying on what appears to be a mortuary slab. Only the body's torso is visible with the head and lower body cut out of the image. Another example is Tess Gerritsen's *Whistleblower* (2008) UK paperback cover which depicts just a hand lying in a pool of blood, with none of the rest of the body visible.

Bibliography

Allen, M. (ed.). 2007. *Reading CSI: Crime Under the Microscope*. London: IB Tauris.

Allue, S.B. 1991. 'Serial Murder, Serial Consumerism: Bret Easton Ellis' American Psycho', *Journal of English and American Studies, University of Zaragoza*, 71–90.

Annesley, J. 1998. *Blank Fictions: Consumerism, Culture and the Contemporary American Novel*. London: Pluto.

Bindel, J. 2007. 'Murder, She Wrote', *Guardian Online*. Accessed on 25 April 2012, http://www.guardian.co.uk/books/2007/jan/31/crimebooks.gender

Brooks, L. 2007. 'Women Innocent of Crime Fiction Charge', *Guardian Online*. Accessed on 25 April 2012, http://www.theguardian.com/books/booksblog/2007/aug/16/womeninnocentofcrimefictio

Carrabine, E., M. Cox, M. Lee, and N. South. 2002. *Crime in Modern Britain*. Oxford: Oxford University Press.

Cole, M. 2009. *Hard Girls*. London: Headline Publishing Group.

Cooper, N. 2008. 'Why are Women Crime Writers ignored?', *Times Online*. Accessed on 25 April 2012, http//entertainment.timesonline.co.uk/tol/arts_and_entertainment/books/article4315389.ece

Cornwell, P. 1990. *Postmortem*. London: Warner Books.

——. 2003. *Portrait of a Killer: Jack the Ripper – Case Closed*. London: Sphere.

——. 2007. *Book of the Dead*. London: Sphere.

Flood, A. 2008. 'Patricia Cornwell gets Tough on Violent Crime', *Guardian Online*. Accessed on 12 June 2010, http://www.guardian.co.uk/books/booksblog/2008/dec/05/patricia-cornwell-crime

Greer, C. 2010. *Crime and Media: A Reader*. Oxford: Routledge.

James, P.D. 2009. *Talking About Detective Fiction*. Oxford: Bodleian Library.

Jarvis, B. 2007. 'Monsters Inc: Serial Killers and Consumer Culture', *Crime Media Culture* 3(3): 326–44.

Johnson, T. 2002. 'The Fear Industry: Women, Gothic and Contemporary Crime Narrative', *Gothic Studies Journal* 4(19): 44–62.

Kierkegarrd, S. 1957. *Concept of Dread*. Princeton: Princeton University Press.

Mann, J. 2009. 'Crimes against Fiction', *Standpoint Magazine*, September. Accessed on 5 February 2014, http://www.standpointmag.co.uk/crimes-against-fiction-counterpoints-september-09-crime-fiction

McDermid, V. 2009. 'Complaints about Women Writing Misogynist Crime Fiction are a Red Herring', *Guardian Online*. Accessed on 25 April 2012, http://www.guardian.co.uk/books/booksblog/2009/oct/29/misogynist-crime-fiction-val-mcdermid

McKay, C. 2008. 'Bloody Brilliant: When it comes to Fiction Crime pays', *The Author* CXIX: 141.

Patterson, J. 1996. *Kiss the Girls*. London: Harper.

Sawday, J. 1996. *The Body Emblazoned*. London: Routledge.

Schmid, D. 2004. 'Murderibilia: Consuming Fame', *Journal of Media and Culture* 7(5). Accessed on 24 February 2014, http://journal.media-culture.org.au/0411/10-schmid.php

Seltzer, M. 1998. *Serial Killers: Death and Life in America's Wound Culture*. London: Routledge.

Shillabeer, R. 2010. 'Female Crime Writers are Pivotal to the Popularity of Graphic Gore in the Twenty-First Century', unpublished MA. Dissertation. Oxford: Oxford Brookes University.

Slaughter, K. 2009. *Fractured*. London: Arrow Books.

Taylor, J. 1998. *Body Horror: Photojournalism, Catastrophe and War*. Manchester: Manchester University Press.

Turner, B. 2003. *The Writer's Handbook: Guide to Crime Writing*. London: Macmillan.

Willis, A. 2009. 'Book Reviewer quits over "increasing sexist violence"', *Telegraph Online*. Accessed on 25 April 2012, http://www.telegraph.co.uk/culture/books/6431386/Book-reviewer-quits-over-increasing-sexist-violence.html

Worthington, H. 2005. *The Rise of the Detective in Early Nineteenth-Century Popular Fiction*. Basingstoke: Palgrave Macmillan.

PART III

DEATH IN VISUAL CULTURE

9

THE POWER OF NEGATIVE CREATION –
WHY ART BY SERIAL KILLERS SELLS

Ricarda Vidal

Introduction

In 2003 the Centre for Contemporary Culture in Barcelona (CCCB) held an exhibition on 'Trash Culture'. A small room in the show was dedicated to art produced by serial killers: seven small paintings and drawings of diverse styles varying from realist horror to abstract expressionism and almost childish felt pen drawings. The works were accompanied by short blurbs which commented on their artistic style but were mainly dedicated to the biography of their creators, the serial killers Charles Manson, John Wayne Gacy, Nicolas Claux, Ottis Toole, Henry Lee Lucas, Richard Ramírez and Eugene Stano.[1] Next to the dates of birth and (in several cases) death, the visitors were informed about the murderer's nickname, the 'artist name' so to say, the number of victims and the punishment. This was followed by a small description of their careers from murderer to painter and some information about the economic value of their works on the serial killer art market. The inclusion of these artworks and their stories into the exhibition paid tribute to the popularity of the serial killer in contemporary society, a popularity which is reflected in adaptations of famous murder cases to novels and films and the fictionalisation of murder in pulp fiction, which also formed part of the show. In chapter 8 of the present volume, Rebecca Shillabeer describes the success of explicitly brutal descriptions of murder and serial murder in crime fiction. The burgeoning number of true-crime shows on TV and the thriving online trade in so-called *murderabilia*[2] further attest to our undeniable fascination with serial murder, which has led Mark Seltzer to call it a 'career option' which has the power to make the perpetrator a 'superstar' (1998: 1f.).

The seven murderers whose works were included in the show at the CCCB are all represented by galleries who sell their work at auctions or online. The gallerists are adamant that neither the murderers nor their relatives make any money from these sales. Instead, all proceeds go to charities of social causes once the galleries have taken off their commission.[3] Most of the works sell for between $300 and $500, but some of them, such as John Wayne Gacy's seemingly innocent and cheerful self-portraits in clown costume, can fetch up to $15,000 at auction. The number of websites dedicated to the sale of these works and the astonishingly high prices people are willing to pay for them raises the question of their symbolic value, for it is this rather than their artistic quality which is for sale. This chapter sets out to explore the peculiar attraction of serial killer art. Why do we consume these artworks – whether in the art gallery or on the web? And why do some of us feel the need to possess them? What does it mean to own these works? In order to find answers to these questions I will first explore our attitude towards death and our fascination with the serial killer and his[4] (usually sexually motivated) violence.

Sex, Death and Violence – Why Serial Killers are Attractive

Much has been written about the disappearance of death from public life and consciousness in the Western world since the arrival of modernity. Walter Benjamin speaks of the elimination of death, which has 'been pushed further and further out of the perceptual world of the living' (1970a: 94). Where once death was at the centre of life, and the dead person was surrounded by family and friends and displayed to strangers who paid their respects, today it is treated like an affliction, an incurable disease which cannot be talked about or shared. In the course of modernity death has generally become institutionalised at the edges of society. However, several authors in the present volume claim that Benjamin's diagnosis of death's disappearance is no longer valid. Instead, they argue that death has returned to public consciousness with renewed power after a period of suppression. While Maria-José Blanco explores the growing number of books about loss and bereavement (see chapter 4) and John Horne looks at the new and intimate visual scrutiny of terminal disease on screen (see chapter 10), Natasha Lushetich's description of her friend's dying party in chapter 16 attests to a return of the old rituals of dying – albeit in a refreshed and updated form. The interest which Briony Campbell's intimate artistic engagement with her father's terminal cancer (see chapter 18) received from art critics as well as the popular press shows that there is indeed a need and a willingness to bring death out of hiding and back into the world of the living. However, as Catherine Jenkins shows, the dying are often still isolated in the sterile heterotopias of hospitals and care homes (see chapter 1). Cemeteries, meanwhile, have been relocated from the centre of town to the outskirts. Philippe Ariès speaks of a loss of death, which has become so regulated and organised by bureaucrats that it 'no longer belongs to the dying man ... nor to the family' (1981: 588).

This exclusion of death from public life and ultimately its denial or suppression can be attributed to the loss of religious belief and the changing perception of eternity which has become increasingly detached from death and its traditional religious framework. Today in Western society a natural death very rarely occurs in public. However, while the individual has lost ownership over their own death as well as their place in public life, curiously it is exactly the public who have taken ownership of death. As Horne argues (chapter 10), death has become 'structurally central to popular entertainment, none more so than in the cinema where [...] the dying individual is screened *for* public view'. Although Horne is mainly concerned with representations of death by terminal illness in feature films, he also points to the very public death of reality-TV star Jade Goody in 2009, whose ultimately futile struggle against cancer was televised and watched by millions. While the high number of spectators who watched Goody's final days is evidence of our continuous need to get close to natural death, it is unquestionably violent death which really attracts the masses – whether to the cinema to watch the latest blood-and-gore splatter movie, to sites of real accidents and violent deaths, or, as Julia Banwell suggests, to the internet in search of endless replays of actual death and injury (see chapter 11). Despite Jade Goody's public death on television and a growing number of films as well as books and artworks such as Campbell's *The Dad Project*, which focus on natural death and give space to grief and mourning, what Geoffrey Gorer diagnosed for the mid-twentieth century continues to hold true: 'While natural death [has become] more and more smothered in prudery, violent death has played an evergrowing part in the fantasies offered to mass audiences – detective stories, thrillers, Westerns, war stories, spy stories, science fiction, and eventually horror comics' (Gorer 1995: 21). Gorer goes on to establish a link between sex and death and eventually between pornography and death:

> There seem to be a number of parallels between the fantasies which titillate our curiosity about the mystery of sex, and those which titillate our curiosity about the mystery of death. In both types of fantasy, the emotions which are typically concomitant of the acts – love or grief – are paid little or no attention, while the sensations are enhanced as much as a customary poverty of language permits. (Gorer 1995: 21)

Death, undeniably, attracts us even as we try to shut it out. 'On the one hand the horror of death drives us off, for we prefer life; on the other an element at once solemn and terrifying fascinates us and disturbs us profoundly', writes George Bataille, that most prolific of writers on sex and death (2001: 45). He traces this ambiguity back to the essential split within human experience between the chaos represented by the animal senses of the body and the order of reason and society. In *The Theory of Religion* (1992) he describes the emergence of the human from the animal state of immanence, unconsciousness and blindness into the consciousness of their own discontinuity within the continuity of nature (19). In *Eroticism* (2001) he postulates that we are aware of the fact that 'for us as discontinuous beings death implies the continuity of being' (82); we are also aware of the violence which is necessary to the flux of life and which brings about the origin of new discontinuous beings through the death of others. Since we cannot deny the violence, we try to shut it out by imposing taboos, by subjecting nature to our profane laws of work and prohibition and by repressing the animal senses inside ourselves. Death and the dead body are thus covered by taboo. So is sex, which, in its ideal form, comes very close to death when the bodies of two individuals merge into one at the moment of climax, when they cease to exist in one form and transform into another. According to Bataille, the human being is constantly torn between the ordered world of work and taboo, which allows self-possession and individuality, and a desire to give in to violence and destruction, fuelled by a longing for annihilation and the unconscious animal state of continuity.

Bataille posits a sound balance between order and chaos, which is achieved through taboos and transgressions, as the fundamental basis for humanity. However, only if we transgress the taboos of society, which impose order through illusion, can we transcend individuation and experience the deepest meaning of life. Of course, this transcendence and experience of continuity can only be of a temporary nature before we have to return to the world of order. Otherwise we would not only risk the death of another but also our own demise. Bataille locates the most profound experience of life in sexual union and, taking it one step further, in witnessing the death of another creature. However, the witnessing must happen within the strict framework of society, either as ritual sacrifice or public execution (2001: 82). Chaos must at all times be contained by order. Hence the taboo of murder keeps violence and the chaos of death at bay and allows humans to concentrate on life and to function as a society. The taboo may only be lifted when murder serves to reaffirm the frameworks of society, as in war, ritual sacrifice or the death penalty. Though sanctioned by society, under these circumstances murder still constitutes transgression. However, as *organised* transgression it allows for the profound experience of life at its most precarious while at the same time confirming the social framework. In *Eroticism* Bataille explores the interdependence of the profane and the sacred and the dependence of the sacred on the taboo, which gives a negative definition of the sacred object and inspires us with awe on the religious plane. Carried to extremes, this feeling becomes one of devotion and adoration. The gods who incarnate this sacred essence put fear into the hearts of those who reverence them, yet men do reverence them, none the less. Men are swayed by two simultaneous emotions:

they are driven away by terror and drawn by an awed fascination. Taboo and transgression reflect these two contradictory urges (68).

The disappearance of taboos naturally leads to a disappearance of the sacred and vice versa. While sex was once subject to the same taboos as death, it has now been integrated more and more within the profane world. However, where sex is still sacred and subject to one of the strongest taboos in our society is in connection with the lust-murder, the 'senseless' murder, which is unmotivated by material gain and committed by the serial killer. As a matter of fact, the serial killer emerges as a figure in cultural consciousness around the turn of the nineteenth century approximately at the same time as taboos on sexuality begin to loosen and death starts to disappear from public consciousness (Seltzer 1998: 2). The *Broadsides* which Shillabeer described in the previous chapter had their heyday around the same time. With their graphic illustrations of sexual violence and murder they can be seen as the harbingers of Gorer's pornography of death.

> [P]eople have to come to terms with the basic facts, of birth, copulations, and death, and somehow accept their implications; If social prudery prevents this being done in an open and dignified fashion, then it will be done surreptitiously. If we dislike the modern pornography of death, then we must give back to death – natural death – its parade and publicity, readmit grief and mourning. If we make death unmentionable in polite society – 'not before the children' – we almost ensure the continuation of the 'horror comic'. No censorship has ever been really effective. (Gorer 1995: 22)

What Gorer says about the horror comic of the 1960s with its splatter and gore aesthetic is true for the nineteenth-century *Broadsides* as well as for the horror movies or novels of our times. It is suppression that lies at the heart of the fascination with violence, murder and the serial killer in contemporary culture.

Elliott Leyton points out the paradox of terror and desire inspired by the serial killer: 'virtually all our multiple murderers achieve true and lasting fame. [...] During their celebrated trials, they may well be surrounded by admiring women who press their affections upon the killer, radiating admiration and even love as they do so' (2005: 27). However, normally such declarations of love rarely occur while a murderer is still at large. Once he is caught, the close encounter with death played out by the admiring public is no more than a sexual fantasy. If the murderer is condemned to death, the pending punishment only adds to his attraction – as object of desire or redemption. He is doubly connected with death as murderer and as condemned, as transgressor and as object of socially sanctified transgression, which will reinstitute the taboo of murder which he has violated. While most people refrain from public declarations of love and admiration, there is clearly a public fascination with the serial killer, which finds its outlet in the consumption of fictionalised versions of murder. As David Schmid has observed, 'characters such as [Hannibal] Lecter allow for the free expression of feelings of fascination and admiration concerning serial killers that are more carefully concealed in other instances' (2006: 23). Fiction allows us to explore our fears, but also our suppressed desires. Here we can indulge in what Bataille calls the animal side of sex, the basest and most primitive desires which would be frightening – and even life-threatening – if translated into reality. Unsurprisingly fictional images of serial killers are usually highly unrealistic. While they answer to our personal fantasies they have very little to do with actual serial killers (Piven 2010: 207). Jack the Ripper is a case in point with his many incarnations in popular culture, from the nineteenth-century *Broadside* to the films, musicals, plays and countless novels that continue to be produced. Jarvis argues that 'at least in the popular imagery, the distinction between historical serial killers and their cinematic counterparts is dissolving' (2007: 328). When it comes to serial killers, history is quick in the making. The already fine line between fantasy and reality is often blurred while the murderer is still at large. Once the killer is caught and screen-writers and novelists have gotten hold of the story, the transition into fantasy is smooth. Fiction, of course, allows us to take control. I will return to this point later.

The Serial Killer as Lawmaker

Bataille describes how organised transgression – in war, public execution, or great feast days – functions as a vent for the suppressed violence imposed by the rules of society which our civilisation is based on. He acknowledges the dark urges within the human psyche, the attraction of uninhibited violence which we suppress, and which the serial killer acts upon. However, the violence employed by the serial killer is never chaotic but always follows a system and often includes ritualistic elements. Sara Knox has described serial killing as an extreme form of collecting. A collection reflects its creator's particular vision of the world; it structures it and gives it a system and an order. She argues that 'the serial killer [can be seen] as someone who has the power, the will, and the dark vision to remake the world' (2003: 295). As collector the serial killer becomes a world-maker who is wholly in charge of rules and regulations. However, in relation to the existing society whose rules he breaks, he becomes a lawmaker. As world-maker he is reminiscent of what Bataille called de Sade's 'sovereign man', who 'knows himself to be alone and accepts the fact; [who] denies every element in his own nature, [...] that is concerned with others than himself; pity, gratitude, and love, for example are emotions that he will destroy' (2001: 172). As lawmaker, in contrast, the serial killer is perceived and perceives himself as part of society and at the same time superior to it. He represents the violence that is at once coveted and suppressed. As Walter Benjamin argues, 'in the great criminal this violence confronts the law with the threat of declaring a new law, a threat that even today, in spite of its impotence, in important instances horrifies the public as it did in primeval times' (1978: 283). Mixed in with the horror is the exhilaration of law-breaking and the admiration for the one who assumes the power of lawmaking. The serial killer acquires the quality of the sacred in the Bataillean sense: like the gods of old he inspires fear and reverence. These religious overtones are also reflected in W.H. Auden's declaration that 'murder is negative creation' and the murderer 'the rebel who claims the right to be omnipotent' (1948). Like a proper craftsman or artist, Auden's murderer is proud of his handiwork and of his rebellion. While Auden writes about fiction, the creator's pride the actual serial killers felt in their crimes is evidenced in the accounts of Leyton, Schmid and Seltzer amongst others. The murderer then becomes not only an admired lawmaker but also a revered creator – albeit a negative creator who works with the dark forces of destruction rather than those of production.

Schmid quotes a passage from Ian Brady's autobiography, where the child murderer writes about his position of total freedom which is paradoxically bestowed on him by being in captivity:

> The certitude of my death in captivity paradoxically confers a certainty of belief, a freedom of thought and expression most so-called free people will fail to experience in their lifetime. Unlike the merely *physically* free individual, no hellish circles of social graces and ersatz respect bind me to censor beliefs. I am not under the least obligation to please by deceit any individual whomsoever. To all practical intents and purposes, I am no longer of your world – if, as you might suggest, I ever was. (Brady quoted in Schmid 2010: 37)

Convicted and incarcerated, Brady no longer needs to act and play the game of moral and social pretence. Rather, he can be entirely himself beyond the restraints of society. However, this mental freedom is, of course, in stark contrast to his physical incarceration. He has in fact completely lost his power over his own body and even his death, which has become the 'property' of the state: Brady has tried to starve himself to death several times but has been prevented from doing so by being force-fed. Perhaps ironically, his punishment for committing murder lies in preventing himself from committing suicide. Still, Brady's notion of freedom and being above the moral code, is an interesting, abstract thought, which adds to the cult of the serial killer as Sadist 'sovereign man'. As Schmid points out, the fact that receiving punishment is as much part of the Sadean concept of pleasure as dealing it out 'renders Sadean heroes untouchable; they cannot be harmed, no matter what happens to them' (2010: 37). The Sadean hero is hence truly beyond the reach of society, superior to it in all ways. However, unlike Sade's fictional libertines, the highly influential and rich protagonists of his books, serial killers are often outsiders with little social power or influence: 'Acutely aware of their status as nonentities, the murderous methods of serial killers become their way of asserting both their identity and their ability to exert some kind of control over their environment' (36).

In fiction as well as in popular press coverage, however, serial killers are usually portrayed like Sadean heroes, i.e. as very intelligent and intellectually superior in the style of Hannibal Lecter. The popularity of actual serial killers (as is obvious in the marriage proposals they receive or the sale of murderabilia) can almost certainly be traced back to the confusion of fiction and reality in the popular imagination. We can here also think back to Gorer's comparison of pornography and death and the objectification of the body inherent to both. The fictional serial killer's victims, the bodies on the screen (or on the pages of a book), become Gorer's 'somebody else [who] is not a person [but] either a set of genitals, with or without secondary sexual characteristics, or a body, perhaps capable of suffering pain as well as death' (Gorer 1995: 22). In particular with regard to serial killer and slasher movies, Dietrich and Fox Hall observe that the protective frame of fiction, in this case the cinema, 'removes any *empathy* with victims' (2010: 98).

Dietrich and Fox Hall also point to the allure of the mystery that serial killers present, the mystery of why they kill – a mystery we need to solve in order to protect ourselves from them. But there is also the mystery of our own attraction to their crimes and to death itself. I would argue that the serial killer also allows us to question ourselves and our own attitude towards death. We may ask why they kill, but we also need to ask why we want to know so much about their murders.

Serial Killer Art

Let us return to the artworks exhibited at the CCCB. With the exception of Claux, the murderers only began to paint in prison – most likely within a programme of art or occupational therapy. One could argue that in some sense the constructive creation of painting replaces the negative creation of murder.[5] However, serial killer art is always consumed as inseparable from the history of its creators and as an intricate part of the negative creation of their crimes. The serial killer's self-declared right to omnipotence paired with his disregard for human life conjures an image of pure evil with all its inherent repulsion and fascination. An art object created by such a man reflects and in some sense retains the negative creation of his crimes and thus becomes a tangible incorporation of evil. The aesthetic pleasure of horror then becomes mixed with something darker and frightening, a fascination with violence which must be suppressed. Engaging in this pleasure entails a transgression of our own, it brings us closer to the killer, closer to death and closer to breaking this ultimate taboo ourselves.

The aura of evil, the repulsion and attraction emanating from the work, paired with a need to understand, is perhaps even greater when the artworks in question are apparently innocent and childlike in style and content. While most serial killer art shows gruesome scenes, several of the above mentioned artists/killers have also produced non-violent works. Most striking among these are probably Eugene Stano's simplistic colour pencil drawings of comic-style bears and other animals and John Wayne Gacy's cheerful self-portraits in clown costume. These works contain the thrill of looking at something banal and everyday, something anyone – a child or perhaps the neighbour from next door – could have painted, but which is at the same time the creation of a killer. Stano killed forty-one women and Gacy murdered at least thirty-three boys and young men.[6] Perhaps more here, in front of these innocent drawings rather than in connection with more explicitly cruel artworks, we can experience Benjamin's aura of authenticity (1970b). Here we become aware of the erstwhile function of the work of art as cult object. It is deeply disturbing but also thrilling to examine the lines traced by the hand of the killer, a hand that strangled, stabbed and murdered. The banal and childish drawings are transformed – they emanate the abject horror of the human monster who created them, but at the same time they are an expression of the artist/murderer as a lawmaker. As such they become the object of fear, but also reverence. When serial killers are elevated onto the superior plane of lawmakers with quasi-divine powers, their possessions and creations attain the status of reliquaries. If the serial killer's artwork is understood as part of the negative creation that constitutes his morbid oeuvre, then buying and claiming ownership of the artwork can become a way of participating in the transgression – even if only on an imaginary plain.

Writing about representations of death in art, Chris Townsend suggests: 'If our death is something so disabling that we cannot lay hold of it, as human subjects who die, perhaps it may be laid claim to by others, or bestowed upon them, even if they misunderstand or misrepresent it' (2008: 2). Townsend is mainly talking about natural death and about the difficulty (and the need) of artists to represent it in their work. However, with Auden's notion of negative creation in mind, it is possible to transfer the status of the artist as painter of death to the serial murderer as creator of death. In some sense, the murderer takes the work of the artist further. The murderer is the one who deals death, who works with death. Through his close connection to the victim, the one who dies, the murderer must know more about death than anyone else alive. Proximity to the murderer can then mean proximity to his knowledge. While such proximity is limited if only experienced via text or screen, murderabilia, or, and perhaps more so, serial killer art, present a tantalisingly close, yet safe, encounter with the murderer, death's willing executioner. The quest for murderabilia and serial killer art can then also become a quest for knowledge, for a piece of 'the real'. Ownership of such work therefore also constitutes a way of taking control over the unfathomable, the violence of murder and ultimately the violence of death itself.

Notes

An earlier and shorter version of this chapter was published as 'Painting Murderers – The Morbid Attraction of Serial Killers and their Art' in *Desipientia* 17:1, April 2010, pp. 12–15.

1. Nicolas Claux was a slightly unusual inclusion in this line-up of illustrious killers, as he only committed one murder. He did, however perform satanic rituals, drank blood he had stolen from a hospital and ate flesh which he cut from corpses in the morgue he worked at as a mortician. He was judged as mentally unstable at the time he committed the murder, which decreased his jail sentence. He was released in 2002 and now lives in Paris where he works as a mortician and artist. The following artworks were exhibited at the CCCB: Nicolas Claux, *Guts*, c.1998; John Wayne Gacy, *Pogo*, c.1978; Henry Lee Lucas, no title (oil painting of human monster with bloody mouth), 1998; Charles Manson, *Abstract*, c.1993; Richard Ramírez, *Dahmer's Fridge*, c.1994; Eugene Stano, no title or year (colour pencil drawing of small blue bear with yellow flower); and Ottis Toole, no title or year (felt pen drawing of man with bleeding axe stuck in split skull). The works are reprinted in the exhibition catalogue of *Cultura Porquería* on pp. 36–39 (see bibliography). Most of them can also be found online.

2. 'Murderabilia' are items that belonged to or were created by murderers or formed part of the crime scene. Some websites also offer fingernail clippings and hair of murderers to willing collectors and fans. Others are dedicated to all sorts of merchandise from coffee mugs to tea towels featuring reproductions of the killers' artworks or of their portraits. These items were also sold via eBay up until 2001, when eBay made such use of its facilities illegal in a reaction to demands from pressure groups of relatives of murder victims.

3. Claux is the exception to this rule. Since his release in 2002 he has been making and selling his works for his own profit.

4. I am deliberately referring to the serial killer as male, since most documented cases of serial killing were perpetrated by men. See Amanda Howard, 'A Timeline of Serial Killers', for a complete list of documented serial killers from 144 BC to 2002 (Howard 2010: 222–25). In the popular imagination serial killers are also almost exclusively male. For a more extensive discussion of the gendering of serial killers (and their victims) in Western society see Downing (2013).

5. It would be interesting to explore the therapeutic value of these artistic creations for the murderers themselves. However, this would be an entirely new chapter.

6. Before he was caught, Gacy performed as a clown for the children of friends at birthday parties or other festive occasions. He was, in fact, the friendly neighbour from next door.

Bibliography

Ariès, P. 1981. *The Hour of our Death*. New York, Oxford: Oxford University Press.
Auden, W.H. 1948. 'The Guilty Vicarage: Notes on the Detective Story, by an Addict', *Harpers Magazine*, May 1948. Accessed on 24 July 2012, http://www.harpers.org/archive/1948/05/0033206
Bataille, G. 1992. *The Theory of Religion*, trans. R. Hurley. New York: Zone Books.
_____. 2001. *Eroticism*, trans. M. Dalwood. London: Vintage.
Benjamin, W. 1970a. 'The Storyteller: Reflections on the Works of Nikolai Leskov', in H. Arendt (ed.), trans. H. Zohn, *Illuminations*. Glasgow: Fontana, pp. 83–109.

_____. 1970b. 'The Work of Art in the Age of Mechanical Reproduction', in H. Arendt (ed.), trans. H. Zohn, *Illuminations*. Glasgow: Fontana, pp. 219–53.

_____. 1978. 'Critique of Violence', in *Reflections: Essays, Aphorisms, Autobiographical Writings*, trans. E. Jephcott. New York: Harcourt Brace Jovanovich, pp. 277–300.

Cultura Porquería: una espeleologia del gust. Exh. Cat., 2003. Barcelona: CCCB.

Dietrich, E. and T. Fox Hall. 2010. 'The Allure of the Serial Killer', in S. Waller (ed.), *Serial Killers: Being and Killing. Philosophy for Everyone*. Chichester: Wiley Blackwell, pp. 93–102.

Downing, L. 2013. *The Subject of Murder: Gender, Exceptionality, and the Modern Killer*. Chicago: University of Chicago Press.

Gorer, G. 1995. 'The Pornography of Death', in J.B. Williamson and E.S. Shneidman (eds), *Death: Current Perspectives*, 4th edition. Moutainview, CA, London, Toronto: Mayfield, pp. 18–22.

Howard, A. 2010. 'A Timeline of Serial Killers', in S. Waller (ed.), *Serial Killers: Being and Killing. Philosophy for Everyone*. Chichester: Wiley Blackwell, pp. 222–25.

Jarvis, B. 2007. 'Monsters Inc.: Serial Killers and Consumer Culture', *Crime, Media, Culture* 3: 326–44.

Knox, S. 2003. 'The Serial Killer as Collector', in L. Dilworth (ed.), *Arts of Possession: Collecting in America*. New Brunswick, New Jersey, London: Rutgers University Press, pp. 286–302.

Leyton, E. 2005. *Hunting Humans: The Rise of the Modern Multiple Murderer*, revised edition. Toronto: McClelland and Stewart.

Piven, J.S. 2010. 'The Thread of Death, or the Compulsion to Kill', in S. Waller (ed.), *Serial Killers: Being and Killing. Philosophy for Everyone*. Chichester: Wiley Blackwell, pp. 206–17.

Schmid, D. 2006. *Natural Born Celebrities: Serial Killers in American Culture*. Chicago, London: University of Chicago Press.

Schmid, D. 2010. 'A Philosophy of Serial Killing: Sade, Nietzsche, and Brady at the Gates of Janus', in S. Waller (ed.), *Serial Killers: Being and Killing. Philosophy for Everyone*. Chichester: Wiley Blackwell, pp. 29–40.

Seltzer, M. 1998. *Serial Killers: Death and Life in America's Wound Culture*. London, New York: Routledge.

Townsend, C. 2008. *Art and Death*. London: I.B. Tauris.

SCREENING THE DYING INDIVIDUAL
Film, Mortality and the Ethics of Spectatorship
John Horne

⬥⬥⬥

Is there no thinking that goes beyond my own death, toward the death of the other man, and does the human not consist precisely in thinking beyond its own death?
— Emmanuel Lévinas (quoted in Robbins 2001: 126)

Bernard Tavernier's 1980 film *Death Watch* posits a near future where dying 'the old way' – through terminal illness – has become a rare event, so rare, in fact, that its presence is seen as suitable subject matter for a media event. When Katherine (Romy Schneider), a middle-aged woman, is given just two months to live, a television network launches 'Death Watch', a reality show following her every movement. Briefed to befriend Katherine, journalist Roddy (Harvey Keitel) permits a camera to be implanted in his brain, allowing continual covert filming of everything he sees. Whilst shying, then running, away from the overt public spotlight placed upon her, Katherine is inescapably captured and framed by Roddy's gaze: as camera and companion he invades her private space so she can be screened for the entertainment, edification and education of television spectators.

What is most absent – and least understood – in this alternate public sphere is terminal illness. As one journalist tells Katherine: '[We need] to come close to someone dying. There's a certain sad fame about it, in dying the old way. Not in flames, or in a crash, or abroad in war … we've had that up to here. But in the way … forgive me … the way it's happening to you. We miss the real thing.' The dying individual has become so unseen a being that their existence needs to be captured and broadcast, and thus mediated, framed and screened. 'Why?' Katherine asks. 'We need it,' she is told.

At the time of *Death Watch*'s production, the idea that death had replaced sex as the great Western social taboo had particular cultural currency, encouraged by the popularity of texts by Elizabeth Kübler-Ross (1970), Ernest Becker (1973) and others.[1] In 1981, Philippe Ariès' not uncontroversial tome *The Hour of Our Death*[2] accorded historical credence to the thesis that death had, over time, become structurally suppressed as the West sought to 'tame' and contain its uncertain and unknowable borders (see also Illich 1977; Elias 1985; Kearl 1989; Bauman 1992; Seale 1998; Kellehear 2007 and 2009). Through institutionalisation, medicalisation and social exclusion, the encounter with the dying individual became increasingly foreclosed and screened away from public view. This sequestration and severing of intersubjective engagement was further reinforced by barriers of taboo. Indeed, Norbert Elias suggested that dying had become seen as 'a deviation from the social norm' (1985: 69). However, death was (and is) structurally central to popular entertainment, none more so that in the cinema where it sustains a visual, often visceral, presence (see Aaron 2014; Hagin 2010). Here, of course, the dying individual is screened *for* public view.

Central to the public projection of the dying individual is Geoffrey Gorer's (1955) concept of 'the pornography of death'. Writing mid-century, he saw that whilst 'the natural processes of corruption and decay [had] become disgusting [...] violent death has played an ever growing part in the fantasies offered to mass audiences' (Gorer 1985: 20–21). As such, the spectacle of death had displaced the natural actualities of illness and the everyday banalities of dying (see also Tercier 2005: 210–15). Indeed, as Vicki Goldberg (1998) suggests, such a notion – of visual culture reframing the day-to-day encounter with death – is an integral development of pre-twentieth-century society.

Writing in the present volume about audience fascination with accidental sporting death, Julia Banwell considers perhaps the pinnacle of contemporary death as both spectacle and spectator sport: the fatal crash of Formula One driver Ayrton Senna in 1994, watched live at the time by millions and then rewatched (and remediated) until the present day, in an almost ritualised manner. For Banwell, the endless replaying of the incident offers the spectator a means of alleviating the 'unsettling' reality that the body of the being they so identified with – Senna – is, like their own, both fragile and mortal. Through slow-motion, multiple camera angles and repeated viewings, Senna's spectacular and destabilising death is safely contained within the contours of the representational frame. Also contained and kept at bay is, arguably, any unsettling sense of responsibility the spectator may hold in having found pleasure in the spectacle of Senna's death.

Gorer's 'pornography of death' thesis is especially pertinent to *Death Watch*. At one point, the television producer even opines: 'Look how shy we've become about death – it's the new pornography'. My interest lies in *Death Watch*'s suggestion that this is not a dystopic projection: that whilst 'we miss the real thing', we seek it out in spectacle, not actuality. Whilst the specifics of *Death Watch* remain, thankfully, science-fiction – although the recent case of Jade Goody's very public dying (see Walter 2009 and 2010; Woodthorpe 2010) suggests the prescience of Tavernier's text – the film raises, for me, several significant questions about how the dying individual is encountered, how they are seen and screened, in contemporary Western media. How, for example, do we typically experience terminal illness in everyday life? Is the dying individual considered an equal within the space of the public sphere? If our formative encounters with dying 'the old way' take place on screen, what are the ethical and political implications of this? Moreover, what is the *responsibility* of the spectator in such a situation?

As Phillip Mellor (1993) observes, Western modernity has structured itself to minimise, perhaps eradicate, threats to our 'ontological security'. Furthermore, as Jackie Stacey argues, 'we are encouraged to think of our lives as coherent stories of success, progress and movement' (1997: 9). Accordingly, the autobiographical impasse of dying, let alone the personal uncertainties of illness, presents a specific challenge to the self. Indeed, the possibility, if not reality, of our finitude is perhaps the ontological challenge *par excellence*. Robert Jay Lifton speaks of this as 'the universal human fear of death without integrity – of a death that is disintegrative in its humiliation, incoherence, absurdity, or prematurity. To imagine such a death is to see one's life in the same terms' (1980: 100–101). Lifton terms this 'death anxiety' (see also Yalom 1980; Piven 2004).

In seeking to shore up our 'ontological security' against the threat of 'death anxiety', terminal illness films perhaps function as spectatorial salves. Spectatorship offers a safe space for the social taboo to be transgressed, whilst concurrently granting the temporary quelling of individual death anxiety. Which is to say that 'we need' the moral solace offered by the sacrificial spectacle of the dying individual: the promise that dying *can* be comprehended *and* made meaningful *and* contained within a framework.

The epigraph by Emmanuel Levinas which opens this chapter indicates the direction we are headed. The quotation stems from Levinas' disagreement with Heidegger, who placed great ontological significance on death as the temporal end of being.[3] In arguing that the death of the other, not the self, was the primary responsibility of being, Levinas moved away from the comforts of ontological security and opened up an anxious and uncertain plane of ethical responsibility. Concisely, Levinas argued for ethics as 'first philosophy' – that is, before ontology – wherein the self held infinite responsibility towards the Other. Ethics, for Levinas, was the process of continually justifying why this infinite responsibility was not being met.

The pertinence of this to the present discussion is the wish to formulate an ethical preface to spectatorship: a momentary space before full submission to the spectacle where the socio-cultural (and thus ethico-political) is instated into the act of watching. That is, I simply intend for ethical responsibility to result in the spectator thinking about the dying individual outside of the filmic frame. In Levinasian terms, this is to conceive the encounter between self and Other as always occurring in the presence of the Third. The Third (crudely, society; that is, the other Others) can, in the context of spectatorship, be seen as the spectacle. The Other is thus the unknown being outside the spectacle for whom the spectator holds, ethically, infinite responsibility.

The dying individual, I argue, is mostly screened for the benefit of the spectator. Furthermore, that spectator is interpellated as an individual who is 'not-dying', which is to say 'living'. Ethical responsibility thus stems from the spectator's recognition of this state of affairs, alongside their reflection on how such spectacle sustains the *status quo*. Accordingly, responsibility requires a shift in the direction of the spectator's subjectivity: away from the self and towards the Other – the dying individual. I use 'dying individual' purely as a rhetorical device. It is meant to encompass both a necessarily fixed theoretical being, whilst also acknowledging the unknowability – the absolute individuality – of each real-world person the term refers to. Responsibility, therefore, also entails the unsettling of totalising frames that seek to strip the agency of the dying individual away, by containing, representing and narrating them through objectifying discourse.[4]

In pursuing this question of spectatorial responsibility, I will chiefly consider three films which stage quite direct encounters between spectator and dying individual. In each, albeit for very different purposes, the spectator is routinely positioned as both camera and companion. Whilst Hollywood melodrama *My Life* (1993) naturalises this dynamic, *Wit* (2001) works to expose the spectator as complicit with the camera in wanting to keep dying framed and at a distance. Finally, *Lightning Over Water* (1980), where documentary and fiction collide, collude and confuse, accords the spectator no safe position from which to watch. Instead, watching itself is presented as a deeply troubled subject position, fraught with unsettling ethical questions that have no necessary solution. As such, it will be argued as an essential text for rethinking how the dying individual is encountered on screen. This argument is not simply made for intellectual and theoretical interest: there is a necessary praxis to the following discussion. *Wit* and *Lightning Over Water* are suggested as particularly useful texts for purposes of death education, in social and medical settings, because they engender an actively ethical subject position. Neither is concerned with 'doing the right thing' but rather in continually questioning what 'doing the right thing' even means.[5]

Although certain theoretical conceits concerning death and the medium of cinema have been foundational to film studies, there has been a surprising absence of work dealing with film and death in general. Within this critical corpus there is little that deals directly with dying, still less that considers terminal illness.[6]

Even within the academy, it seems, there is a preference for spectacle, or at least a distancing from the actualities of natural death as experienced by the dying individual. I am using 'spectacle' quite specifically, in order to recall Guy Debord's (1967) definition: 'The Spectacle is not a collection of images; it is a social relation between people that is mediated by images' (Debord 1983: 7). As such, I am arguing that the contemporary encounter with the dying individual has to be thought of as a mostly mediated event, and, more importantly, that this has certain real-world political consequences.

John Tercier argues that the act of watching death and dying on screen produces a physical response – 'a *frisson*' – which marks the pleasure of transgressing social taboos. He speaks of the typical spectatorial dynamic in terms of how 'We make of the dead *things*, distancing ourselves from them, not just to achieve the emotional detachment necessary to go on living [...] but so we might apprehend what we as survivors are graced with and sentenced to – life' (2005: 216–17; emphasis in original). The climax to My Life captures this dynamic well, and thus serves as a paradigmatic text for terminal illness films as a whole. The film spans the period between protagonist Bob Jones receiving a diagnosis of cancer and his ultimate death. Bob's wife, Gail, is pregnant, prompting him to make a video record for his unborn child, consisting of life-lessons and biographical asides. Following Bob's death, the film cuts to a close-up of a TV screen playing a video of him reading a children's book aloud. The camera slowly zooms out, revealing Bob's infant son enjoying the story and taking comfort from the encounter (see Fig. 10.1). Gail, sitting to one side, draws similar solace.

This scene could be considered for its mending of the patriarchal gap that Bob's death opened up, or its quasi-religious promise of life extending beyond the mortal boundaries of the body. What concerns me is a different, although not unrelated, concern. This scene, not even Bob's death, is what the film has been building to. Within the private family context of the diegesis, the last thing Bob's wife and child want is to only ever be encountering him in recorded form; however, it is a salve and it is all they have. The film's spectator, however, has been cued throughout to anticipate this moment. From the opening moments of the film, Bob is seen recording himself speaking to his unborn child. These scenes are framed from the perspective of the video camera. Or rather, the film's spectator is interpellated as Bob's ideal spectator: his child. Indeed, the autobiographical stories Bob imparts function throughout as narrative exposition.

In this final scene, therefore, the spectator gets to take a step back and is moved precisely because they have spent the past two hours routinely imagining themselves in the intimate space where the child is now sat. The spectator's entertainment is thus entangled in Bob's dying. Or, to rephrase that, the spectator's price of submission to the spectacle is their disavowal of any complicity in anticipating – and speculating on – Bob's suffering. As a dying individual, he is made into a '*thing*': an audiovisual object sacrificed for the self-centred interests

Figure 10.1 Bob, on screen, reads his son a story in *My Life* (1993, USA, Capella Films, Columbia Pictures Corporation, Zucker Brothers Productions), film still.

of the spectator. Furthermore, whilst a wealthy middle-aged married man is an unusual protagonist, *My Life*'s narrative varies little from many other dramas of terminal decline. The spectator expects to end the film shedding and sharing tears with the dying individual's family and friends on screen.

Fran McInterney's survey of terminal illness films offers a useful expansion on this point. Whilst she mainly considers mainstream American fictional film, her conclusion is worth citing at length:

> the dying are passive players; their agency is of the sacrificial endurance kind and the narrative focus is principally on survivors. The dying journeys depicted are largely linear; traversing a 'diagnosis-to-death' trajectory in a 100-minute span leaves little time for oscillation. [...] Ceding to cinematic aesthetic requirements, overt bodily disintegration is seldom depicted. [...] Cinematic dying, enacting the narrative imperative for a 'happily ever after', promulgates passivity, linearity, beauty, resolution and salvation in the face of mortality. (McInterney 2009: 213)

Having watched the films McInterney considers, I concur with her observations.[7] There are, however, some significant limitations. The absence of non-American cinema, as well as documentary and experimental film, is problematic and will be addressed below. Also, whilst McInterney does note the preponderance of dying middle-class, white mothers, and the corresponding absence of elderly deaths, she fails to significantly explore some essential political questions, which are particular pertinent given the popularity of the texts she examines. Specifically, to draw on Judith Butler's (2004) term, there is the question of how the cinematic frame helps to construct and govern what society considers a 'grievable life'. That is, does film collude in wider ideological formulations by presenting the death of certain bodies and beings as more tragic, more deserving of our grief, than others, whether that be regarding age, gender, race, nationality, sexuality, disability, or so forth. There is not the scope to explore this further here; however the precise makeup of the dying individual in audiovisual discourse certainly warrants further study. Equally, the cause of death deserves attention: does cinema exaggerate the prevalence of certain conditions (such as brain tumours and leukaemia) whilst excluding others (such as colorectal cancer, respiratory disease and, indeed, the co-morbidities of old age)?[8]

The lack of non-English language films, particularly those which have been both acclaimed and well-circulated in the Western marketplace, is a problematic absence in many respects.[9] In such films, there is often, although not always, a 'narrative imperative' for tragedy-ever-after. Moreover, operating under different 'aesthetic requirements' and tenets of realism, such films frequently present the body in decline much more graphically than their Hollywood counterparts (a similar distinction could be made regarding 'independent' productions). Yet this is still wedded to spectacle. Whilst we might consider an axis of alleged actuality, between, say, Jennifer's beautified body in *Love Story* (1970) and the tangible corporeality of *The Death of Mr. Lazarescu* (2005), or between the mawkish melodrama of *Stepmom* (1998) and the inexorable stasis of *La Gueule ouverte* (1974), these films have all been carefully constructed to achieve their desired ends. Furthermore, all offer the spectator the comforting container of narrative and the security that any performance of dying is only ever just pretend. Such displacement sustains distance: the messy everyday of actuality is smoothed over through submitting to the appealing sheen of spectacle. It is precisely this which *Wit* works to unpick.

Wit is a 2001 television adaptation of a Pulitzer Prize winning play. Emma Thompson plays Vivian Bearing, a professor of English literature, who is dying of ovarian cancer. The film's narrative – diagnosis, decline and death – mirrors many a melodrama. What differs here, however, is Vivian's solitude. The film opens with a set of jagged, jarring chords on the soundtrack, followed by an imposing extreme close-up of a doctor announcing 'you have cancer'. That is, diagnosis occurs before Vivian is even seen. The doctor is standing, looking down at Vivian. In the reverse-shot that reveals her, taken from his point-of-view, Vivian looks directly into the camera. From the outset, then, the spectator is aligned with the clinical position. This shot, where Vivian's look unsettles the diegetic boundaries of the frame, establishes a prising apart that occurs throughout the film.

This prising apart becomes much more explicit in the scenes that follow. Vivian enters hospital for treatment and begins narrating her story to the audience. Across the flashbacks of the film's first half, Vivian seems to be literally steering the chronological presentation of events. She interacts both directly with the spectator and within the diegesis. This all conveys the impression, so to speak, that Vivian is framing herself. The spectator is thus interpellated, through Vivian's direct address, as her only companion, separate from the totalising clinical and institutional confines.

These confines are initially the stuff of content, but they soon take on the tenor of form. As she begins to physically weaken, Vivian's narrative agency diminishes. That is, she increasingly becomes the subject – or rather object – of the narration. This is first figured midway following a fade-to-black. The soundtrack reprises the jagged chords from the opening and the black screen cuts to a very sick Vivian being readmitted to hospital. The scene that follows bears no indication of Vivian's narratorial control – not even a look to camera. Whilst her direct address subsequently returns, the film now follows a linear progression towards Vivian's death. Whereas before Vivian's mental recollections were shared with the spectator, introduced with lines like 'I can recall…', now the film simply intrudes on them. This intrusion is dramatised when a nurse, who has arrived to take Vivian away for a test, appears within the once safe space of her mind's-eye. With this comes an increase in Vivian's allusions to the artifice of dramatic representation. Earlier, for example, she observes how the film is only showing the 'interesting' moments of her hospital stay and not adequately conveying the tedium she experiences. She remarks: 'If I were writing this scene it would last a full fifteen minutes. I would lie here and you would sit there'.

This revelation of artifice reaches a crux in a scene where she is left alone, awaiting an ultrasound, and begins to address the audience. The camera slowly approaches Vivian until she is framed in tight close-up (see Fig. 10.2). She says: 'My next line is supposed to be something like this: "Oh, it is such a relief to get back to my room after those infernal tests". This is hardly true. It would be a relief to be a cheerleader on her way to Daytona Beach for spring break. To get back to my room after those infernal tests is just the next thing that happens'.

The film then suddenly cuts to Vivian, falling back into her hospital bed, giving a deliberately exaggerated line reading: 'Oh God, it is such a relief to get back to my goddamn room after those goddamn tests'. This produces a fracturing of the spectatorial contract which is never fully mended. Whereas before the spectator was welcomed as companion to Vivian's dying, here they are left bereft of any certainty that such a welcome was genuine or scripted. Or rather,

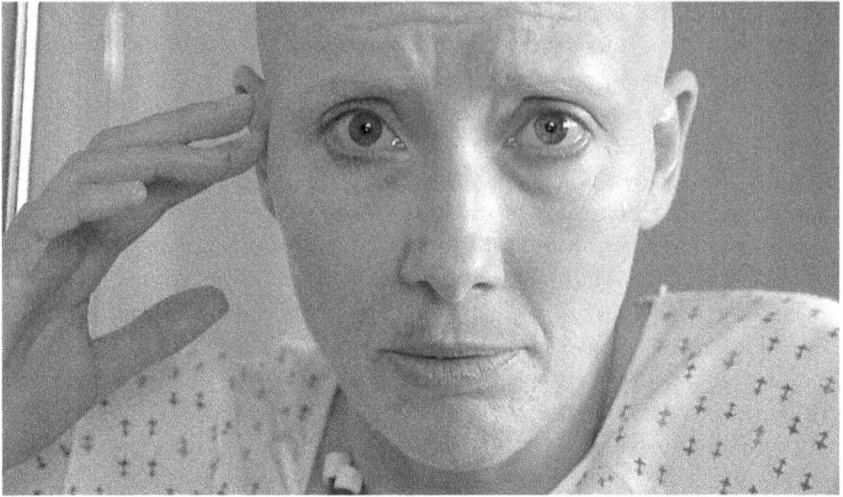

Figure 10.2   Vivian addresses the spectator in *Wit* (2001, USA, Avenue Pictures, HBO Films), film still.

the spectator's responsibility becomes about much more than mere presence in the encounter. It becomes instead about accountability for spectatorial demands, which have become explicitly linked with dehumanising medical discourse and, more subtly, aligned with the spectator's need for Vivian's dying in order to provide them with a narrative to watch. This specific revelation of Vivian's subordination to narration – and thus to the spectator – is the culmination of the prior thematic and formal prising apart. What results is a distrust of narration – which nevertheless is all there is. However, the spectator's price of submission – complicity in Vivian's subordination to object status – has been exposed.

I am arguing, then, that *Wit* works to unsettle the cinematic frame which always-already contains the dying individual, objectifying them through the camera's totalising lens. That is, it both exposes and traffics in the production of dramatic interest and acts of narrative containment which stage the fictional encounter for the benefit of the spectator. Moreover, it seeks to reveal the formal fabric of disavowal, through which the spectator typically submits to the cinematic spectacle. We thus have in *Wit* an encounter concerned explicitly with the violence that representation – as characterisation and narration – does to the dying individual, which is furthermore concerned with revealing the same effect of institutionalisation and medicalisation. The spectator is seated in a position of complicity, whose only recourse is a reconsideration of that role. Or rather, the spectator's responsibility is awakened in a perpetual reflection on their reduction of Vivian to an object of perception. Concern thus shifts to the construction of Vivian's – fictional – dying, which has been witnessed, rather than simply watched and walked away from.

Accordingly, *Wit* provokes the questions of spectatorial responsibility raised at the start of this chapter. It refuses to let the spectator rest as both camera and companion. Rather, the violence of the former is revealed and left exposed, a revelation which the spectator must either disavow or somehow accommodate (and justify). As such, *Wit* not only muddies the sheen of the spectacle, it undermines the pretence that the dying individual can be encountered on-screen without the spectator ceding certain ethical responsibilities. *Wit* sets out to do this; it is structured to give a strong inkling as to what the right response is. *Lightning Over Water*, on the other hand, flat out refuses.

Before turning to *Lightning Over Water*, the final limitation of McInterney's survey of terminal illness films needs to be addressed: the absence of documentary.[10] Whilst films which take actuality as source material are clearly distinguished from their fictional counterparts, when considered in relation to how they screen the dying individual, certain similarities remain. Namely, the fundamental spectatorial dynamic in documentary is no different to its fictive equivalent: the dying individual is mediated, framed and screened for the benefit of the spectator. Indeed, in many respects, documentary, whilst introducing reality into the equation, simply accentuates, rather than undoes, the pretence of actuality which the spectator clings to.

Vivian Sobchack notes the morally charged nature of documentaries which offer a direct gaze upon real dying.[11] She also observes how few documentary representations there are of natural death. For Sobchack this is partly because:

> gradual, natural death allows time and space for the ill-mannered stare to develop and objectify the dying. The filmmaker's ethical relation to the event of death, the function of his or her look, is open to slow scrutiny by the spectator. [...] The viewer (both as filmmaker and spectator) bears particular subjective responsibility for the action marked by – and in – his or her vision. (2004: 242–43, 248)

Therefore it is essential that the viewer's gaze on real dying is structured as welcomed and invited (254). As an example, the footage and photography that Briony Campbell presents of her dying father in 'The Dad Project' is offered (and constructed) as consensual: her very personal framing (re)assures the spectator that it is okay to watch. Campbell discusses the project in the present volume, describing the dual roles she found herself performing. She writes of feeling 'resigned to the fact that documenting [my] dad's death was as instinctive to me as experiencing it,' adding that this triggered both pride in demonstrating an 'innate' photographic ability, and shame that she 'was thinking so objectively' through such an emotional time (see p. 248 of the present volume). These struggles articulate a tension between Campbell's presence as both companion and camera to her father's passing, a binary she punctures in the project through the inclusion of self-portraiture. Campbell's willingness to enter the representational frame she otherwise constructs – not to mention her tangible sadness and supportive presence – adds a personal, subjective texture to the lens through which her dying father is encountered, shielding the spectator from concerns which she was clearly wrestling with.

Although there are clearly differences between documentary and fictional figurations of dying, I suggest that they both function similarly. Whilst documentary amplifies the 'subjective responsibility' of the spectator, both it and fiction are typically concerned with mitigating or disavowing what that responsibility entails. For Sobchack, 'as the filmmaker watches the dying, we watch the filmmaker watching and judge the nature and quality of his or her interest' (2004: 243). What does get disavowed is the spectator's responsibility for 'the nature and quality' of *their own* interest. Michele Aaron asserts that real and fictional representations of suffering can be placed 'at either ends, of some kind of continuum of spectatorship'. The spectator to both is engaged in an act where he or she is 'looking on' at the suffering of another, which surely raises 'questions of personal and social response and responsibility' (Aaron 2007: 122). That is, the dying individual, in both documentary and fiction, is framed in a manner which keeps those spectatorial questions of responsibility at bay. Questions which would otherwise address the social positioning and ethical entanglements of the spectator are rejected in preference of self-interest.

Lightning Over Water began as a collaboration between directors Wim Wenders and Nicholas Ray, who was dying of cancer. The initial, fictional idea was scrapped due to Ray's ill health. Instead, the two improvised scenes where they played themselves, performing the very roles they were actually in: Wenders, a director, who had come to make a movie with Ray before his death. Tom Farrell, Ray's assistant, constantly shot video footage of the proceedings. Ray's condition worsened and shooting was abandoned. Wenders filmed some more footage before abandoning the material to his editor. The result, entitled *Nick's Movie: Lightning Over Water*, played at Cannes in 1980; however, Wenders was not happy with the result.[12] He felt it told a story in the 'third person' which should have been in the 'first person'. He spent three months re-editing it, adding a voice-over and giving it a stronger chronological and linear narrative. His – definitive – version, now simply *Lightning Over Water*, was released in 1981.[13]

The finished film charts Wenders's arrival at Ray's apartment, the difficulties they faced in making a film, the declining state of Ray's health and finally a wake, on board a boat, held by Wenders and his crew. Jon Jost, in a scathing article (based on the original cut), accuses Wenders of refusing Ray 'love', and instead '[seeming] to perceive life only through the mechanical devices of film.' He goes further: 'They rolled [Ray] over with a movie-making machine and now they even choose to display the carnage' (Jost 1981: 96). This attack hides a personal bias (Jost wanted to make a final film with Ray), but it usefully articulates the particular fear which haunts Wenders – an anxiety which is expressed literally and structurally throughout the film. He renders this terror visually in a dream sequence midway through the film. In voice-over, he comments on how the cinematic apparatus, and the daily logistics it demanded, consumed his time, 'rather than being concerned with Nick'. Even in sleep, Wenders says, 'the camera would always be there'. This is followed by shots of Ray superimposed onto the camera on the deck of the boat carrying Ray's ashes (see Fig. 10.3).

The film thus stages the encounter between spectator and Ray wholly within the framing imposed by Wenders. The film's indexical instability is further troubled by its temporal doublings. The performative nature of the footage is undercut by the past-tense of Wenders's voice-over. Furthermore, the ugly, draining palette of the video-footage contrasts troublingly with the bright, clean sheen of the film. The film therefore refuses a stable viewing position. The only stability in the encounter is the fact that it is always mediated, ever shifting. However, this banality, accentuated by the ongoing moral anxieties expressed by Wenders, constantly unsettles the frame. In doing so, it ruptures the shared contract of subjective responsibility between spectator and filmmaker, and creates the conditions for a new one – between spectator and Ray – to emerge. In this new contract, the watching conditions are remarkably different. Spectatorship here becomes a performative act, posthumously producing Ray's existence against that which seeks to contain it. Equally, this opens the film up to Ray's creative contribution.[14]

Figure 10.3 Wim Wenders's nightmare in Lightning Over Water (1980) sees Nicholas Ray super-imposed on a camera. Germany/Sweden, Road Movies Filmproduktion, Wim Wenders Produktion, Viking Film, film still.

Here, the spectator and Wenders find a point of contact: the film is replete with moments of Wenders watching Ray's work, in film, as a theatre director and as an actor. The spectator becomes a guarantor that Ray achieves the restoration of 'self-image' he sought. However, there is no guarantee that this is the 'right' response and particularly in the video-footage of Ray, that watching is at all welcome (and *vice versa*). This constant negotiation of response, however, and the continual cycling between performance, actuality and potential exploitation, begins to reveal the formal fabric of spectatorial disavowal. That is, it brings to the fore the usual means of filmic relief – the defacement of the dying individual – and reveals the ethical price it comes at. The spectator, in becoming more concerned with Ray than in shoring up their 'ontological security', rubs against the grain of the frame and suggests another way of watching.

I want to conclude by returning to *Death Watch*. Late in the film, Roddy confronts the consequence of his dual role as camera and companion. Entering a pub, he sees a television which is screening Katherine in the show 'Death Watch'. We share Roddy's perspective as he re-experiences a private encounter he recently had with her, now being broadcast for the entertainment of millions. Seeing this triggers a breakdown. Roddy blinds himself – thereby destroying the camera – and reveals the truth to Katherine. Together, as true companions, they try to evade the gaze of the production company. In the television executives' most cynical revelation, we discover that Katherine, initially, was never dying. The diagnosis of terminal illness was a lie, intended simply as a stunt to provide ratings. However, the drugs she was prescribed as part of the pretence are, in fact, slowly killing her. Ultimately, Katherine takes her own life.

This is, perhaps, a despairingly cynical note on which to end, suggesting that the only escape from spectacle involves the ultimate severing of spectatorship: to stop watching; and that the only hope for the dying individual to achieve agency from the self-interest of the spectator watching them is through suicide. But such ruins offer the opportunity for the spectatorial contract to be rebuilt: for the spectator, at a minimum, to recognise that the dying individual is being screened for their benefit and that such self-interest does real-world violence. This – precisely this – is the foundation for an ethics of spectatorship in the encounter between spectator and dying individual. Such an awakening of ethical responsibility cannot bear the burden of further dictates: it is not about the spectator being instructed on what the moral thing to do is, but rather perpetually thinking through what doing the right thing even means. As such, *Wit* and *Lightning Over Water* offer themselves as vital texts in the service of death education, for a multitude of social, medical and political purposes. The hope is that there can be a restructuring of the *status quo*, so that the dying individual will cease to suffer the inequities and inequalities of stigmatisation, isolation and abandonment so as to appease the death anxiety and shore up the ontological security of the so-called 'living'.[15]

Notes

1. See also Lynne Simpson's chapter in the present volume (Chapter 2), which situates the work of Kübler-Ross and others in the context of a century of scholarship indebted to the legacy of Freud's work on grief.

2. See for example Allan Kellehear's critique (2007: 172–84). As Tercier notes, however, Ariès' thesis, 'is in its broad sweep, in most authors' opinions, valid' (2005: 11).

3. Limitations of space preclude a detailed engagement with Levinas's thought here. For relevant discussions, see Gibson (2001), Davis (2004) and Downing and Saxton (2009) regarding film, Levinas and the 'face' of the Other; see also Keenan (1999), Cohen (2006) and Townsend (2008) on Levinas and death.

4. I explore this question of 'responsibility' towards the dying individual in the context of photography, end-of-life care reforms and notions of citizenship in Horne (2013).

5. This is thus to draw on the distinction between 'morality' and 'ethics' made by Aaron (2007), Saxton and Downing (2009) and others.

6. See however: Aaron (2014), Grønstad (2008), Hagin (2010), Sobchack (2004), Gibson (2001), Oeler (2009), Knox (2006), Tercier (2005), McInerney (2009), McIlwain (2005), Russell (1995) and Davis (2004).

7. Alongside the films studied by McInerney, and staying within the domain of mainstream American terminal illness film, I have also watched *Unstrung Heroes* (1995), *The Mighty* (1998), *Autumn in New York* (2000), *My Life Without Me* (2003), *Henry Poole is Here* (2008) and *Things Fall Apart* (2011); as well as *Last Holiday* (2006), *The Guitar* (2008) and *50/50* (2011) where a potentially 'dying individual' is granted a complete cure in the closing act. See also the films cited in the notes below.

8. Equally, of course, is the question of how film might facilitate the construction of 'illness as metaphor' (see Sontag 2002).

9. For example, *Ikiru* (1952), *Cries and Whispers* (1972), *La Gueule ouverte* (1974), *The Barbarian Invasions* (2003), *Le temps qui reste* (2005), *The Death of Mr. Lazarescu* (2005) and *Biutiful* (2010).

10. For example, *Near Death* (1989), *Silverlake Life: The View from Here* (1993), *Sick: The Life and Times of Bob Flanagan, Supermasochist* (1997), *Dying at Grace* (2003) and *How to Die in Oregon* (2011).

11. Sobchack actually uses the term 'ethically charged' (2004: 248).

12. That version, according to Kathe Geist, was characterised by '[e]xtreme disjunctive editing and longer speeches, which tended toward obscurity' giving it 'a highly personal, ultimately morbid quality' (1981–1982: 48). Ivone Marguilies also notes that it 'avoids the linearity that would signal a fictional construction' (1993: 55).

13. For more on *Lightning Over Water* see especially Burnett (1981), Chamberlin (2005), Corrigan (1985), Geist (1981–1982), Jost (1981), Margulies (1993), Russell (1995: 67–104), Scheibler (1993) and Naremore (1988: 19–21).

14. Ray and Wenders together scripted, and/or improvised, with Ray directing Wenders, all the scenes in which they appear together (with the exception of the scene when Ray is in hospital). Carloss Chamberlin, in one of the few critical readings emphasising Ray's creative role, sees it in these terms: '[t]he plot of the film is the story of an actor (Ray) controlling the director (Wenders) through the brilliant use of his weakness. Wenders' benign sadism, the sadism of all directors who have to get the shot, is his performance' (Chamberlin 2005).

15. Special thanks to Michele Aaron for her invaluable comments on several drafts of this article during its development.

Bibliography

Aaron, M. 2007. *Spectatorship: The Power of Looking On.* London: Wallflower.
_____. 2014. *Death and the Moving Image: Ideology, Iconography and I.* Edinburgh: Edinburgh University Press.
Ariès, P. 1981. *The Hour of Our Death,* trans. Helen Weaver. New York: Barnes & Noble Books.
Bauman, Z. 1992. *Mortality, Immortality & Other Life Strategies.* California: Stanford University Press.
Becker, E. 1973. *The Denial of Death.* New York: The Free Press.
Burnett, R. 1981. 'Wim Wenders, Nicholas Ray and *Lightning Over Water*', *Cine-Tracts* 14/15(2/3): 11–14.
Butler, J. 2004. *Precarious Life: The Powers of Mourning and Violence.* London: Verso.
Chamberlin, C.J. 2005. 'Regarding *Bitter Victory*: Hollywood's Philoctetes in the Desert or *La Politique des Comédiens*', *Senses of Cinema.* Accessed on 17 February 2014, http://sensesofcinema.com/2006/38/bitter_victory/
Cohen, R.A. 2006. 'Levinas: Thinking Least about Death: Contra Heidegger', *International Journal for Philosophy of Religion* 60(1/3): 21–39.
Corrigan, T. 1985. 'Cinematic Snuff: German Friends and Narrative Murders', *Cinema Journal* 24(2): 9–18.
Davis, T. 2004. *The Face on the Screen: Death, Recognition and Spectatorship.* Bristol: Intellect Books.
Debord, G. 1983. *The Society of the Spectacle,* trans. K. Knabb. London: Rebel Press.
Downing, L. and L. Saxton. 2009. *Cinema and Ethics: Foreclosed Encounters.* London: Routledge.
Elias, N. 1985. *The Loneliness of the Dying,* trans. E. Jephcott. Oxford: Basil Blackwell.
Geist, K. 1981–1982. 'Lightning over Water', *Film Quarterly,* Winter, 35(2): 46–51.
Gibson, M. 2001. 'Death Scenes: Ethics of the Face and Cinematic Deaths', *Mortality* 6(3): 306–20.
Goldberg, V. 1998. 'Death Takes a Holiday, Sort Of', in J.H .Goldstein (ed.), *Why We Watch: The Attractions of Violent Entertainment.* New York: Oxford University Press, pp. 27–52.
Gorer, G. 1985. 'The Pornography of Death', in J.B. Williamson and E.S. Shneidman (eds), *Death: Current Perspectives,* 4th edition. California: Manfield Publishing Company, pp. 18–22.
Grønstad, A. 2008. *Transfigurations: Violence, Death and Masculinity in American Cinema.* Amsterdam: Amsterdam University Press.
Hagin, B. 2010. *Death in Classical Hollywood Cinema.* Basingstoke: Palgrave Macmillan.
Horne, J. 2013. 'Unsettling Structures of Otherness: Visualising the Dying Individual and End of Life Care Reform', in M. Aaron (ed.), *Envisaging Death: Visual Culture and Dying.* Cambridge: Cambridge Scholars Publishing, pp. 224–242.
Illich, I. 1977. *Limits to Medicine: Medical Nemesis: The Expropriation of Health.* Middlesex: Pelican.
Jost, J. 1981. 'Wrong Move', *Sight and Sound,* Spring, 50(2): 96–97.
Kearl, M.C. 1989. *Endings: A Sociology of Death and Dying.* New York: Oxford University Press.
Keenan, D.K. 1999. *Death and Responsibility: The 'Work' of Levinas.* Albany, New York: State of New York University Press.
Kellehear, A. 2007. *A Social History of Dying.* Cambridge: Cambridge University Press.
_____. (ed.). 2009. *The Study of Dying: From Autonomy to Transformation.* Cambridge: Cambridge University Press.
Knox, S.L. 2006. 'Death, Afterlife, and the Eschatology of Consciousness: Themes in Contemporary Cinema', *Mortality* 11(3): 233–52.
Kübler-Ross, E. 1970. *On Death and Dying.* London: Tavistock.
Lifton, R.J. 1980. *The Broken Connection: On Death and the Continuity of Life.* New York: Touchstone.
Margulies, I. 1993. 'Delaying the Cut: the Space of Performance in *Lightning Over Water*', *Screen* 34(1): 54–68.

McInterney, F. 2009. 'Cinematic Visions of Dying', in A. Kellehear (ed.), *The Study of Dying: From Autonomy to Transformation*. Cambridge: Cambridge University Press, pp. 233–52.

McLlwain, C.D. 2005. *When Death Goes Pop: Death, Media and the Remaking of Community*. New York: Peter Lang.

Mellor, P.A. 1993. 'Death in High Modernity', in D. Clark (ed.), *The Sociology of Death: Theory, Culture, Practice*. Oxford: Blackwell, pp. 11–30.

Naremore, J. 1988. *Acting in the Cinema*. California: University of California Press.

Oeler, K. 2009. *A Grammar of Murder: Violent Scenes and Film Form*. Chicago, Illinois: University of Chicago Press.

Phelan, P. 1997. *Mourning Sex: Performing Public Memories*. New York: Routledge.

Piven, J. 2004. *Death and Delusion: A Freudian Analysis of Mortal Terror*. Greenwich, Connecticut: Information Age Publishing.

Robbins, J. 2001. *Is It Righteous to Be? Interviews with Emmanuel Lévinas*. Stanford, California: Stanford University Press.

Russell, C. 1995. *Narrative Mortality: Death, Closure, and New Wave Cinemas*. Minneapolis: University of Minnesota Press.

Scheibler, S. 1993. 'Constantly Performing the Documentary: The Seductive Promise of *Lightning Over Water*', in M. Renov (ed.), *Theorizing Documentary*. New York: Routledge, pp. 135–50.

Seale, C. 1998. *Constructing Death: The Sociology of Dying and Bereavement*. Cambridge: Cambridge University Press.

Sobchack, V. 2004. *Carnal Thoughts: Embodiment and Moving Image Culture*. California: University of California Press.

Sontag, S. 2002. *Illness as Metaphor; AIDS and its Metaphors*. London: Penguin.

Stacey, J. 1997. *Teratologies: A Cultural Study of Cancer*. London: Routledge.

Tercier, J.A. 2005. *The Contemporary Deathbed: The Ultimate Rush*. Hampshire: Palgrave Macmillan.

Townsend, C. 2008. *Art and Death*. New York: I.B. Tauris.

Walter, T. 2009. 'Jade's Dying Body: the Ultimate Reality Show', *Sociological Research Online* 14(5).

———. 2010. 'Jade and the Journalists: Media Coverage of a Young British Celebrity Dying of Cancer', *Social Science & Medicine* 71(5): 853–60.

Woodthorpe, K. 2010. 'Public Dying: Death in the Media and Jade Goody', *Sociology Compass* 4(5): 283–94.

Yalom, I.D. 1980. *Existential Psychotherapy*. New York: Basic Books.

Filmography

Death Watch (aka: *La mort en direct*). 1980. Director: B. Tavernier. France, West Germany, UK: Films A2, Gaumont International, Little Bear, Sara Films, Selta Films, Société Française de Production, TV13 Filmproduktion.

Lightning Over Water. 1980. Directors: W. Wenders and N. Ray. USA: Road Movies Filmproduktion, Viking Films, Wim Wenders Productions.

My Life. 1993. Director: B.J. Rubin. USA: Capella Films, Columbia Pictures Corporation, Zucker Brothers Productions.

Wit. 2001. Director: M. Nichols. USA: HBO Films, Avenue Picture Productions.

THE BROKEN BODY AS SPECTACLE
Looking at Death and Injury in Sport

Julia Banwell

Advances in visual technologies allow sports spectators to enjoy a privileged view of events through close-ups and slow-motion replays, and YouTube has made it possible to access and repeatedly view footage of unpredictable and disturbing occurrences. Death and serious injury in sport destabilise the notion of the excellence and toughness of the sporting body and expose it as breakable and vulnerable.

This chapter will explore the potential for reading the repeated viewing of real and reported death and injuries in sporting contexts as ritualistic. It will examine the location of death in contemporary visual media cultures, taking as its focus the visual representation and reporting of death and injury in two heavily viewed sports: football (soccer), and Formula One motor racing. Analysis of two examples will be undertaken, with attention first being given to English footballer David Beckham's foot metatarsal injury, sustained on 10 April 2002 during a Champion's League match against *Deportivo La Coruña*. Discussion will then focus on Brazilian Formula One driver Ayrton Senna's fatal crash on 1 May 1994 during the San Marino Grand Prix. Analysis will centre on the ways in which the sporting body is represented and subsequently colonised by different types of gaze: the gaze of the sports and news media with their medicalisation of reporting sports injury, and the gaze of the viewers of sports. I will devote attention to the uneasy, destabilising modes of spectating that occur when looking at death and injury in sport as unpredictable events that heighten and intensify the spontaneity of live sport and the voyeurism inherent in watching sporting bodies as they engage in the rituals of competition and performance. The function of the body as metonym will also be explored. Drawing on theories of spectatorship of sport, suffering and of the representation of death in contemporary visual cultures, I propose that there are multiple potential readings of this kind of viewing. The following exploration into the repeated viewing of such unsettling events in the news and other visual media, and whether it may be seen as ritualistic, will be framed by three principal questions. Firstly, can viewing be seen to transcend the supposed dislocation and distance between the viewer and the viewed, or to increase it? Secondly, does the location of elite sporting bodies such as those of Beckham and Senna within celebrity culture have any particular effect on the way(s) in which such bodies are viewed when they experience pain and suffer trauma? And, finally, does the threat posed to notions of the integrity of the physical body by death in its imagery and representations become more, or less, disturbing within the context of viewing elite sporting bodies?

The term 'ritual' has two potential applications in sporting contexts. The first describes sports as performative practices whereby the game or race is undertaken following a set of prescribed rules, and the second (which receives attention in the following discussion) relates to the viewing of events by spectators, in the sense that multiple sensory and emotional engagements with the scene through actions such as replaying footage ritualise the act of looking through repetition.

The presence of physical violence, injury and death, either accidental or deliberate, in sporting practices across multiple cultural contexts is well documented and is certainly no recent phenomenon. Examples include fighting to the death in Roman gladiatorial combat, the ball game of *pelota* practiced by pre-Hispanic Mesoamerican civilisations such as the Maya and the Zapotec, and the rituals of European medieval tournaments which were, as Guttmann notes, designed to mimic war at a time when, he asserts citing a study by Charles Haskins in 1927, 'the major sport [...] was war, with its adjuncts the tournament, the joust and the judicial duel' (in Guttmann 1998: 15). There are also many more recent instances of competitive physical practices where violence is integrated into, and indeed forms a central component of, the contest, such as boxing, wrestling, and cage fighting, and of course, martial arts, some forms of which have been practiced for hundreds of years. In the case of martial arts, however, it must be pointed out, that the violence of the practice is rooted in a philosophy and regulated by complex rules, so violence, though sometimes bloody, may not be seen as arbitrary or gratuitous in the way it can be perceived to be in other physical cultures. In football and motor racing, however, injury and death are not taken to be integral to the practice as in aggressive contact sports, though it may be acknowledged that they are risks associated with participation, particularly in the case of motor racing. Nonetheless, I would suggest that death and injury are not comfortably incorporated into the performative aspect of the physical practice, and instead occupy a highly destabilising position. The two aforementioned sports are reported and analysed widely by both the visual and print media and are therefore highly visually present and accessible to large numbers of readers and viewers. Furthermore, both football and Formula One racing are heavily marketed and extremely lucrative sources of revenue for corporate sponsors (take for example McDonalds' – arguably rather ironic – sponsorship of the 2010 football World Cup held in South Africa), as well as for venues, broadcasters and media providers.

There is a wealth of literature dealing with the depiction and representation of dead and broken bodies in visual cultures such as cinema, fine art and photojournalism, and discussing questions of spectatorship of these phenomena, but relatively little scholarly attention has been given to the visual location of death and injury in sporting cultures. Existing studies in this field have tended to focus on aggressive contact sports such as wrestling. For example, Curry and Strauss argue in their 1994 photoessay entitled 'A Little Pain Never Hurt Anybody', which documents the treatment of, and attitudes towards injuries sustained by wrestlers, that injury has arguably become 'normalized' in this kind of sporting context. In their view, injury in this setting occupies a far less threatening position than the risk of injury in, say, football or motor racing. In their case study, an athlete's ability to withstand both minor and more serious injuries strengthens rather than destabilises perceptions of their physical toughness and sporting prowess.

It is possible to say that injury and its treatment have to some degree also become normalised in other sports, thanks to ever-watchful pitch- and track-side cameras which show the injury and subsequent first aid and physiotherapy treatments as they are administered, and follow players who have suffered more serious injuries as they are stretchered off the field of play. In this way, the visibility of injuries in close-up could be argued to have a normalising effect, making visible events that can later be replayed and examined by commentators and spectators. A crucial distinction to be drawn at this stage is that between injury resulting from deliberately enacted, performed violence, and injury that is accidental, that is to say, unintended as either a function or an outcome of the physical practice. The latter occupies an uneasy space both in terms of how we look at such events, and also how we can talk about the act of looking at such events. I would posit in the first instance that the way we view injury in sport varies broadly according to various factors: its seriousness (impact on the body), its impact on an athlete's career, and the sporting context within which it occurs. It would be erroneous and reductive to assume simply that spectators enjoy looking at violence in sporting contexts where it is a part of the contest, and are not interested in looking at violence outside these parameters. The issue of enjoyment, or otherwise, of looking at real and represented injury and death is, of course, highly complex and problematic in its own right, and has been extensively theorised. Georges Bataille, for example, has devoted much attention in his writings to the mingling sensations of fascination and disgust arising in an individual when confronted by a profoundly unsettling experience such as the sight of a corpse. Julia Kristeva explores the notion of the abject as something that disturbs and unsettles the individual and is yet inextricable from our bodily and psychological selves, proposing that death, specifically the physical evidencing of death as corpse, is 'the utmost of abjection. It is death infecting life' (Kristeva 1982: 4). The corpse thus not only reminds us troublingly of the inescapable materiality of the body, and its destructibility, but also by extension stands metonymically for death itself. Metonymy, according to Lakoff and Johnson's (1980: 35–42) definition, is a process by which a part may not only stand for the whole but also provide understanding. In this way, an object such as a body or body part may function not only as a form of rhetorical shorthand, but also as part of a symbolic system by which meanings are transmitted, so that, for example, a corpse may come to stand not only for one dead individual, but for other dead people and even for death itself. However, as Bataille, Kristeva and others have noted, coupled with revulsion and the instinct to turn away, is the compulsion to look. Viewers of bodies that are broken or dead may thus be both disturbed and fascinated.

Any attempt to fathom and theorise the internal experience of individual spectators of death (or, indeed, of any phenomenon) is, however, fraught with seemingly irresolvable complications. As Kennedy has observed, the spectator is 'a corporeal presence but a slippery concept' (Kennedy 2009: 3), and we should not treat individual spectators within a collective audience as though they lack autonomy in their perceptions of, and reactions to what they watch: 'Audiences are not (and probably never have been) homogeneous social and psychological groups [...] and recording their encounters with events, regardless of the mechanism used to survey or register them, is usually belated and inevitably partial' (Kennedy 2009: 3).

This is especially tricky when considering the spectatorship of potentially unsettling events. But can we assume that seeing injury and death in a sporting context will have an unsettling effect on spectators? Theorists have identified several types of gaze through which spectators may subject viewed events, and it goes without saying that these may be enacted in combination with one another. But, of course, not all viewed events are the same, and ideas that work in cinematic spectatorship theory cannot necessarily be directly applied in a sporting context.

Analyses of sports photography have examined the viewing of sporting bodies in the languages of race, sex and gender discourses. Rowe's 1999 study, for instance, draws parallels between sports photography and pornography, both of which 'are fixated on the body, minutely examining its performative possibilities and special qualities. Both are concerned with arousal – either of the photographic subject straining to perform at their best or of the viewer in deriving pleasurable excitement from the image before them' (Rowe 1999: 148). According to this view, the visual positioning of sporting bodies involves a degree of objectification by the gazes of camera and spectator. The analysis of the role of the 'gaze', a mainstay of psychoanalytic theory since its first applications to cinematic texts during the 1970s (most famously by Laura Mulvey's 1975 essay 'Visual Pleasure and Narrative Cinema'), has also been a subject of study in the field of sports spectatorship. Duncan and Brummett's 1989 essay, 'Types and Sources of Spectating Pleasure in Televised Sports', examines three types of spectatorship, which they define in the following way: 'Voyeurism, or illicit looking at some object, usually another person; fetishism, or fascinated looking at a spectacle that is intended to be observed; and narcissism, or looking that elicits identification' (Duncan and Brummett 1989: 199).

There is some debate around the limitations and usefulness of psychoanalytic approaches to the analysis of sport spectatorship, which have been read as downplaying or ignoring the importance of its social and collective aspects. Rose and Friedman, for example, reject the notion that the gaze of the sports spectator is voyeuristic and objectifying, arguing that 'Television sport seems to invite the viewer to engage in distracted, identificatory and dialogic spectatorship [...] The sports fan is like the brother on the sidelines: he shares the greater wisdom and perspective of the commentators, whilst identifying alternately with players, coaches and fans' (Rose and Friedman 1994: 25–26).

Kennedy also draws a distinction between spectatorship of sports and of other activities such as theatre, asserting that sports fans are expected to actively encourage athletes by cheering and clapping, as opposed to sitting quietly, which may certainly be seen as a mode of spectatorship involving an amount of participation, if not in the actual game or contest then by way of, as Kennedy puts it, 'civic or tribal investment in the team' (2009: 156). This may be demonstrated by the possession of a season ticket, a team shirt or scarf worn whilst watching a match at the stadium or at home, or by placing bets on the outcome of matches.

Whilst I agree that the spectators' gaze may be identificatory, I would suggest that the way in which sports are broadcast, replayed and reported effectively positions the spectator as voyeur. In this way, a tension may be identified between different spectator positions. For example, a spectator of televised sport may identify with other fans through a shared enjoyment of looking, while also being interpellated into the authoritative position of analyst through the use of technologies such as replay and slow motion, which identify key moments in the contest and pinpoint them as foci for detailed discussion in the televisual dissection of sports commentators.

In her discussion of repetitive viewing of images of death, Vicki Goldberg argues that any threat is neutralised by the spectator's control over how and when to view such images: 'knowing when the violence and death will turn up allows a certain monitoring of one's own emotions' (Goldberg 1998: 39). To play and re-play a video clip of a motor racing accident or a clash of bodies on a football pitch could, if we follow Goldberg's line of argument, be seen as an attempt to exert some control over the unpredictable and uncontrollable, to make uncomfortable realities seem less threatening to our own bodies. This ritualisation of viewing disturbing events through repetition of the act of looking may be seen as a mechanism for coping with trauma through an act of empowerment in rejecting the instinctive urge to look away – with both the real trauma of seeing bodies broken, and the imagined trauma of the possibility that our own bodies may also undergo such damage.[1] The act of viewing seen from this perspective is a form of meditation, of trying to make sense of the chaos, destabilisation and disorder that injury and death imply. It is, however, ultimately rendered futile by the displacement inherent in the experience of spectatorship of death. It is the great unfathomable reality, and therefore impossible to 'know' directly simply by seeing. Looking at death and injury is, let us not forget, also fraught with complexities and contradictions, so that coupled with the notion of control of or meditation on disturbing realities, there may also be a perverse pleasure in the act. Voyeurism is inherent in the act of looking and looking again at events both as they unfold and later in replays and close-ups that fragment and distort not only the bodies of the athletes but also, as noted by Margaret Morse, the sense of the passing of time in the match or the race. As Duncan and Brummett assert: 'As one of the few "live" programs left on television, sport offers many unexpected opportunities for uninvited, illicit, and therefore voyeuristic looking' (1989: 203).

The notions of fetishism and voyeurism are particularly applicable to a highly visible and much commented upon figure like David Beckham. Beckham is the archetypal celebrity sportsman whose body has been commodified by the media, that is to say, following Duncan and Brummett's definition of body commodification, treated as 'goods to be closely examined, appraised, and assessed' (1989: 199). Beckham possesses, as Garry Whannel posits, 'all the attributes of a golden boy' (Whannel 2001: 138), and is consequently exposed (some might say overexposed) to scrutiny not only of his performance as an athlete but also in advertising images and in the pages of glossy celebrity magazines where he is often pictured accompanied by his wife, the former Spice Girl and archetypal WAG[2] Victoria. Beckham is arguably responsible for the adoption of the word 'metatarsal' into common usage in English in the UK. The caption underneath an image on the footy-boots.com website, reads 'Before 2002, most of us thought metatarsal was a cheap, Greek brandy'. The image[3] itself is a computer-generated picture of a foot resting atop a football in a pose familiar to any spectator of the sport. This foot, however, is stripped of boot, skin, and flesh, and referencing the England team colours of red and white, the bones of the skeletal foot are white, with the metatarsal marked in red. The association of the colour red with the England football team thus becomes conflated with its connotation of blood, danger, transgression of bodily boundaries, but in a curiously detached and sterile way owing to its being computer-generated. Of particular fascination in this and other such images is that the viewer is allowed to visually explore a bloodless though highly suggestive fantasy of transgression of the boundary between the interior and exterior of the sporting body from a safe position, that is, one unthreatened by the sight of real bodily injury and its untidy effects evidenced by blood, skin, pain. The image described above is, of course, a simulation, not Beckham's actual foot. However, given the extent to which the footballer's name has become symbolically linked to the word 'metatarsal', the image can be taken to stand as a metonym for the body of the man. Newspapers reporting the injury contained information on how to find your foot metatarsals alongside diagrams of the skeletal structure of the foot, bringing the technical language of medical discourse into the realm of mass media sports reporting. Articles such as the one in the *Guardian* newspaper on 11 April 2002, entitled 'Beckham's Injury Explained', provide evidence that the fragmentation and colonisation of Beckham's body has transcended the boundaries of the body itself. Both the interior and exterior are now, it seems, fair game for scrutiny, the fetishising gaze even penetrating flesh.

Advances in visual technologies, such as telephoto lenses, allow sports analysts and spectators (though it could be argued that in some ways these positions are one and the same, as sports spectators are interpellated into a privileged position of authority and knowledgeability) to enjoy extreme close-ups of sporting action, and events on pitch and track are told and re-told in slow motion and vivid still images taken from multiple camera angles. The intense scrutinising gaze of these visual technologies, coupled with verbal input from commentators on location and pundits in the television studio, positions the home viewer as knowledgeable sharer of this privileged viewpoint, in on all the action with nothing being missed, thanks to the plethora of viewing technologies being employed. Slow motion, in addition to allowing repeated viewing of the action, also has an aestheticising and beautifying effect upon what is shown, so that, as Margaret Morse observes, 'the slowness which we associate with dignity and grace transforms a world of speed and violent impact into one of a dance-like beauty' (Morse 1983: 49). Spectators are thus placed in a position of knowledge, and arguably, power, invited to share the privileged gaze of the cameras and enter into a lingering contemplation of the bodies on display. The medicalised language of injury reporting further enhances this sense of power, as now spectators may share in the authoritative gaze of the medical professional, fetishising the body by intensely focusing on fragments of it. Repeated viewing of footage or still images also enables a controlling gaze, through which the beautiful body in pain may thus become an object of voyeurism that borders on the sadistic. What happens, then, when the horrifying is aestheticised by the cameras' gaze?

Brazilian Formula One driver Ayrton Senna's fatal crash at the San Marino Grand Prix at Imola, early in the third race of the 1994 season, put a premature and violent end to a successful and high-profile racing career that had spanned a decade, and is undoubtedly one of the most famous disasters in sport. Senna, born in 1960, won the Formula One championship three times, and is regarded as one of the most talented drivers the sport has produced, and his life and death continue to fascinate, as Asif Kapadia's critically-acclaimed feature-length documentary *Senna*, released in 2010, testifies. Senna's death, however, was not the only fatality to occur at this event: during a qualifying session, the Austrian driver Roland Ratzenberger was also killed in a crash, and the previous day, another driver, Rubens Barrichello, had been seriously injured in a crash and was left unable to race. Following a further accident at the start line of the race, there was a restart, shortly after which Senna's car careered off the track at a corner and hit a concrete wall at over 100 miles per hour. Senna suffered skull fractures which were to prove fatal and he was pronounced dead in hospital in Bologna at 6.40 P.M., two hours after doctors had declared that he was brain dead and being kept alive only by life support machines.

There has been significant controversy surrounding various aspects of this tragic case, ranging from uncertainty about the cause of the crash, to court cases following the event (one accused Williams, with whom Senna had just signed in 1994, of manslaughter, although the charges were later dropped). By far the most disturbing controversy, though, centres on the previous day's crash involving Roland Ratzenberger. According to Italian regulations at the time, if the Austrian driver had been declared dead at the scene of the crash, the track would have had to be closed and the Grand Prix could not then have gone ahead. Senna drove to the scene of Ratzenberger's crash to see for himself the track and the remains of his car, based on the condition of which he believed that Ratzenberger had died instantly. Indeed, if Ratzenberger had been pronounced dead at the scene of his accident, Senna's death would have been prevented (which, of course, does not preclude the possibility that he could have fatally crashed on another occasion). It is believed by some that Senna died instantly from his injuries and should have been pronounced dead at the track-side. Two uncomfortable questions are raised here, around the ethics of showing such events in the media, and also, if we believe the conspiracy theory outlined above, the ethical implications of the power of big money over sporting events to the potential detriment of safety.

As we have seen, sports reporting in the media benefits from a range of advanced visual technologies that allow repeated viewing of the action, including events such as the ones discussed above. Death in sport is mercifully rare. Senna's crash was shown by media across the world, and the footage is still available on YouTube, so that spectators may look at his death as many times as they wish. There are many clips of the crash itself, and also various e-memorials created by fans. One such home-made tribute, uploaded on 11 April 2009, is seven minutes long and contains the crash footage as part of a montage of other images such as stills of Senna, set to music.[4] This kind of personalised memorialisation has been discussed by Marguerite Helmers in relation to e-memorials to Diana, Princess of

Wales, who was killed in a car crash on 31 August 1997. Such tributes, she argues, are acts of public mourning that speak to the fact of Diana's life as spectacle. Media such as the Internet allow members of the public to engage actively with individuals they never come into contact with: 'Thus, mass media provides citizens with common stories, shared cultural memory, and mandatory rituals. The web memorials position viewers as members of a temporal, yet temporary, public sphere that shares awareness of the media event' (Helmers 2001: 450).

In the case of Senna's crash, although the man's dead body is not visible, it is enough to see the broken, fragmented car, which becomes a metonym for the broken body. The relationship of looking at death in this way to sports spectatorship arguably indulges, encourages or perhaps even exaggerates voyeuristic and sadistic looking by visually presenting the abject within a viewing context where looking is encouraged and expected. Susan Sontag links death and the erotic using the example of the car crash (a connection also explored in fiction by J.G. Ballard in his 1973 novel *Crash*, and its later film adaptation by David Cronenberg). Sontag argues that 'Everyone knows that what slows down highway traffic going past a horrendous car crash is not only curiosity. It is also, for many, the wish to see something gruesome. Calling such wishes "morbid" suggests a rare aberration, but the attraction to such sights is not rare' (Sontag 2003: 85). The compulsion to look at disturbing events perhaps partially explains the proliferation of videos of the Senna crash on YouTube. The other key factor is that Senna was a high-profile, highly visible and popular sporting celebrity, and his death was emotionally upsetting to fans of motor racing, so that despite the fact that the man was not known to them personally, individuals were motivated to produce highly emotive memorials.

It is pertinent to enquire whether looking at death and injury in sport may be seen to decrease or to increase the presumed distance between the viewer and the viewed. Although sports spectatorship is far from passive, the viewer is still not physically a part of the game, so there is certainly a physical displacement; however, this operates on multiple levels of physical involvement according to whether the event is viewed from pitch- or track-side, at home alone or accompanied, in another place that is public yet removed from the viewed events, such as a sports bar, as the action happens or at a later moment. Due to the active and engaged nature of sports spectatorship, however, the physical displacement between players and spectators does not negate any sense of involvement on the part of spectators. This characteristic of sports spectatorship could be seen to expose spectators to potential psychological trauma through their receptiveness and reactivity. Under typical viewing circumstances, reactions to what happens on-screen (or for spectators at the event, at a comparatively short physical distance) may manifest in expressions of extreme emotion such as shouting, crying, or physical movements such as jumping up, throwing arms into the air, etcetera. On the other hand, it would be a gross oversimplification to surmise that repeatedly looking at disturbing images such as an eye-watering football tackle or a high-speed car crash causes spectators to become desensitised or emotionally unaffected by what they see, but as Goldberg argues, the fact that viewing can take place under completely controlled circumstances renders the threat more safe. In this sense, the physical displacement between spectator and action provides a buffer between the broken body of the performer and that of the spectator. If this notion is applied to the motivation to memorialise and repeatedly view the Senna crash, it may be argued that such acts function as mechanisms for coping with trauma, both the psychological trauma of viewing death, and the emotional trauma of grief, without the risk of bodily fragmentation or of pollution by the corpse. Death is the great unfathomable, unknowable reality, and it is possible that ritualising, that is to say, repeating the act of viewing such unpredictable events is a search for reassurance, a humanising expression of curiosity, yet at the same time the viewed is abject and disturbing, and also fascinating. The heightened visibility of sporting bodies intensifies the conflict between looking and not looking at them in situations of pain and suffering.

The spontaneity of live sport, which is so attractive to spectators, sometimes gives rise to unsettling events, such as injury and death, to which the spectator is thus exposed. The fascination of looking at images of death and horror, a cultural phenomenon much discussed in visual cultural studies, can also, I would suggest, be identified in looking at death and injury in sports as they are reported in the news media, and is derived from human beings' curiosity and deep fear of phenomena which threaten boundaries and structure. Death and injury unsettle and fragment the body itself, and also destabilise the image and the notion of the elite sporting body as invincible. In this way, the idea of the sporting body as the embodiment of excellence and a commodified site of aspirational fantasy by the spectator is thrown into question and, ultimately, disturbingly undermined. The moment at which a sportsperson is injured or killed marks an uncomfortable nexus between the fetishisation of, and identification with, the other's body. It is precisely this that is so unsettling. As Bataille and many others have noted, to look at the death and destruction of the body is to be confronted by our own fragility and mortality, and the inescapable materiality of our own bodies. Herein lies the fascination of injury in sport; it threatens the apparent perfection of elite bodies. The act of repeatedly watching and examining slow-motion replays of a disastrous tackle on the football pitch or a fatal crash on a motor racing track aestheticises and dramatises the fragile physicality that is common to us all.

Notes

1. See also John Horne's chapter for a detailed discussion of death as spectacle, and of spectatorship as a safe place from which to observe death.

2. WAGs is the acronym for 'Wives and Girlfriends', a term commonly used in the print press and celebrity magazines in the UK and applied to women who become romantically involved with high-profile sport stars, usually football players on the England national team.

3. Accessible at: www.footy-boots.com/craig-johnston-in-stud-release-plea-7353/

4. It can be accessed at http://www.youtube.com/watch?v=svDuPAThOlc

Bibliography

Carlisle Duncan, M. and B. Brummett. 1989. 'Types and Sources of Spectating Pleasure in Televised Sports', *Sociology of Sport Journal* 6: 195–211.

Curry, T.J. and R.H. Strauss. 1994. 'A Little Pain Never Hurt Anybody: A Photo-Essay on the Normalization of Sport Injuries', *Sociology of Sport Journal* 11: 195–208.

Goldberg, V. 1998. 'Death Takes a Holiday, Sort Of', in J.H. Goldstein (ed.), *Why We Watch: The Attractions of Violent Entertainment*. Oxford: Oxford University Press, pp. 27–53.

Guttmann, A. 1998. 'The Appeal of Violent Sports', in J.H. Goldstein (ed.), *Why We Watch: The Attractions of Violent Entertainment*. Oxford: Oxford University Press, pp. 7–26.

Helmers, M. 2001. 'Media, Discourse and the Public Sphere: Electronic Memorials to Diana, Princess of Wales', *College English* 63(4): 437–56.

Kennedy, D. 2009. *The Spectator and the Spectacle. Audiences in Modernity and Postmodernity*. Cambridge: Cambridge University Press.

Kristeva, J. 1982. *Powers of Horror: An Essay on Abjection*. New York and Chichester: Columbia University Press.

Lakoff, G. and M. Johnson. 1980. *Metaphors We Live By*. Chicago and London: University of Chicago Press.

Morse, M. 1983. 'Sport on Television: Replay and Display', in E.A. Kaplan (ed.), *Regarding Television: Critical Approaches – An Anthology*. Frederick, MD: University Publications of America Inc. in association with the American Film Institute, pp. 44–66.

Mulvey, L. [1975] 1999. 'Visual Pleasure and Narrative Cinema', in L. Braudy and M. Cohen (eds), *Film Theory and Criticism: Introductory Readings*. New York: Oxford UP, pp. 833-44.

Rose, A. and J. Friedman. 1994. 'Television Sport as Mas(s)culine Cult of Distraction', *Screen* 35(910): 22–35.

Rowe, D. 2004 [1999]. *Sport, Culture and the Media: The Unruly Trinity*, 2nd edition. Maidenhead: Open University Press.

Sontag, S. 2003. *Regarding the Pain of Others*. London: Penguin Books.

Whannel, G. 2001. 'Punishment, Redemption and Celebration in the Popular Press: The Case of David Beckham', in D.L. Andrews and S.J. Jackson (eds), *Sport Stars: The Cultural Politics of Sporting Celebrity*. London: Routledge, pp. 138–50.

12

DEATH ON DISPLAY
The Ideological Function of the
Mummies of the World Exhibit

Diana York Blaine

In 2010, the California Science Center in Los Angeles hosted the world premiere of *Mummies of the World*, an exhibition featuring the desiccated corpses of both human and non-human animals. Using words like 'groundbreaking' and 'breathtaking', American Exhibitions Incorporated, the marketing firm in charge of producing this travelling event, described it as 'the largest exhibition of mummies and related artefacts ever assembled', and promised to transform 'audiences into amateur "mummyologists™"'. The public responded eagerly to this forceful rhetoric, showing up in droves and paying nearly $18 per ticket. So great was the demand that people had to be admitted in timed windows, and just seven weeks after opening, the exhibition welcomed its 100,000th guest, a fact trumpeted in the local media. *Mummies of the World* ultimately became one of the museum's most successful draws ever, eclipsed only by Gunther von Hagen's *Body Worlds*, which also made its US debut at the Center in June 2004. As well as having their overwhelming popularity at the Los Angeles museum in common, *Body Worlds* and *Mummies of the World* both share one other crucial similarity: they permit visitors to gaze directly upon the dead bodies of other human beings. Given that thanatologists from Ernest Becker to Geoffrey Gorer and beyond have argued that humans deny death, what accounts for the intense interest in being in its physical presence – and paying good money for the privilege?

This chapter examines the contemporary fascination with observing human corpses in entertainment venues, looking at how such events provide the opportunity to acknowledge mortality as a natural component of human existence and ultimately stabilise the transgressive irruption of death into the public sphere by ordering the representations along normative ideological lines. I have isolated six dominant narratives through which mainstream American culture currently interprets death: scientific, sentimental, mystical, heroic, monstrous and commercial.[1] Each of these six provides a way of making death comprehensible, either by placing the audience in the superior position over the dead object, as in the case of the scientific, sentimental, monstrous, and commercial narratives, or by offering the promise of transcending death altogether, as in the mystical and heroic ones. While examples can be found of these operating in isolation, the categories often merge, creating a hybrid metanarrative which allows the viewer to enjoy, for example, the materialistic pleasures of modern capitalism while simultaneously believing both in the empiricism of science and the existence of metaphysical deities. *Mummies of the World* constructs precisely this type of hybrid, combining elements of mysticism, science, sentiment, monstrosity and consumption, which, when taken together, guarantees visitors the opportunity to stand in the presence of corpses yet ultimately reject the reality of their own mortality.

The mummy exhibition presents its dead bodies in an objective manner, using what I call the forensic gaze to situate the viewer as active scientist poised over the passive corpse, here interpellated as specimen. Alongside this presentation of the corpse as evidence, however, exists a simultaneous positioning of some of the mummies as belonging to a normative, extant human community rather than as mysterious and exotic traces from the past. Thus I argue that by the end of the exhibition, visitors have not only learned about processes of mummification from around the globe, as promised, but also of the superiority of modern European man, even when those symbolic representatives of Western society are long dead. As I will show, *Mummies of the World* ultimately spins a regressive romance of colonial occupation and penetration,[2] valorising the rational white male who heads a Christian nuclear family. As he is encouraged to identify with this subject position, the viewer finds himself positioned as the possessor of the gaze, rightful inheritor of the world's resources, and capable of transcending death itself.

The Exhibition Structure

As soon as visitors approach the exterior of the exhibition, they see commodified representations of human subjects presented as spectacular objects. Massive posters adorn the outside of the hall, each offering representations of one of the mummies deemed particularly fascinating. Thus humans become the object of the gaze, which immediately distances guests and specimens, even as these posters resemble advertisements for films featuring living actors. One of these celebrity images, that of an ancient female corpse with tattoos and bared breasts (see Fig. 12.1), is featured prominently throughout *Mummies of the World*, in

Figure 12.1 Marvelling at the tattooed mummy. Photograph by Robyn Beck, (c) Getty Images (purchased with kind support from Dornsife College, University of Southern California).

promotional materials such as a gigantic poster, interactive scientific displays inside the exhibition hall, and in the accompanying documentary material. Clearly an over-determined symbol of mortality, this mummy is used to produce multiple intersecting narratives of male dominance.

While the exhibition, set up in a special section of the California Science Center, operates in many ways as a conventional museum, with objects on display and textual accompaniment, it also projects an aura of mystery that belies the otherwise clinical nature of such institutions. The lighting is low, a barely perceptible soundtrack hums in the background; the feeling that one has entered a church is heightened by the image of a stained glass rose window in one of the rooms. The first mummy encountered is that of a small child, alone in a box near the beginning of what will ultimately be a labyrinthine journey. The presentation of the tiny body, suspended in a Plexiglas box, shocks the senses. Around a corner, one encounters an African mummy of a monkey, elaborately dressed and resplendent in feathers, another shocking site this time suggesting occult ritual and adding to the strangeness of the experience. Our minds are meant to be boggled rather than enriched.

The presentation of these two objects at the beginning has no apparent logic save the fascinating visual and exotic aspects of the baby and monkey. The rest of the exhibition follows two parallel trajectories, both suggesting progress:

the movement from animal to human and the movement from dark peoples to light ones. After the ritual monkey display, and the chance to touch simulated preserved skins, visitors enter a room of mummified animals designed to educate museum attendees about the particulars of decomposition. But among the interactive displays in this area, we again encounter the image of the tattooed woman, this time on a huge lighted screen. Signs encourage visitors to expose the results of various experiments performed on her corpse by clicking on labels superimposed on her body. After leaving this area, visitors enter a narrow hall of human heads, featuring a number of skulls in clear boxes on high pedestals. The striking effect is one of crown jewels on display, with a hushed majestic aspect to the darkened narrow room. This demarcates the passage into rooms containing adult human specimens, first a massive Egyptian exhibition, followed by South America, Oceania, and finally Europe. Each area features mummies that dominate the view, selected for their visual interest and/or scientific oddity. While these sections are partitioned, creating the impression of separate rooms, only one area is completely walled off, thereby obscuring any view of its contents. A sign warns visitors that 'foetal specimens' lie ahead and urges viewers to 'exercise caution'. Beyond this ominous side-show, two European mummies lie side by side in a recreated chapel. Finally, visitors pass a Bulgarian family, dad, mom, and two children, charmingly displayed in period costume. We exit through the gift shop.

Metanarratives on Display

Mystical

Scholars in the field of museum studies note that exhibitions carry powerful ideological messages.[3] In the case of the *Mummies of the World* exhibition, these messages reflect current beliefs regarding the nature of death and the ostensible ability that normative humans have to transcend their own mortality. The mummy permits viewers to feel a fantasised power over death, as they arrive with preconceived notions of its supernatural powers, an association that has a long history in Western civilisation.[4] In the popular imagination, mummies are connected to the occult; thus attendance at such an event signals the desire to experience a form of the sublime, to resist the normative epistemologies of modernity that foreground reason over other types of knowledge. Instead of seeing the human body as waste material, and death as a natural organic process removing humans from the community, visitors to this exhibit experience the human subject as permanent, greater than nature and signalling the existence of a metaphysical beyond. Mummies in Western cultures have long served as sources of titillation, associated with the failure of the grave to contain its contents. Interrupted from eternal sleep, they have been represented in books and films as carriers of disease and death, visiting curses upon those who would disturb them in the name of profit. Given the longstanding association between mummies, defilement and death, their popularity would seem hard to explain, but the charge in encountering them comes from the very taboo they manifest. According to Jasmine Day: 'mummies are outlets for an unconscious expression of anxieties about death'. 'What is most feared', she adds, 'is pollution's threat to a hygiene-obsessed, antiseptic society – and the ugliness with which old age makes a travesty of Western ideals of youthful beauty' (Day 2006: 113). Here people desire to encounter what they fear the most, a compulsion not easily explained by appeal to reason, although perhaps a by-product of its dominance. A central portion of the main hall is given over to a display of the Egyptian Book of the Dead, suggestive of a modern fascination with occult ritual and the ability to transcend mortality by appeal to mysticism.

Scientific

However, because this encounter takes place in a museum, not a haunted mansion, the experience also reflects a post-Enlightenment belief in the power of science. Far from cancelling one another out, these competing metanarratives work together at the *Mummies of the World* exhibition, creating an aura that infuses both with the power of the other. Science benefits from the sexiness of the mummy while its occult world receives authority from the legitimising status of the institution.[5] Instead of revealing one's conscious desire to view corpses out of an unconscious fear of death, attending this exhibition seems instead to be the logical act of a modern citizen, because museums are recognised as 'credible and controlled environments for the pursuit of systematic investigations of selectively introduced materials' (Arnold 2006: 28). Curators lay heavy emphasis on the scientific aspects of this exhibition throughout, encouraging viewer participation in the role of scientist, going so far as to bestow them with the title of 'mummyologists™' and offering opportunities to reveal the results of prior experiments on the bodies as if we are somehow involved in the empirical method rather than simply being tourists of darkness.

Sentimental

And yet the objects being experimented upon are human beings, a fact that threatens to collapse the distance between the viewer and what is viewed. Thus two other closely related narrative strains emerge that serve to contain this threat: the sentimental child and the monstrous other. The auditory self-tour and the signage accompanying the displays encourage viewers to apprehend the mummies of women and children as particularly touching. For example, we are told that one child was 'treated with tender care in death' (*Mummies of the World* self-guided tour audio) although there is no evidence to prove that this ancient corpse had been handled any differently than had the adults. Another display depicts a mother cradling her children, but the sign explains that experiments had proven that one of the mummies was actually 500 years younger than the 'mother'. Just as with the tiny infant at the beginning of the exhibition, who turns out to be a much larger child with missing limbs crammed into a tiny case, reality belies the sentimental visual offered to the viewers. The story of another mummy, this one buried with a child's tooth in each of its hands, is described on the *Mummies of the World* DVD as a 'sweetly poignant mystery'. Such pathetic appeals emotionally charge the corpses; this seems to conflate differences between the viewer and what is viewed, but sentimentality actually works as a form of alterity, turning a person into a thing to be adored, a beloved object not a human subject.

Monstrous

The handling of the mummified foetuses reveals another form of objectification, turning a person into a monster. While the notion of the monstrous obviously infuses the entire exhibition, as mummies have been traditionally associated with defilement and horror in Western popular culture, the treating of the foetal mummy as obscene renders it unspeakable. An object of horror and not sentiment, it apparently holds the power to harm those who gaze upon it as the sign at the entrance suggests: 'This area contains artefacts which show foetal specimens in various stages of development. They were used in scientific studies to advance technology and our understanding of disease. Please exercise caution if you have sensitivity to this subject'.

The corpses of other young humans throughout the exhibition were either sentimentalised via their association with a maternal narrative, real or imposed, or presented as wondrous commodities, like the 6000-year-old Detmold child, as shiny and lacquered as the amulet displayed alongside its tiny body. But in this case, the corpses are treated as horrific; for all the careful handling, and perhaps because of it, a freak-show feeling dominates the small area displaying two tiny foetal mummies. Although the explanatory materials reassured viewers that these foetuses – one of whom had anencephaly – were likely miscarriages, clearly the overarching threat is that of the female who aborts her children, betraying both the illusion of transcendence cultivated in Western definitions of the self as well as the potency of patriarchy, destabilised by the woman who refuses to nurture. This tiny reminder of the transient nature of all humans will ultimately be overwhelmed by the much louder insistence upon the immutability of the Western Christian nuclear family throughout the remainder of the exhibition.

Consumerist

While *Mummies of the World* offers thrilling tales of horror, love, and science, its popularity also reflects the desire of museum-goers to be entertained, a status marker for those who have leisure time and income in the consumer-oriented United States. From their inception, museums have offered their visitors the opportunity to satisfy a curiosity about other peoples and the past, and in spite of some concerns about their ability to attract customers in a world rife with more attractive choices, museums became increasingly popular destinations in the twentieth century, with millions of visitors showing up to study the objects on display. This popularity reflects the modern museum's role as a 'stable founda-tion for the newly emerging culture of factual curiosity' (Arnold 2006: 23). For museums are, and have been since their seventeenth-century emergence in early modern form, about objects which purport to offer knowledge through the obser-vation of them. Museums originated in the leisure pursuits of the aristocracy who collected material possessions to prove their own social status and demonstrate their hold over the material world; they also received them as gifts, another sign of these early collectors' powerful social standing. Following the revolutions in England, however, the elitist aspects of collecting were sublimated. What emerged in their wake was the pursuit of collecting as an educational good. Many pamphlets on educational reform in the seventeenth century advocated the use of actual objects to foster knowledge, and so children were taken to museums in order to study things exhibited there. As is clear from any visit to a museum, this practice continues today. *Mummies of the World* clearly cultivates this audi-ence, even generating a Guide for Parents to help them explain the disturbing exhibition to their children.

Stabilising the Imperial Subject

At *Mummies of the World*, the objects designed to foster knowledge are literally other people, and as such, they hold the possibility of granting that most sacred of wisdom: the fate of mortal human beings. Like all objects in museums, mum-mies are signs, placed there to speak of a world beyond their materiality, yet mummies also point to themselves – they are their own referent. And so what do mummies signify? They seem to defy eternity, flesh that does not melt. Thus vis-iting an exhibition to gaze upon them has a theological aspect to it, inherent in the origin of the museum as a place of wonder, but exacerbated here by the pres-ence of dead, yet apparently vital, people. A form of dark tourism, *Mummies of the World* gives access to these corpses in a modern society that generally forbids contact with the dead. Visitors gazing upon the mummies have the opportunity to satisfy a desire to learn about the fate of the human after death, yet in the case of the mummy, they are on display not only because they are dead, but also because they seem to defy death's finality. Hence the thrill of viewing a mummy: in many ways, though no longer alive, it appears uncannily similar to the viewer. This thrill also contains a threat, for if the mummy seems like the human viewer, and the mummy is also a corpse-object, then the mummy stands in for the corpse-object of the viewer, bringing the inevitability of mortality into view even as the intactness of the body on display would seem to deny it.

However, while mummies offer the comforting presence of eternal human beings, they also signify lack. These 'fragments of mortality', as one nineteenth-century newspaper columnist described them, may be freakishly fresh and familiar looking, but it is this very freshness that disturbs, for while they may seem viable with their fleshed skeletons and full heads of hair, they are also no longer humans but exotic spectacles (Wolfe 2009: 105). The corpse's refusal to be either subject or object is why Julia Kristeva selects it as the ultimate site of abjection. The dead body's inability to act as a 'clean and proper' subject forces the viewer to acknowledge her own relationship to this most sickening of wastes (Kristeva 1982: 72–73). 'The corpse', according to Kristeva, 'seen without God and outside of science, is the utmost of abjection' (4). In the case of the mummy, this corpse appears all-too-human at the same time that it manifests the utter absence of life. A protruding tooth in an otherwise fleshly face serves as a jarring reminder to the observer that all that separates our own seemingly discrete bodies from decay is the passage of time.

Thus, this titillation originally offered by gazing at the mummy becomes horror over the abject status of the human-object. But instead of emphasising this parallel between the viewer and the viewed as its educational message, the *Mummies of the World* exhibition instead propagates conventional Western ideological hierarchies affirming the power of the rational white male and the heteronormative Christian nuclear family, the very 'science' and 'God' that Kristeva argues we need to mitigate the corpse's threat. Out of the collapse between the subject and the object that occurs when confronted with a dead body, a collapse reflecting the reality of the observer's own provisional status, the exhibition produces knowledge that stabilises human identity as transcendent, using both theological and philosophical beliefs in order to do so. The exhibition operates on a series of binaries found in both Judeo-Christianity and Western Enlightenment epistemology to create a subject who is not-animal, not-pagan, not-foreign, not-child, not-woman, and ultimately, not-dead. Thus the spectacle places the viewer in the powerful position of a possessor of the gaze, the seemingly natural inheritor of the world's rich resources, here offered as a form of knowledge that I will call museum-commodity-science. Ultimately, instead of confirming the visitor's status as mortal, the *Mummies of the World* narrates a regressive romance of colonial occupation and penetration, establishing each visitor as fully, normatively alive and empowered.

As promised by the title of the exhibition, it displays mummies from all over the world, but the representation of them is by no means balanced either in terms of number or handling. In fact, while the presence of mummies from Europe might seem to have the effect of providing a revisionist view of the otherwise heavily orientalised mummymania that swept the West over the last three hundred years, the handling of these white bodies only ends up exacerbating the presumed differences between superior Europe and inferior Africa and Asia. For example, the layout of the exhibition takes visitors from rooms of non-human animals to Egyptian, Asian and South American specimens, finally culminating in two featured rooms of European mummies. Paralleling nineteenth-century displays in ethnography museums that moved from the dark skinned to the light skinned in order to demonstrate a purported evolutionary movement forward towards white man (Sherman 2008: 250–88), *Mummies of the World* leads up to the Westerners, constructing a schematic move away from the exotic East and towards enlightened Europe that also implies an ontological difference.

The layout of the exhibition is not the only way in which vast differences between the Eastern and Western humans are indicated. Several dark-bodied Egyptians are presented without clothing, including one featuring a prominent erection. Embalmers in ancient Egypt often preserved the penis in this position, so it is not unusual to discover an erect mummy, but codes of dress in modern Western culture – particularly in the puritanically Christian United States – require the covering of genitals. E.J. Bickerman notes that 'In a "clothed" society, where garments are a social obligation, nakedness is an exception, and as such a monstrosity' (in Barcan 2004: 143). And indeed the sight of the visible and prominent penis on this Egyptian mummy caused powerful reactions in the viewers, many of whom pointed and giggled, uncomfortably titillated by the spectacle of what appeared to be a naked black man's genitals.

Notably only the dark male bodies were exposed in this way, thus associating them with a primitivism that the European specimens were spared. Near the end of the exhibition, visitors encounter another naked male mummy, but in this case a cloth draped across the lap of the specimen elides *his* genitals from the visitor's gaze. Signage explains that this European seventeenth-century baron was buried in his family crypt where environmental conditions naturally preserved his corpse (as well as those of a number of family members). A descendent loaned his body, and that of a female relative, to the exhibition, and so she and the baron are identified by name as their lineage is traceable through the family records. Unlike the anonymous male Egyptian specimen who is described in coldly anthropological terms as a 'high status male', the corpse of Baron von Holz is granted nominal subjectivity as well as the dignity afforded him by the covering of his penis. He could just as accurately be described as a 'high status male', and also be fully exposed to the audience's gaze, but since he is not, the exhibition draws an accidental opposition between the two men. Nudity reflects 'deeply ideological and power-laden processes by which people find themselves divided into categories: most fundamentally of all, the human and the non-human, but also male/female; adult/child; civilised/savage; ideal/abject; human/ animal; human/machine; insider/outsider; familiar/alien' (Barcan 2004: 72). Thus the marked difference between the presence and the absence of the penis of the two male specimens re-enacts, as Donna Haraway has said of primatology, an orientalist 'appropriation of nature in the production of culture, the ripening of the human from the soil of the animal, the clarity of white from the obscurity of colour, the issue of man from the body of woman, the elaboration of gender from the resource of sex, the emergence of mind by the activation of the body' (1989: 11).

Ironically, the Egyptian mummy with the visible penis becomes feminised by the production of the virilised Western male. Von Holz's corpse gains status not only by this obfuscation of his genitals, but also by his association with white wealth, baronial power, Christianity, and a physical prowess signified not by a visible penis but by his phallic leather boots, which, we are told, he was buried in. At a special session featuring the mummy's descendent, the Baron von Crailsham, von Holz's mummy was described approvingly by the current Baron as over six feet tall and 'very macho to say the least'. The attribution of virile masculinity to a four-hundred-year old corpse would be inexplicable were it not to produce a transcendent subject position for European man, one composed in binary opposition to the naked – and in a sense more visibly virile – corpse of the exotic other.

The religious context of Baron von Holz and the female relative lying next to him also go unmentioned, granting greater power to Christianity than to the spiritual practices of other cultures described in the exhibition. While these two mummies are positioned in a small room suggestive of a chapel, with a visible cross on the wall and light from an imagined stained glass window adding a sacred aspect to the scene, none of the explanatory material discusses Christianity or *its* sacred theological text containing ritualised accounts of what happens after death. This absence shows the stark contrast between this display and those of other exhibits, which include extensive discussion of the Egyptian Book of the Dead as well as references to rituals and amulets in Egypt, Africa and South America. As the normative religion, Christianity is invisible, needing no interpretation. Thus it gains ideological power over other metanarratives in this ostensibly global affair, further serving to humanise and empower the high-status Baron and his female relative. They are clearly subjects, not objects, naturalised by the privacy cloths, the nomenclature, the aristocratic lineage, and the totalising presence of Christianity. The tourist will not note what is not noted, hence the institutionalised racism of American culture is promulgated.

This interpellation of white Western corpses as normative continues in the final exhibit, allowing museum visitors to end not with monstrous, occult narratives, but those of post-Enlightenment Christendom. This display appears to be of a nuclear family: father, mother, and two children. Clad in the period garb of eighteenth-century Hungary, the Orlivitz family died and were buried in the local church where their bodies were preserved through natural means rather than intentional mummification. Again, because of the availability of church records, these bodies can be identified with names; the dead bodies are humanised by this signage as well as by their appearance as fully-dressed, intact members of a family. But the fine print at the display notes that these clothes are actually reproductions. The mummies were actually naked when they were discovered. Presumably created by curators in Hungary in order to enhance the educational value of the display, the clothes also 'carry something not only of personality but also of humanness itself' (Barcan 2004: 123). Again, we witness a difference between the exposed bodies of the non-Western mummies throughout the exhibition and the fully dressed members of this group. Even though the clothes themselves are fake, the impact on the viewer is powerful: these corpses appear as members of human society. And another fiction lurks behind this intact surface. The museum catalogue, a 384-page volume that goes into great detail about a number of mummies, including those not featured in the travelling exhibition, notes that Mr Orlovitz preceded his wife in death, after which she remarried. So the apparent nuclear family that closes the entire exhibition is itself a simulacrum – naked dead bodies of people who were not married to each other are presented as a fully clothed intact and stable unit, blessed by the Christian God and outlasting death itself. Only someone willing to read the massive catalogue will find this information. Again institutionalised normativity trumps reality.

Besides this fetishising of heteronormative coupling and maternal devotion, the use of gender as an ordering feature abounds throughout the exhibition in other ways as well. Elisabeth Bronfen (1992) has demonstrated a link between the female and death in Western representations, both as mother and as object of desire. One of the most prominent images used in the exhibition and as a marketing tool features the corpse of a female with a full head of hair, her tunic open to reveal desiccated breasts. Tellingly, this tattooed woman is described in promotional materials as having the power to 'enchant visitors', associating a mystical power with the dead female and eroticising the specimen (see Fig. 12.1).

By repeatedly emphasising the attractiveness of this mummy, the curators invoke the trope of romance fiction, which Nicholas Daly has noted was the generic response to the end of England's empire. As Jasmine Day explains, nineteenth-century fiction 'subjugated threats posed to European economies by the material seductions of oriental products, including mummies, by gendering the mummy as female and her lover as male. The unruly mummy is finally re-objectified (turned into a sex object) when the hero seduces her, or the possibility of such seduction is raised' (Day 2006: 40). We can see precisely this objectification occurring in the exhibition as the repeated use of the tattooed woman's image and the insistence that she possesses an unearthly attractiveness positions this mummy as the object of Western male desire. For example, in a special session before an invited audience at the museum, American Exhibition Vice President James Delay described her as 'striking'. This mummy was also selected as the final image in the *Mummies of the World* DVD produced to accompany the exhibition. In the last three minutes of an hour-long documentary, which is otherwise focused on the practical aspects of gathering the specimens from various institutions, the topic finally turns to the inevitable fact that these mummies are humans, as are we, the viewers.

This dangerous admission, with its collapse between the subject/object binary that has been developed by the exhibition, is followed by a narrative attempt to contain the horror of mortality by using heavily figurative language taken from the natural, non-human world: sentimentalising the category of mother; and eroticising the female body. As the camera pans slowly up the exposed torso of the mummy, lead scientist Rosenthal asserts that informing people about the inevitability of death is the 'main educational part of this exhibition'. And yet while this male voice intones about the cycle of birth and death, we gaze upon the eerily un-dead remains of an eroticised female, lit and posed to perfection. The program ends with a freeze upon her face, head cocked to the side, hair cascading down onto her shoulders. In this way, she appears to offer herself up to our penetrative stare, naturalising our colonial possession of her as we project the mystery of death onto the deadly female body: 'The subjectification and sexualisation of corpses in the popular imaginary [distracts] from the possibility of interpreting romance as necrophilia [...] whether corpse or woman, the mummy [assents] to be looked at/unwrapped/penetrated, just as the orient/oriental woman was imagined to consent to conquest by Europeans' (Day 2006: 41).

Ultimately we find the horror of human mortality contained in this exhibition by associating it with the non-human, the child, the woman, and the ethnic other. The ideologies of mainstream Western society, particularly as practiced in the United States, order the exhibition in such a way as to stabilise the values of white Western Christian patriarchy, indeed to produce it out of its opposites, including the pagan Egyptian handling of death, with its mummified cats, naked black men and Book of the Dead; the 'nubile savage' tattooed woman, a corpse who is romanticised in order to sanction Western domination; the abjection of the foetal mummies who appear only behind a privacy screen complete with a warning to those who might be 'sensitive', presumably a nod to Christian sensibility but one that elides the reality of our provisional status as humans; and finally, perhaps most importantly, the commodification of death as it appears here offered up for a ticket price, neatly packaged for consumption, along with a coffee-table book, DVD, and gift shop filled exclusively with Egyptian souvenirs. Visitors cannot buy tiny corpses of Baron von Holz; no foetal mummy key chains are for sale. But beautiful shiny exotic orientalist objects abound. What better way to keep death at bay than to get yourself that shiny gold sarcophagus paperweight catching your eye as you exit?

Notes

1. Since the writing of this chapter, I have added the category *erotic* and dropped *commercial*. In consumer culture, all representations of death are embedded within the cash-nexus and so no representations of death in the mainstream can be considered non-commercial. Additionally some images of death connect mortality primarily with sexuality, hence the need for this additional descriptor.

2. These ideas originate in Nicholas Daly's scholarship on the nineteenth-century English romance. See Day (2006: 30–44) and Daly (1999: 1–29 and 84–116).

3. See for example Bennett (1995).

4. For a comprehensive view of 'mummymania', the Western fascination with all things Egyptian, see MacDonald and Rice (2003).

5. Day notes that museums need to compete with other more attractive forms of entertainment and have taken to 'yucksploitation' (2006: 155) in order to sell tickets. She argues that 'death has become the new sex in museums' (157). Mummies, happily for curators, can offer both.

Bibliography

Arnold, K. 2006. *Cabinets for the Curious: Looking Back at Early English Museums*. Aldershot: Ashgate.

Barcan, R. 2004. *Nudity: A Cultural Anatomy*. Oxford: Berg.

Bennett, T. 1995. *The Birth of the Museum: History, Theory, Politics*. London: Routledge.

Bronfen, E. 1992. *Over Her Dead Body: Death, Femininity and the Aesthetic*. Manchester: Manchester University Press.

Daly, N. 1999. *Modernism, Romance and the Fin de Siècle: Popular Fiction and British Culture, 1880-1914*. Cambridge: Cambridge University Press.

Day, J. 2006. *The Mummy's Curse: Mummymania in the English Speaking World*. London: Routledge.

Haraway, D. 1989. *Primate Visions: Gender, Race, and Nature in the World of Modern Science*. New York: Routledge.

Kristeva, J. 1982. *Powers of Horror: An Essay on Abjection*, trans. Leon Roudiez. New York: Columbia University Press.

MacDonald, S. and M. Rice. 2003. *Consuming Ancient Egypt*. London: UCL Press.

Sherman, D. 2008. *Museums and Difference*. Bloomington: Indiana University Press.

Wolfe, S.J. 2009. *Mummies in Nineteenth Century America: Ancient Egyptians as Artifacts*. Jefferson, North Carolina: McFarland.

PART IV

CEMETERIES AND FUNERALS

13

The Romanian Carnival of Death and the Merry Cemetery of Săpânţa

Marina Cap-Bun

The Romanian mythology of death and the corresponding funerary ritual are complex and captivating, a privileged territory for research in anthropology. Not only did the world famous Romanian historian of myth, ritual, and religion Mircea Eliade find them fascinating – he wrote a number of essays about them – but Arnold Van Gennep also expressed his regret about not knowing Romanian mythology and ritual practices before writing his seminal work *Les Rites de Passage*. The creator of French ethnography was so enthusiastic about 'the richness of Romanian folklore' that he wanted to create a department of comparative history of civilisation and general ethnography at Bucharest University and to organise there the second world congress of ethnology and folklore (Van Gennep 1996: 179–83). Unfortunately, he did not get the support of local authorities to do this, so we kept most of that richness within the borders of a 'small' language, which was one of the principal factors preventing a more extended analysis.

That is why I decided to address some old elements of the Romanian traditional mythology of death, and the particular contemporary evolution they underwent at the Merry Cemetery of Săpânţa. After first visiting this graveyard, in the autumn of 2002, I had the feeling that everything I have learned theoretically, by scholarly research, about the mythology of death was not enough to enable me to fully understand this intriguing phenomenon. So I continued to go there, copying the epitaphs and photographing the images in order to comprehend and culturally contextualise it. In this chapter, I summarise my conclusions so far.

The traditional Romanian funerary ritual, which was practiced well into the first half of the twentieth century, is a complex scenario, particularly abundant in carnivalesque details and conducted over a period of three days (Marian 1995: 128–46), like carnivals in many other cultures, or like the Greek Dionysia. During the funeral, the village becomes a live theatre, in which 'actors' wear special clothes, and even if the vivid colours are replaced with black, this still signifies a symbolic change: each participant in the funeral becomes a mourner, all the social and cultural differences are chromatically abolished and the whole environment surrounding the deceased looks like a land of shadows, where every member of the community performs a temporary theatrical role (Vulcănescu 1985: 190–94).

The concept of free communication between the worlds of reality and magic is customary during carnivals. A similar temporary abolishment of the border between the worlds occurs during the Romanian funeral rituals, as the deceased is metaphorically described as a traveller between the White World (of the living) and the Dark World (of the deceased) (Pop and Ruxăndoiu 1978: 203). But in the carnival-like atmosphere of the ritual, the dress code is turned upside-down: living creatures are wearing black veils, while the deceased is allowed to wear colourful clothing, even a wedding outfit in cases of pre-marital death (Vulcănescu 1985: 194). The best clothes are carefully kept for the funeral in the same manner in which the wedding garments are prepared a long time in advance (Marian 1995: 47).

In Romania, the language used during the funeral is strongly ritualised: nobody can say anything bad about the deceased, they must be praised for their deeds (Lambrior 1976: 172–90; Marian 1995: 99) and even the usual greeting formulas are replaced with the expression 'Dumnezeu să îl/o ierte!' ('May God forgive him/her'!) (Burada 1882: 13; Marian 1995: 99). The journey to the cemetery used to be a carefully directed parade, with a precise route, stops and ritual offerings at crossroads, where every participant would kneel down (Marian 1995: 163–99). Everybody meeting a funerary parade was supposed to stop as though hypnotised, even if they did not know the deceased. If they carried a bucket of water they had to throw it away. Since the latter half of the twentieth century, drivers meeting a procession in traffic in urban areas turn on the lights. Although stopping and kneeling down is no longer practiced, ritual offerings are given in the church, during the religious ceremony and in the graveyard, where coins and sweets are thrown to children.

What makes the Romanian funeral rites singular is probably the mixture of cultural strata, from the Thraco-Dacian belief in immortality, to the Roman and then the Slavic influences, and the evolutions they underwent over time. In 440 BC, in the fourth book of his *Histories*, the Greek historian Herodotus[1] documented the local attitudes towards death, especially the Dacians' ritual of laughing loudly and expressing their joy whenever one of them died, believing that the deceased was going to a better world, to meet their god Salmoxis. Later on such beliefs were confirmed by Ovid[2] who was exiled at Pontus Euxinus and lived for many years among the Dacians while writing his famous *Epistulae ex Ponto*. After the Roman conquest of the territory in 106, the funeral ritual changed dramatically: the public exteriorisation of grief became compulsory

(Marian 1995: 95), and strong theatrical components were added to the funerals. The Roman ritual was sophisticated, from the masks of the family's ancestors, and the luxurious chariots that accompanied the deceased on his/her final journey, to the paid dirge singers, dancers and mimes that completed the spectacular parade (Toynbee 1996: 43–44). These conflicting cultural codes seeped into the local melting pot to form the spectacular Romanian funeral rituals.

In 1892, the priest scholar Simion Florea Marian produced the most complex monograph of the Romanian funeral rites, Înmormântarea la români (Romanian Funeral Ritual), in which he proved the Roman origins of Romanian culture and the addition of Christian elements to the old pagan practices. Throughout the twentieth century, many of the practices described by Marian were still in use, but others were lost, or replaced with different perceptions of death. An interesting illustration of local transformations of the funeral ritual in the last century is the Merry Cemetery of Săpânţa, located in the extreme Northern part of Romania.[3] The particular aspect that I want to address here is the carnivalesque component of the traditional Romanian funeral rites, as described by ethnologists, and its possible connection to this unique graveyard, founded in 1935 by the wood sculptor Stan Ion Pătraş, with its hand-carved oak crosses. He painted each cross blue, and included a scene from the deceased's life or death and an autobiographical poem.[4]

The creator of the graveyard died in 1977, after carving his own cross, but his work has since been continued by his apprentices. At the Merry Cemetery of Săpânţa the mythology of death is still a living creation and the disappearance of some of the carnivalesque props of the traditional ritual was compensated by naïve pictures painted in vibrant colours (blue, yellow, red, white and green), with geometrical and floral decorations on the borders, and tragic-comical epitaphs that totally ignore the grammatical rules of literary Romanian language (Cf. Bilţiu and Man 2009). The traditional Romanian carnival of death was ingeniously reinvented in a visual way.

Romanian traditional ceremonial songs collected by Marian, Lambrior, Burada and many other scholars at the end of the nineteenth century always spoke of posthumous existence: death was envisioned as a great journey to the other world for which the deceased, called 'dalbul de pribeag' ('the pure white traveller'), was washed, dressed, counselled and guided, and properly mourned and honoured (Marian 1995: 77–97; Pop and Ruxăndoiu 1978: 209). The organising principle was to pay tribute to the deceased by recollecting their life and by emphasising the great loss that the family and the society had to endure (Pop and Ruxăndoiu 1978: 202). Sometimes professional dirge-singers were hired, which proves a strong Roman influence (Cantemir 1978: 193; Vulcănescu 1985: 190).

Some of the traditional ceremonial songs were spectacular, implying a sophisticated performance. Cântecul zorilor (The Dawn Song),[5] which was sung twice, before the dawn of the second and the third day of wake, was performed in chorus by a group of women. The first part of the ceremonial song was performed outdoors, around the house, and addressed to the dawn, while the second part was sung inside the house[6] to the deceased (Pop and Ruxăndoiu 1978: 214). This chorus had the same theatrical function as the Greek tragedy chorus, which was supposed to express the collective feelings of the audience, but also to communicate with gods and ask for their mercy. In Transylvania, dawn was asked to hurry so that the deceased might return to light. On the contrary, in the region of Oltenia, dawn was asked not to hurry so that the family of the departed could properly prepare the funeral banquet (an oven full of bread, nine barrels of wine and brandy, and a fatted cow), the wax candles, the chariot for the parade, and letters for relatives to invite them to the ceremony (Pop and Ruxăndoiu 1978: 206). In spite of local variations, the basic symbolic structure of this rite remains the same: the community is trying to help the deceased to fulfil the ritual passage to the other world, by negotiating with the time figure of dawn. As in many carnivals, time is symbolically asked to modify its regular rhythm, in order to cope with the temporary disorder that the absurd event of death brings about.

Another ceremonial song, *Cântecul bradului* (The Fir Tree Song),[7] was sung in chorus by two groups (Cf. Brăiloiu 1981) who responded to each other like the semi-choruses of Greek tragedy. Pop and Ruxăndoiu explained that one of the groups represents the mourners, while the other gives voice to the fir tree, the vegetal double of the deceased (Pop and Ruxăndoiu 1978: 215–16). The absent voice of the deceased was thus symbolically replaced without altering the dialogical structure. I believe that at Săpânța, the missing voice was recreated through the first-person epitaphs telling the story of the deceased's life and death. But while the dirge singers used the second person (directly addressing the deceased) and idealised the story of his/her life, the epitaphs engraved on the crosses are cruelly realistic. The family of the deceased cannot influence the text, which tells the exact details memorised by the collective oral memory of the villagers. The epitaphs clearly replaced the functions of traditional songs, which were no longer regularly practiced by the time the cemetery of Săpânța was created.

Traditional ceremonial songs used to be sung only during the day, between the dawn and the sunset (Marian 1995: 79; Pop and Ruxăndoiu 1978: 224), while the night wake interestingly allowed the famous Dacian 'joy of death' to survive camouflaged in the masked comic games, mimes, and dances, which Marian documented as being still practiced by the end of nineteenth century (Marian 1993: 128–46). Wearing masks and costumes, the participants of the ceremonial night wake abandoned their real identity, pretending to be somebody else, playing a role. The household of the deceased literally turned into a theatrical stage on which anybody could pretend anything, however absurd, to recall the absurdity of death itself. The mourners became 'actors' in the carnival of death and pretended to enjoy it.

The allegorical transformation of the traditional funeral ritual into a carnival becomes even more prominent if we consider other details, documented by the Romanian anthropologist Romulus Vulcănescu, in the last decades of the nineteenth century, in his *Romanian Mythology*: during the mandatory night wake the participants were wearing scary masks which protected them from being recognised by the evil spirits who were trying to steal the soul from the body they watched (Vulcănescu 1985: 192). In this disguise, they spent their time playing games that usually implied hide-and-seek techniques, ritual beating, hoaxes, cheating and lying contests or even imitations of animal sounds (Vulcănescu 1985: 168–209). Marian specifically calls them 'comic games' (Marian 1993: 129). They also sing 'wild, mournful songs' with pipes and trumpets and sometimes dance around a fire in the yard (Marian 1993: 128–46). Vulcănescu also documents a specific ritual, practiced during the last night wake, in which young men make 'an allegoric mask of death, which figures it as a skeleton with a scythe in its hands' and after they perform a 'macabre dance around the body', they play a pantomime in which death cuts down the deceased's life with the scythe (Vulcănescu 1985: 192). Such rituals were no longer documented after the end of the nineteenth century. Modernisation of the ritual during the twentieth century erased these carnivalesque features, but at Săpânţa they spontaneously came back to life in different forms of expression. On the crucifix placed at the entrance of the Merry Cemetery, Pătraş painted a creepy figure of death holding the scythe (Cf. Bilţiu and Man 2009). It seems that the complex carnivalesque performance was replaced by a picture of that performance which keeps the symbolism alive.

Death and carnival have always been metaphorically consubstantial. Like carnival, death brings about a disorder in the social and psychological balance of the community, and in order to cope with this temporary imbalance, local complexes of rituals developed, based on complicated systems of concepts, attitudes, and beliefs. Also like carnival, death obliges us to say farewell to something we love and enter into a mourning grey period. Death itself is very much present in the whole symbolism of the European carnivals, from the puppets that are publicly 'killed' in various ways, to a variety of scary masks and costumes. The Romanian 'Geamala' (Burada 1975: 67) and 'Cucii'[8] (Burada 1975: 71) are representative examples of terrifying, noisy creatures that parade during the winter or spring local carnivals. Burial rituals are not uncommon during carnivals, especially in Eastern Europe. The Hungarian masked figures Busójárás, for instance, perform a burial ritual to symbolise the end of winter at the Mohács Carnival.[9] But, while medieval carnivals were associated with important astronomic or religious transits that were relevant to communities, the carnival of death is connected with a tremendously important personal passage. In both cases, the parades of richly adorned chariots (with flowers, torches and eye-catching items) allegorise this passage as a symbolic journey in space and time (Marian 1995: 163–86).

Death reminds us of how incongruous life is. It brings about a state of confusion, ambiguity and absurd contradiction, but once the ritual is correctly fulfilled, we can go back to where we started from, we forget the absurdity and meaningless of life, and play the game of living as if nothing had happened, as if we had already forgotten that death exists.

If the conventional black is still more or less present in the dress code of contemporary funerals, the masks, the mimes and dances, and the comic games were totally lost in the course of the twentieth century. Nobody practices them today, although jokes are still told during the wake and the funeral banquet, and people laugh, which contrasts with the family's grief.

At Săpânţa, the joyful aspect of the cemetery, with its vivid colours and its tragic-comical epitaphs, fully recovers the carnival-like atmosphere of the traditional funeral rites. During my research visits to Săpânţa, I was told that the name of 'merry cemetery' was given by a group of French tourists in the 1970s, and immediately adopted by the locals. It is unlikely that the foreign visitors understood the textual messages on the crosses, so it was probably the visual component that gave them the idea for such a strange name for a cemetery. The colourful pictures are complemented by epitaphs which sometimes provide quite humorous details. Some villagers were truly devoted to their professions and daily work, but others spent their entire life in a perpetual carnival: partying, singing, dancing, and drinking.

We can see and hear about bartenders cheating their drunken clients, next to drunkards who wasted their lives in the local pub, or even moralising poems about the excess of alcohol: 'Plum brandy for some is poison / And becomes the road to sorrow / It only filled my life with torment / And placed me under your feet. / Those who love the plum brandy / listen / Learn from my experience and death / As I hold tight to my bottle'*.[10] Others have no regrets and plan to go on drinking even in the afterlife: 'Buried here is Pop Mihai / And dear uncle Mihai too. / I have come to keep you company / And see what I have brought for you. / It's a bottle of plum brandy / To chase away the morning dew. / So let us raise a glass together, / As we lie here, just us two. I left this life at 42 years.'*

By treating death as just another fact of life, as natural as eating or drinking, an infallible tragic-comical effect is created, with its corresponding catharsis. The community needs to symbolically re-ensure the departed of the continuation of life after death.

A mother of five forgives her husband, putting all the blame on wine: 'Griga, husband, be forgiven / For all the grief you have given / In the evenings, by wine driven.'* On the contrary, other wives had no understanding for the carnival-like existence: 'While I was young and unmarried / I used to dance to violin music. / But after I got married my wife wouldn't let me dance anymore. / I also had a child with her / and I was very happy to raise him. / Sorinel, my son, I waited /

and longed for you to come near my death bed, / but your mother wouldn't let you / and I died very upset / and I left this life / at only 38 years.'[11]

Violin singing and dancing are also customary themes for both pictures and epitaphs. Here is a veritable *carpe diem*: 'Here lies Ilie Petrenjel, / The oldest man in the village. / I danced to the folk-tunes, / Played on the violin / By the brothers Petreuş. / They took me to Baia Mare / And also to Bucharest. / I danced the old Romanian dances, / So, please dance like me / And live until ninety-six.'* Who could regret such a life?

One exception from the first-person rule is to be found in a comic epitaph of a wicked mother-in-law, recalling the local lyrical poetry, which elaborated on the theme of the conflict between mother and wife: 'My poor mother-in-law / Under this heavy cross you lie, / And yet, if you'd had three days more, / You'd be here to see me die. / So, passer-by do not disturb her / For if she were to come again / We'd never stop her tongue from wagging, / Her words and curses fell like rain. / I will keep quiet, please do so too / And she'll not wake to curse all you.'* The picture on the cross shows an authoritative woman strongly indicating her son what to do. So, the combined information of text and image makes it clear why the daughter-in-law does not want anyone to 'disturb' her mother-in-law and make her 'come again'. In spite of the traditional rule of praising the deceased, at Săpânţa, fake sorrow is no longer necessary.

Another example of a comic message is 'And now, I tell you good bye! / See you all at the Resurrection.' (The Romanian text is also available in audio version in Ardelean 2006.) This type of black humour is not uncustomary in Romanian mentality. I distinctly remember my own grandfather smiling during his last moments and telling my grandmother: 'Well, my dear, I have to go now. If you miss me you know where to find me.' Such apparently comic messages express both the Christian believe in resurrection, and the certitude in the continuation of life after death which is also a focal point of the pre-Christian local mythology. This is not a desecration of death, but rather a carnival-like mingling of the sacred mythological elements with the profane vision of Pătraş and those who continued his work.

Bruno Mazzoni noticed that the content of the epitaphs is sometimes inspired by traditional funeral texts and songs, which explains their nostalgic tone (Cf. Mazzoni 1999). However, Pătraş is unlikely to be fully aware of the rich and dramatic mythology of death documented by ethnologists. Andrei Iustin Hossu suggested that Pătraş was incapable of falsifying a true life-story by an 'aesthetic lie' (Hossu 2000: 31). From the local authorities I have learned that Pătraş went to school only for a few years, so his vision was not influenced by an erudite awareness of the funerary ritual. He only knew what he had learnt from his parents and grandparents and from witnessing the funeral rituals of his village, as in small rural communities everybody attended such events. His creation of texts and images is definitively spur-of-the-moment and is based exclusively on oral culture, which was enough to intuitively reactivate some of the mythical structures accurately described by Mazzoni.

All the professions are represented in the graveyard, but shepherds represent a particularly interesting case study. Like everyone else, they are portrayed as continuing their profession after death. The theme is very strong in Romanian oral culture (Marian 1995: 161), due to its presence in the ballad *Miorița* (the ewe lamb). Mircea Eliade reproduced the most famous variant of the text, published by Vasile Alecsandri in 1850:

> the lamb warns its young shepherd that his companions, jealous of his flocks and his dogs, have decided to kill him. But instead of defending himself, the shepherd-boy addresses the lamb and tells it his last wishes. He asks it to say that he is to be buried in his own fold, so that he will be near to his sheep and can hear his dogs. He also asks it to put three shepherd's pipes at the head of his grave. When the wind blows it will play on them, and his sheep will gather around and weep tears of blood. But above all he asks it to say nothing of his murder; it must say that he has married, and that at the wedding a shooting star fell, that the moon and the sun held his wedding crown, that the great mountains were his priests and the beech trees his witnesses. But if it sees an old mother in tears, looking for a 'proud shepherd', it must tell her only that he has married 'the peerless queen, the bride of the world, in a beautiful country, a corner of paradise'; but it must not tell of the falling star or the sun and moon holding his crown or the great mountains or the beech trees. (Eliade 1972: 227)

I reproduced the entire summary, as I intend to discuss here some intriguing correspondences between this ballad, imbued with Romanian funerary mythology (Eliade 1972: 234, 238), and the Merry Cemetery of Săpânța. The first striking resemblance is the ostentatious disguise of the funeral ritual. In *Miorița*, the dark carnival of death is allegorised as the luminous carnival of wedding (Eliade 1972: 242). The old mother is not to be told all the details of this metaphor, as she might understand the unbearable truth. The same allegory of marriage as death explains the bridal garments of the unmarried deceased (Marian 1995: 47; Vulcănescu 1985: 194); the event of marriage has to be symbolically recuperated, as it is an important rite of passage that has to be consumed between birth and death. 'No life is complete without marriage [...] In Romania the ritual of posthumous betrothals is very widely disseminated' – explained Eliade (1972: 248).

The shepherd of *Miorița* explicitly asks that his tools of trade (flute, pipe, horn, bugle, axe, lance, etc.) be placed on his grave, as a symbolic prolongation of his activity. Eliade commented that 'the shepherd hopes to enjoy a post-existence resembling the life he has lived' (246). In the same vein, Pătraş painted favourite objects or professional tools on each cross, thus reassuring the relatives that the deceased can symbolically continue their daily activities in the afterlife.

There is a huge symbolic richness in this, as the painted images become part of the cosmic integration of the deceased, ensuring the ritual post-existence. In *Miorița*, the blowing wind is supposed to moan, making the flute, the pipe and the bugle sing and thus induce the sheep to lament their shepherd's death in a very natural way. At the Merry Cemetery relatives will also be moved to mourn by the images on the crosses. They retell the story of the deceased's life and thus death temporarily loses its immediate meaning, it is contested and transgressed through the celebration of life, and it is this paradoxical unity of life and death that asserts man's victory over his mortal condition.

Acceptance of death becomes possible as the pictures and epitaphs prove that man cannot defend himself against fate, however absurd. In the same manner, the shepherd of *Miorița* is not fighting his destiny; he is only concerned that his passage rituals of marriage and death should be performed correctly, so that he can enjoy his post-existence. Eliade explained that 'In the universe of folk values the shepherd's attitude expresses a deeper existential decision: *man cannot defend himself against fate as he can against enemies; he can only impose a new meaning on the ineluctable consequences of a destiny in course of fulfilment*' (252, Eliade's italics).

As a consequence, he simply tries to integrate death into his life project. His serene first-person speech about his own death undoubtedly inspired Pătraş to create his carved epitaphs, which endorse the idea of communication between worlds. The picture and the autobiographical poem are actually a visual adaptation of funeral wailing. Like the Mioritic shepherd, the villagers of Săpânța hope to enjoy a post-existence that resembles the lives they have lived. This whole repertory of text, image, symbols, and colours create a cosmically structured image of death. A wholly different spiritual horizon is accessed so that the brutal, incomprehensible death makes sense and becomes acceptable. Meaning is imposed on the absurdity of death.

There are lots of shepherds buried at Săpânța. Pop Gheorghe, the orphan, is just one example: 'Here I rest / Pop Gheorghe is my name / I came near my mother as she / had left me while I was very young / I lived as I could and I've achieved all I needed / I raised cattle and sheep / and I enjoyed doing that / But I left this life at 74'. He seems to have enjoyed his solitary shepherd life, but the afterlife gives him the opportunity to reunite with his mother, who must have been missing him like the mother in *Miorița* does.

Another epitaph, from 1943, reads: 'Alas, I cannot rest in peace,/ Saulic Ion is my name./ Whilst I fed my sheep in the garden of Belmezau / A terrible thing occurred. /A Hungarian shot and beheaded me. / May he be cursed for his cruelty / That sent me here.* The story is confirmed by the two images on the cross, sequentially representing the shooting and the decapitation. The first one embodies Saulic tending his sheep and the aggressor shooting him from behind. The second one is even more dramatic, recalling the religious representations of the beheading of Saint John the Baptist: Saulic's decapitated body is laid on the ground, while the Hungarian kneels down holding the head. There is symbolic transparency here: due to the mutilation of his body he 'cannot rest in peace' so he is cursing his killer. The resemblance with the Mioritic plot is obvious, as *Saulic Ion* is killed in a natural setting (the garden of Belmezau / the 'corner of paradise'), proper to his pastoral profession, by a bad Hungarian (the ethnic conflict is also present in *Miorița*). Nevertheless, his death is not 'aesthetically falsified' by allegories, but presented as a crude fact of life; there is no poetic interpretation of the crime story, no mythical projection of the 'creative' violent death, and no mercy for the weeping mother. Death must be faced as such. But even in *Miorița*, death is the inevitable 'bride of the world'.

At Săpânța, all the cases of premature death make reference to the suffering parents, sisters, brothers, and friends, but nobody invokes the possibility of avoiding a tragic fate, however cruel and absurd. Pre-marital deaths sometimes allude to the marriage to death motif by indicating that the deceased died instead of getting married. Here is just one example: 'Please do not pass me by, / Know that once I saw the world. / I loved to dance in my brothers' band / And died before I was ever old / Just to be married, I came to my end, / Sorrow and tears for family and friends. / We did not have a farewell kiss / So, I must ask you – remember this.'*

The epitaphs and the images are simply rememorising the story, without aesthetic artifices, but there is always an embedded symbolic dimension. The dirges sung during the traditional funeral ritual also rememorised the life of the deceased, but they were supposed to idealise it, to ignore unpleasant details, not to upset the deceased. We find no such concerns at the Merry Cemetery.

The dialogic structure of the Romanian funeral songs reconfirms the carnivalesque scenario, through the permanent dialogue between the audience and the deceased, who is supposed to hear and understand everything (road directions for the underworld, instructions on how to use the money put into the coffin to pay the taxes etc.). The deceased are also advised to open their eyes and to thank those who are performing the night wake, but because they cannot, they ask God to thank them in return (Pop and Ruxăndoiu 1978: 208–13). The painful truth of death is thus contested as are all truths during the carnival. The physiological reality of death is transgressed through a complex theatrical scenario in which the departed is the interlocutor of the ceremonial songs; he is advised to prepare his journey properly, and to deliver messages to the dead relatives. I have already discussed Pop Mihai's epitaph, in which the traditional textual message was comically replaced with 'a bottle of plum brandy' for his uncle.

In his own epitaph, Pătraş does not refer to the act of writing/carving, but to the act of speaking and listening: 'Now I beg, lend me your ears / I tell no lies, so have no fears'*. Modest, he does not write or paint anything about his art, but on his wife's cross we can read that she enjoyed watching her husband working. He does not need to enter into details as the whole environment tells the story of his creative effort. He simply painted his portrait in traditional costume, as if to suggest that he was only perpetuating old traditions, even if he did it in an innovative form. Like the shepherd of Miorița, who planned to listen to his dogs barking, his flutes singing and his sheep weeping, he is buried among the objects he created, where he can hear all the bitter laments that will be performed in 'his' cemetery.[12] (After 1990, his work became a museum and tickets are sold at the entrance gate, which is unheard of for Romanian cemeteries.) His life story is depicted as a tragic one: 'And yet in my life there was sorrow / Hard days I had, many a morrow'*. We cannot help but wonder: was his life so difficult because he decided to spend it fighting death and the common perception of it? He definitely won this battle; he became immortal by tricking death and teaching all his fellow villagers to do the same. He seems to have instinctively reinvented the forgotten games in which tricking contests functioned as an effective way in which to deal with the unexpected and perplexing phenomenon of death.

In traditional funeral songs, the deceased were prepared for a great journey 'to the gates of Heaven' (Brăiloiu 1981: 109). The belief in this posthumous journey was reinforced by the baking of bread in symbolic forms, such as a key from the Heaven's gate, stairs to Heaven, a soul-bird, a hook, an archangel, a doll and various other shapes (Marian 1995: 115). In some rural areas, the family of the deceased still bakes such offerings in symbolic shapes, but in the cities the bakery was simplified in the last decades. Bakeries offer special forms of breads for funerals, called 'colaci' but they are usually no more than round, decorated white breads.

In Northern Moldovan villages the ritual offerings are still hung into 'the tree of the deceased' (Marian 1995: 67–76), which consists of a branch of an apple tree decorated with fruits, sweets and baked goods that accompanies the funeral parade to the graveyard. This tree is a reminiscence of the Tree of Life and acts as a symbolic substitute of the scale to heaven. The same Tree of Life was painted by Pătraş on the pillars supporting the gate of the Merry Cemetery. The soul-bird is present on almost all the crosses, and winged dolls are often represented in lively colours on children's crosses.

Objects or plants, too, are integrated into the belief system of the Romanian funeral ritual. Vulcănescu documented the ritual of the symbolic brotherhood between the new born baby boy and a fir tree planted to celebrate his birth, proving their consubstantiality (Vulcănescu 1985: 194–96). If the boy/man dies unmarried, the fir tree becomes his symbolic bride. A group of men goes to the mountains to choose the tree 'which best resembles the deceased', cut it, and place it near the head of the deceased. The fir tree is tricked to believe that it has been cut for a wedding ceremony, not for a funerary one, and that is why the cutters have to mime joyfulness while singing the Song of the Fir Tree (Vulcănescu 1985: 185–86).

Clear echoes of this ceremonial song are to be found in the following Săpânţa epitaph: 'Here I rest / And Gheorghe Pop is my name / Like a handsome mountain fir / I was in my parents' yard / Young and kind-hearted / There were not many like me in the village / When I finished the army / I bought myself a car / And the whole country I toured / Many friends I found / Many friends that were kind / The way I liked / When I was to live my youth / In the earth I rot.'

At Săpânţa, the funeral rites are no different from those in the rest of the country. In 2007, during one of my visits to the Merry Cemetery, I witnessed a burial ceremony of an unmarried young man, during which an old woman suddenly began to sing a wedding song (chiuitură), which proves that the mythology of marriage to death is still well known to the villagers. However, the joyful aspect of the monuments is new and striking. The life-story is a realistic one, highlighting both professional and the personal status. The crosses evoke humorous aspects of daily life, especially vices. Their comical effect is enhanced by the total abolishment of grammar, which is the case whether the crosses mark the grave of someone with a college education or no education at all. This obvious disrespect for the rules of written language not only reaffirms the oral character of the textual messages on the crosses, but also harmonises with the carnival-like ambiance. The paintings and the epitaphs are made in such a manner as to make the family smile or even laugh out loud when they visit their deceased loved ones.

The fact remains that the deceased is no longer idealised as the perfect man or woman; at Săpânţa the truth was expected, in the same manner in which comical unpleasant truths are told publicly at parties while the person is still alive. Death is not only diminished in importance but presented as a natural and acceptable part of daily life. The Merry Cemetery defies death by pointing out man's existence in his community as it really was, and thus becomes a place of public celebration of life.

All this, in my view, proves that at Săpânţa we are in the presence of a still living creation of the funeral rites which affirms the power of folk creativity, even in the era of the Internet. In spite of the naïve creative process that produced the cemetery, which sometimes ignores the possible mythological projection of many of these tangible individual destinies, the phenomenon illuminates the changes in mentality imposed by the historic and regional circumstances. The Merry Cemetery of Săpânţa, listed as a heritage site by the UNESCO and probably one of the most visited graveyards in the world, is unique in many ways. Here, the imminence of death is accepted as a fact of life, actually the one and only certitude that life offers. It provides us with an important lesson on the necessity of celebrating both life and death.

Notes

1. Herodotus provides the first insights into the Thraco-Dacians' religion, collected from the Greek Ionians living at the coast of the Black Sea: 'They think that they do not really die, but that when they depart this life they go to Salmoxis', their one and only god. Their belief in immortality was often mentioned by various sources and it explains their rituals of human sacrifice, also documented by Herodotus, in sending a messenger ('the best and the bravest of them all') to their god, Salmoxis: 'at intervals of four years they send one of themselves, whomsoever the lot may select, as a messenger to Salmoxis, charging him with such requests as they have to make on each occasion; and they send him thus: – certain of them who are appointed for this have three javelins, and others meanwhile take hold on both sides of him who is being sent to Salmoxis, both by his hands and his feet, and first they swing him up, then throw him into the air so as to fall upon the spear-points: and if when he is pierced through he is killed, they think that the god is favourable to them; but if he is not killed, they find fault with the messenger himself, calling him a worthless man, and then having found fault with him they send another: and they give him the charge beforehand, while he is yet alive' (Herodotus, *Histories*. Accessed on 24 May 2013, from http://ancienthistory.about.com/library/bl/bl_text_herodotus_4.htm).

2. 'Illi, quos audis hominum gaudere cruore' (*Tristia*, IV, 4, v.61); 'Aque mea terra prope sunt funebria sacra' (*Tristia*, IV, 4, v.85), in Publii Ovidii Nasonis. 1652. *Operum* Tomus I-III. Amstelodami: Typis Ludovici Elzevirii.

3. For details on location, see http://en.wikipedia.org/wiki/S%C4%83p%C3%A2n%C5%A3a, accessed on 23 May 2013.

4. A few pictures are available at http://www.sapanta.mmnet.ro/, accessed on 23 May 2013.

5. Versions of this ceremonial song are available at http://www.youtube.com/watch?v=MfpxRwHSch4, accessed on 23 May 2013, and http://www.youtube.com/watch?v=1Kca_Mep2OE, accessed on 23 May 2013.

6. A version of the song of the dawn from inside the house is available at http://www.youtube.com/watch?v=8pXdMHMSXJA, accessed on 23 May 2013.

7. Versions of this ceremonial song are available at http://www.youtube.com/watch?v=td2S7krUEYc, accessed on 23 May 2013, http://www.youtube.com/watch?v=-OhBJYtolys, accessed on 23 May 2013, and http://www.youtube.com/watch?v=dvVsxUNLmfE, accessed on 23 May 013.

8. Pictures of contemporary processions of Cucii are available at http://www.youtube.com/watch?v=aCCICW4R8eY, accessed on 23 May 2013.

9. More information can be found at http://en.wikipedia.org/wiki/Bus%C3%B3j%C3%A1r%C3%A1s, accessed on 23 May 2013.

10. Texts marked with * are translated by Ovidiu Tămaş, in the photo album *Maramureş. Săpânţa*.

11. Unmarked texts were transcribed and translated by myself during my research visits at Săpânţa.

12. A few samples of lamentations can be seen at http://www.youtube.com/watch?v=t4sNuGTpxKo, accessed on 23 May 2013.

Bibliography

Ardelean, T. 2006. *Merry Cemetery of Săpânţa* (audio book), voices: Victor Muşeteanu, Sorin Tănase; violin: Ioachim Fat. Timişoara: Cartea sonoră Publishing.

Bilţiu, Pamfil and Grigore Man. 2009. *Maramureş. Săpânţa*, photo album, photographs by Gabriel Motica, Felician Săteanu and the archive of the Romanian Orthodox Parish of Săpânţa, English translation of the epitaphs by Ovidiu Tămaş. Baia Mare: 'Proema' Publishing.

Brăiloiu, C. 1981. 'Ale mortului din Gorj', in *Opere*, vol. V. Bucharest: Musical Publishing House, pp. 107–14.

Burada, T.T. 1882. *Datinile poporului român la înmormântări*. Iassy: Tipografia Naţională.

_____. 1975. *Istoria teatrului în Moldova*. Bucharest: Minerva Publishing House.

Cantemir, D. 1978. 'Despre obiceiurile de îngropăciune la moldoveni', in *Descrierea Moldovei*. Bucharest: 'Ion Creangă' Publishing House, pp. 192–94.

Eliade, M. 1972. 'The Clairvoyant Lamb', in *Zalmoxis, the Vanishing God. Comparative Studies in the Religious and Folklore of Dacia and Eastern-Europe*. Chicago and London: The University of Chicago Press, pp. 226–56.

Hossu, A.I. 2000. *Cimitirul vesel nu este vesel*. Baia Mare: Gutinul Publishing House.

Lambrior, A. 1976.. 'Obiceiuri şi credinţe la români. Înmormântările', in *Studii de lingvistică şi folcloristică*. . Iassy: Junimea Publishing House, pp. 172–90.

Marian, S.F. 1995. *Înmormântarea la români*. Bucharest: 'Grai şi suflet – Cultura Naţională'.

Mazzoni, B. (ed.). 1999. *Le iscrizioni parlanti del cimitero di Săpânţa*. Pisa: Edizioni ETS.

Pop, Mihai and Pavel Ruxăndoiu. 1978. *Folclor literar românesc*. Bucharest: Editura didactică şi pedagogică.

Toynbee, J.M.C. 1996. *Death and Burial in the Roman World*. Baltimore: Johns Hopkins University Press.

Van Gennep, Arnold. 1996. *Riturile de trecere*. Iassy: Polirom.

Vulcănescu, R. 1985. *Mitologie română*. Bucharest: Romanian Academy Publishing House.

14

IN THE DEAD OF NIGHT
A Nocturnal Exploration of Heterotopia in the Graveyard

Bel Deering

~~~~~~~~~~~~~~~~~~~~~

Introduction

The photograph below shows a visitor to a Hallowe'en graveyard event.[1] Hundreds of flickering tealights lit up the tombstones, while storytellers enthralled the crowds with ghostly and ghastly tales. Having attended this annual event for several years I noticed that it attracted people from all over the city and beyond.

Figure 14.1   Hallowe'en in a churchyard. Source: photograph owned by author.

On a night when there are myriad pop-up cultural events on offer, what could possibly be the lure of a dark and gloomy graveyard? This chapter explores the phenomenon of nocturnal graveyard visits and interrogates the motivations and experiences of the visitors. The study forms part of a larger PhD research project looking at leisure and spatiality in cemeteries, work that initially identified cemeteries as places of otherness and difference. This research found that leisure visitors engaged with cemeteries through a range of different activities, each governed, to a degree, by the perceived sense of place of the burial ground. What became apparent from participants' accounts was that they did not view them as 'normal' public spaces and that they struggled to articulate how these spaces felt. In addition, visiting at different times of year, in different weather and at different times of day seemed to influence the experience of place. In this chapter, I explore the impact of darkness on cemetery visitors in order to better understand the ambiguous relationship between people and place in the graveyard.

Data from daytime visits to the graveyard led me to agree with Foucault (1986) that cemeteries and graveyards are heterotopias. In this chapter, I show how darkness increases the intensity of heterotopic qualities, which in turn exacerbates the potential for fear and excitement in this liminal zone. I interviewed graveyard visitors by day and night as we walked amongst the gravestones in four different cemeteries and churchyards in England. In daylight hours, participants in my research variously described these deathscapes as peaceful, natural, beautiful and melancholy. When night fell, however, something changed and participants' language reflected this in the prevalence of adjectives such as creepy and spooky. Although participants showed wide variation in their reaction to the space, all recognised the potential of the sites to engender fear. While many linked this directly to the role of the imagination rather than to the reality of the situation, people were of the opinion that the cemetery itself was an unusual space, and that darkness heightened this sense of unsettling 'otherness'.

Heterotopia and the Cemetery

Cemeteries and churchyards are much more than merely burial spaces for the deceased. They offer a community greenspace for a variety of leisure activities, from dog walking to drinking (see Deering 2010; Dunk and Rugg 1994; Linden-Ward 1989). Despite being used for a range of what appear to be normal leisure activities, participants confirmed that burial grounds did not feel like normal, everyday spaces, being somehow different to parks, playgrounds and gardens. The idea of difference from the norm resonates with Foucault's writing on heterotopias. Foucault uses the term heterotopia to describe strange spaces of 'otherness' which are neither here nor there, being both physical and mental at the same time. He asserts that all societies have, and indeed need, heterotopias, and outlines six principles that describe them. He attributes significance to the fact that such spaces accommodate those members of society who do not fit soci-etal norms and suggests that communities make use of heterotopias in different ways at different times. Foucault also describes how a heterotopia can embody many different and potentially contradictory spaces and that these sites come to full power either at an absolute break in, or layering of, time. Time is highly significant in the burial ground, with dates of death recorded on gravestones as a way of marking the rupture of time at an individual level. Other layers of cir-cadian and ecological time ebb and flow around this static time of the dead on a daily or yearly basis, creating a juxtaposition of different times that participants in this research recognised and responded to. Access is also important to the concept of heterotopia, which may have very specific ways of opening and clos-ing. Foucault's final proposed role of heterotopias is in relation to all other space around them. He described this as follows:

> Either their role is to create a space of illusion that exposes every real space, all sites inside of which human life is partitioned, as still more illusory […]. Or else, on the contrary, their role is to create a space that is other, another real space, as perfect, as meticulous, as well arranged as ours is messy, ill constructed, and jumbled. This latter type would be the heterotopia, not of illusion, but of compensation. (1986: 27)

Despite some concerns over the weaknesses and lack of intellectual rigour in the concept of heterotopia (McNamee 2000; Johnson 2006; Saldanha 2008), many disciplines have appropriated the concept and added new interpretations and uses (see for example Allor 1997; Hall 2004). Foucault specifically names the cemetery as a heterotopia in his writings and outlined how it fits the model. He contends that whilst burial grounds used to be the sacred heart of a city, they were subsequently banished to the suburbs or beyond, due to society's fear of death and disease. As a result, cemeteries have become separate cities where families may visit the dead rather than hold them close by. Cemeteries appear to be a good fit for the model of heterotopia, adhering closely to the principles of ruptured time, controlled access, and societal norms. The model of heterotopia also recognises that the use of the space evolves through time; this is especially relevant to the cemetery where we find both changes in appearance and use with the passage of time (Rugg 2000). Furthermore, it is insightful to consider dead spaces as a juxtaposition of contradictory places. This is a reminder that they are perceived and experienced differently by different visitors.

Meyer and Woodthorpe argue persuasively in favour of cemeteries as heterotopias even though they recognise that 'Foucault's analysis overlooks the dissolution and disappearance of living beings (and their substantive remains) which are deeply embedded (both symbolically and physically) in the setting of the cemetery landscape' (2008: 6). Despite this issue they raise the point that at the heart of what Foucault is saying is a simple recognition that these are different spaces and that gathering them together under an umbrella term helps to conceptualise the role they play in society. Further support comes from Shackley who identifies English cathedrals as heterotopias by virtue of their being 'a ritual space that exists out of time' (2002: 345). This final example resonates with the similarly sacred qualities and notion of respect for the resting place of the dead that some people recognise in churchyards and cemeteries (Shackley 2001; Deering 2012). I believe that, in spite of its shortcomings, heterotopia is a useful concept that can aid our understanding of the cemetery space both by day and by night. It expresses the sense of alterity that participants in this research certainly reflected as they struggled both to describe the site and to pin down how they felt when they were there.

Taking Part

Four burial grounds were used for this research project, all located in southern England. Two of the sites were non-denominational municipal cemeteries, one in a busy residential part of the city and one in a quieter suburban area of a town. The other two sites were Church of England churchyards, and while there was again a split with one being in a town and the other a city, both had busy central locations. These sites were selected for research because they were accessible for leisure users, and provided a contrast between secular and religious burial. In addition, they were wholly or partly disused for burial, meaning that visitors were predominantly there for recreation rather than mourning. Whilst the sites were varied in location and appearance, they were all recognisably places of death and burial. Indeed, participants in my wider PhD research frequently referenced the appearance of the tombs as contributing to their perceived sense of place. One woman, for example, commented during an interview that 'The shape of stones connects to what they say. The gothic ones are all about hellfire and brimstone. That's quite a scary attitude.' This suggests that the appearance of the burial grounds, which was influenced by their ethnic and religious roots, had an effect on the way in which the landscape was experienced. This research, with its focus on just four burial grounds, cannot therefore capture a definitive sense of the graveyard after dark. It implies that burial grounds associated with different faiths, religions and cultures may engender a different response because of their different appearance, but further work would be needed to confirm this.

At the heart of this research is the issue of how such deathscapes feel after dark. To gain insight to this question I recruited participants who were either willing to visit a burial space at dusk or at night, or who could describe a prior visit. From the thirty participants that contributed to my PhD research study of the leisure uses of cemeteries, fifteen shared their nocturnal experiences with me in interviews and informal conversations. Pseudonyms are used in this work to ensure the privacy of participants, who came from a range of different backgrounds with regard to the cemetery and churchyard sites. They included churchwardens, vicars, Friends Group committee members, tourists, regular visitors and patrol/ranger staff. Some were recruited opportunistically at churchyard events and others through contacts made within the church community or local authority.

The choice of location for the interviews and conversations varied between each site. Participants took an active part in deciding on the location and the choice in many cases reflected the nature of the site, weather conditions and their own personal obligations and commitments on the day. Whilst I attempted to ensure the comfort, privacy, safety and convenience of the participants, in reality, graveyards varied widely in their suitability and presented unique issues and problems in several cases. In many instances the cemetery or churchyard itself formed the location, which enabled participants to point out specific features and increased the sense of connection to the data being generated during the interview. Many participants were keen to take me on a walking tour and used this to prompt their memories, descriptions and stories of events they had experienced or observed. Whilst this was a very useful way of bringing the research alive, colder and wetter days sometimes prematurely curtailed interviews. In a couple of instances, the interview moved from graveyard to car park when the participants became too nervous of the dark.

Groping around in the Dark

Whilst some participants were openly nervous of the dark, others recognised that it felt different by night, but enjoyed this contrast. The fact that sense of place changed between day and night offers support for Hanyu's (1997) argument that the appearance of a place influences human experience and emotions. Both Pink (2008) and Tuan (2008) also emphasise that it is sensory encounter and experience that are crucial in forming a sense of place. This suggests that where the sensory input changes – for example when vision is reduced by night – the sense of place will change. Cloke et al. (2005) suggest that our imaginations shape the physical reality of landscape around us – an effect which may be given freer rein by night. It therefore seems that there is a reciprocal relationship whereby people influence place and place influences people. Whilst I am more attentive to the issue of place affecting people in this chapter, the influence of people on place could be very interesting to explore in a burial ground. By asking participants about the nocturnal cemetery experience I build on the link between time and heterotopia described earlier and examine how the diurnal cycles of day and night influence perception and sense of place.

In the cemetery at night, the aspect of the experience subject to the most observations was the condition of darkness itself. Participants made comparisons with their experience of the site during daylight hours and were sometimes surprised by the way in which a familiar site could appear to be so different. Robinson's (2009) work on nightspaces used by young people also found this duality between night and day, in which public space became transformed into an intimate and private space as darkness fell. Darkness was central to one of my participant's, Mitzi's, description of how she felt in the graveyard. In the daytime she felt secure in such a public place but at night it became a space that she felt did not belong to her or welcome her:

> It is creeping me out – I actually feel quite nervous. Not because it is a graveyard, but because it is dark. We are two women alone in a dark place where something untoward could happen. Ahh – Jesus Christ we have only been here two minutes, and I want to go. Shall we maybe go and sit in that thing [the lychgate] with our backs to the wall? I am actually surprised at how I don't like it. I thought it would not be a problem, but I take it we are going back to the car. I am really surprised at how I feel – it is the dark though. (Mitzi in interview with author)

Several other participants shared Mitzi's unease. They described how their inability to see clearly in the darkened landscape inspired fear, supporting previous work by Jones and Nasar (1997) about fear and safety in night-time environments.

Night-time fears were often understood to be irrational, but participants felt that they were not in control of their imagination and this was where the thoughts of ghosts, vampires and the dead rising from the grave came from. Another participant, Charm, sums this up neatly when she says 'Do I believe in vampires? No. Does my imagination believe in vampires? Yes!' This lack of control over the imagination – which participants such as Charm and others felt, was responsible for their feelings in the dark – was attributed to three main causes. Firstly, participants felt that, as their senses were restricted, their minds tried to fill in the gaps in the data received and sometimes made simple errors – for example identifying the shadow of a moving branch as a person's arm. Secondly, many participants felt that their imaginations had been conditioned to be fearful of the dark through childhood fairy stories and a later diet of horror films and books. Thirdly, some participants described having had seemingly supernatural encounters on a previous occasion. For two interviewees, these encounters were understood as real supernatural interactions, and for several others they were interpreted as imaginary, but had 'spooked' them and made them more nervous of the dark. Luther recognised the emotional dimension of the cemetery, relating it to human physiology by saying:

> People have emotional reactions to being in different places – some churchyards or graveyards get a feeling there, like serenity, but I don't know how that is cre-

Figure 14.2 Shadow in a churchyard. Source: photograph owned by author.

ated. In woodland or shady areas you can feel the change of temperature, light and humidity. That has a fundamental effect on the body so maybe it creates the sense of place from this, from a really physiological perspective. (Luther in interview with the author)

Mitzi and Joan were among the participants who echoed Luther's idea that place could have an effect on the physical body. Mitzi's nervousness was quite apparent and she articulated exactly how she was feeling when we were in the churchyard, relating her physical symptoms to the tension she felt in the overwhelming darkness of the churchyard, saying 'D'you know what – my heart rate is actually quite fast – is yours? [Bel – laughs] I feel quite uugh. My mouth is dry, I would never have anticipated that. Honestly I feel quite heebee-jeebie. Let's have a fag and chill out.'

Fear has been shown to be a stressful experience (Rigor 1985) and stress can have mild physical symptoms or possibly lead to more serious disease (Cohen, Janicki-Deverts and Miller 2007). Figure 14.2 serves to further illustrate this point about how the perceived landscape can influence the mind and body. The image was captured during a visit to a churchyard when a participant pointed out how the church floodlights actually made their vision worse; in the light we were blinded, and out of the light our eyes struggled to adjust. The powerful lamps cast huge shadows and if these were glimpsed out of the corner of the eye as we walked along, they hinted at the movement of some other presence in the churchyard. Joan was not alone in this research in finding the shadows disorientating and fearsome.

Morris refers to the experience of visual deprivation in her exploration of a night-time art installation, highlighting how it can have many effects on the body and the senses. She describes how 'At night new orders of connection assert themselves: sonic, olfactory, tactile. The sensorium is transformed. Associations swarm out of the darkness. You become even more aware of the landscape as a medley of effects, a mingling of memory, movement, life. The landforms remain, but they exist as presences: inferred, less substantial, more powerful' (Morris 2011: 315). She asserts that while there is the potential for disorientation and fear, darkness also offers something positive, akin to exercise, for the other bodily senses. I have mentioned here how darkness can both rob the sense of sight of its ability while enhancing the power of the other senses. Participants experienced a range of sensory distortions and mysterious apparitions in the cemetery that they found unsettling. Charm and Joan both refer to this in their interviews. Charm asks 'What's that light down there? I want to know what that light is – I need to know but at the same time I am slightly concerned with what is behind us. Are you ok? [Bel – I'm ok] Oh, do you know what? It is just the moon. I'm not sure I would be this calm by myself here!' Referring to an inscription that is something of an optical illusion when caught between the shadows and the floodlighting, Joan describes how 'the writing inverts and looks like it is coming out when it is going in… woooooo… [laughs nervously] Although we are in the light, when you see that, it gets scary again.'

Darkness therefore has a significant impact on participants' experience of the cemetery and changes the sense of place they perceive. Night brings fear and mystery and intrigue along with sensory deprivation and the next section looks more closely at the links between fear and fun and why it sometimes seems to attract people to the cemetery. This sense of thrill-seeking links the experience of being in a cemetery after dark with the literature of legend tripping and edgework.

Fear, Edgework and Legend Tripping

Faced with the question of what causes fear in the cemetery, the almost instinctive answer would seem to be the undeniable presence of dead bodies. Certainly in popular fiction the dead bodies are frequently the reason for the fearful nature of burial grounds, as they are attributed with the power to rise out of the grave and enter the world of the living (Breslin 1995; Cascone 1997; Stine 1999). Historical accounts of death suggest that whilst the moment of physical death itself may not have been feared as much in past times, there was a fear of 'bad' death preventing the deceased from resting in peace, and bad behaviour condemning the dead to hell (Aries 1994). Today, there is no consensus in the death literature as to whether or not death is something feared, taboo, or sequestrated in society (Gorer 1965; Walter 1994; Woodthorpe 2010) and indeed society's relationship with death has been argued to have changed through time (Berridge 2002; Walter 1991). This suggests that there is no clear societal-level agreement

that death, and by extension, graveyards are to be feared. In this research, however, participants felt that it was normal to have some degree of fear of death.
This was partly because death could be sudden, brutal and unwanted in sepa-
rating families and loved ones, and also because even for those of faith, it was
unknowable. Death was seen as being potentially physically painful and involving suffering for the dying and the bereaved, and this pain was thought by some
to have the potential to last beyond death and into the grave. While fear in many
cases was attributed to the possibility of vampires, ghosts and malevolent spirits,
it was also linked closely to this concern for future pain and loss. Whether death
is feared or taboo it cannot be avoided in the cemetery where it dominates the
landscape. For some participants in this research, for example Sylvie and Mina,
the fact that it is a burial ground is attractive, encouraging visits and recreation
that include the more sensational forms such as ghost tourism or legend tripping
(see Bird 1994 and 2002; Ellis 1994; Holloway 2010; and Holly and Cordy 2007).
Figure 14.3 shows a queue of visitors lining up for a graveyard storytelling event.
Visitors waited patiently for over twenty minutes to gain access to the storytelling circle and their chance to be regaled with tales of mystery and intrigue: fear
does not repel, but in fact can be a strong force of attraction.

On closer examination of the concept of fear, many research participants
confessed they were scared or anxious about being in a cemetery in the dark,
but were divided as to whether it was the living or the dead that would bother
them. Both living and dead had the potential to 'lurk' (a term much used by
interviewees) thus their real or imagined presence rendered the site perceptually
less safe. Joan voiced a commonly-held opinion as to why it was a scary place to

Figure 14.3   Queue for ghost stories at a Hallowe'en churchyard event. Source: photograph owned
by author.

go at night, saying 'It's dark and has got dead people in it. I think if they happened to wake from the dead they would obviously be quite upset and would come and harass you in some way'. Several participants said that although logically they knew there was nothing scary there, their imagination could not be tamped down. In the words of Imogen: 'Maybe I watched too many horror films but [I thought the dead bodies] were all going to come up'. Whilst Imogen was deterred from going into the graveyard because of her fears, others claimed that they actively sought this feeling of heightened sensation and emotion. Pewter said that she 'came here a lot as a child – mostly to spook each other out' and described leaping out on her friends and pulling pranks on people to scare and surprise them. Sylvie's experiences echoed those of Pewter in that she too had chosen to visit the churchyard because it felt like a more exciting place than any other part of the town. She describes her experiences, saying: 'We used to hide behind the gravestones and spook people at night. We would wait outside the church until there was a quiet bit in the service and then knock on the door or windows. It was like our patch, for our gang.'

Bird (1994) underlines the playful nature of such cemetery visits and asserts that the emotional power is co-created by the combination of place, stories, and actions. For Sylvie and for Pewter here, they remembered the fear as being fun and part of the reward for the activity. Being in a cemetery with dead bodies and sensing the otherness of the place heightened the experience for them. Some of the recreation that reportedly took place in churchyards and cemeteries, such as drinking and partying, was illicit and exciting in itself. For more mundane activities, the fact that they took place in a graveyard gave them an edge, an extra potency that they would otherwise have lacked. Mina talked about how her group of friends used to visit the graveyard at night and described some relatively innocent behaviour that was given much higher status because the site was a graveyard: 'when people come in you can hide behind the gates and rattle them'. The significance of it being a burial ground was that 'there are lots of dead people under you […] skeletons clinking around […] it is scary and exciting'. Bird (2002) explains the importance of a sense of danger and the need for bravery as part of the power of the legend trip. Although teenagers and Goths are usually seen as the stereotypical legend trippers, the term is not exclusive to these groups (Holly and Cordy 1997). A legend tripper is usually a thrill-seeker who visits sites that are rumoured to have magical or paranormal interest and enacts rituals aimed at invoking the supernatural. Interestingly, whilst not all the experiences recorded in my research are a perfect fit with legend tripping itself, they do share many characteristics, including the telling of the story to reminisce and recreate the original excitement.

The recounting of stories – both of graveyard visits and the legends or spooky stories attached to these visits – is an important feature of this activity. During interviews, every participant independently chose to tell me about a mysterious experience they had previously had. Charm shared the story of her mother's ghost who was always seen about the house, Mitzi told of being saved from falling by what seemed to be a ghostly hand, and Joan recounted a scary encounter with someone in a Scream mask. Ellis (1994), writing about horror legends and fear-motivated visits, argues that storytelling is an essential part of testing and challenging our social world. Somers adds to this: 'It is through narrativity that we come to know, understand, and make sense of the social world, and through which we constitute our social identities' (1997: 83). Somers asserts that storytelling can play an important role in our individual and community identity, whilst Bird extends this and explores why some places make better storytelling fodder than others: 'Why is it that some places seem to invite the telling of stories? Unusual houses, cemeteries, and lonely bridges are the kinds of places around which legends cluster [...] at the heart of many local legends is an attempt to explain ambiguity – something does not quite seem to belong or stands out from its surroundings' (Bird 2002: 525).

In the case of the cemetery perhaps this ambiguity is the very essence that the term heterotopia is trying to capture. And because the place and feeling is so hard to grasp and understand people keep going back to try and pin down this unsettling quality. Mina's 'scary and exciting' experience also articulates something of the essence of Warner's argument that fears can serve a positive role. Warner explains her understanding of this phenomenon: 'That children's word "scary" covers responses ranging from pure terror to sheer delight, and the condition of being scared is becoming increasingly sought after not only as a source of pleasure but as a means of strengthening the sense of being alive, of having a command over self' (2007: 6). Amongst others, Mina and Pewter separately described graveyards as exciting. Berg and Heijne (2005) reinforce this view with their argument that fear can be positive as it can have the capacity to invigorate and fascinate even whilst it causes stress and heightens emotions. It would seem to be no surprise then that a graveyard could be a leisure or tourist attraction.

Seeking fear and that elusive thrill of being alive is the sensationalism at the heart of edgework, described by Lyng as voluntary risk taking activities that 'involve a clearly observable threat to one's physical or mental well-being or one's sense of an ordered existence [...] the "edge" or boundary line, confronted by the edge worker can be defined in many different ways: life versus death, consciousness versus unconsciousness, sanity versus insanity, an ordered sense of self and environment versus a disordered self and environment' (Lyng 1990: 857). In the edgework model the experience of taking a risk creates high levels of stimulation and so the participant gains a sensory reward for the activity. Like the thrill of legend tripping, Lyng describes how a person reaching the height or the 'edge' of the experience finds that their perceptual field becomes highly focused, that time slows and that they experience a strong connection to their environment. I suggest here that the edgework model has parallels with the deliberate fear-seeking activities of those people who visit cemeteries for legend tripping and also explains the sensation of my participants who had different motives in visiting a graveyard but the same outcome. In this hypothesis graveyards validate the aliveness of visitors, helping them to be in the now and grooming the visitor for an edgework-esque thrill. This buzz can be augmented through thrilling activities which serve to exacerbate the edgework effect.

Conclusion

This nocturnal study was part of a broader exploration of the way in which cemeteries are perceived, experienced and used. The aim of this individual element of the research was to understand the experience of being in a graveyard at night, an activity that had been identified by participants as being different from a daytime visit. Interview data clearly showed that darkness increased emotional intensity, with imagination, storytelling, fear and excitement as clear themes. By day these themes were also present but on a more subdued level; for participants in this research, darkness seemed to magnify feelings, emotion and imaginings. At night the storylines prescribed by tombstones were obscured, thus control of the site was ceded to the visitor's imagination.

As heterotopias, cemeteries are already configured as places of otherness. They are the separate cities of the dead that both Foucault (1986) and Aries (1994) describe as being outside of the normal and everyday world. This separation contributes to the ambiguity of burial grounds as places, which in turn stimulates imagination and storytelling as tools to make sense of the mystery and explain the unknown (Bird 2002). Bringing darkness into this place already rich in alterity, further increases the ambiguity and thus potential for imagination and stories. As darkness sits within the surrounding frame of light it may be that this simple juxtaposition, or splintering of the familiar, catalyses the imagination and moves people into heterotopic other-worlds.

Imagination and storytelling formed a core part of the way in which participants related their experiences and described how they were feeling both during the interview and on previous occasions. Participants regaled me with a variety of tales, including personal legends about spooky experiences, and even where these were generally mysterious or uncanny and unrelated to the cemetery, they did serve to heighten the atmosphere that we felt there and made us alert to every sound and flicker of light that our eyes could pick up. It appeared that darkness did not obscure death, but escalated its impact through heightened excitement or fear. As a response, fear is partly rational, since we are more vulnerable in the dark (Hanyu 1997) and partly a response to the changing sensory landscape, in which optical illusions sparked imagined sightings and glimpses of the unknown (Morris 2011).

Both Charm and Joan tap into Ellis's theories about the social role of fear, horror legends, and the stories people tell. Ellis asserts that these kinds of tales 'allow participants to experiment with a social taboo; violating it, respecting it or compromising with it' (1994: 70). Indeed, I contend that it is the heterotopic quality of these spaces that underlies their richness for storytelling, for being taboo and for inspiring fear. Storytelling is also a way to articulate and make sense of the ambiguity of heterotopias and to explain a fear that seems so irrational. However, their narratives expressed an unresolved tension between the experience of logic and of imagination, and between reality and the supernatural. Joan was, unwillingly, very fearful in the cemetery, and identified the cause quite simply when she said 'Imagination versus reality? Imagination is much more powerful.' Participants felt that their living bodies were at the heart of the cemetery experience; their sensory limitations in the dark fed into the power of their imagination and caused illusions, fear, and wild imaginings beyond their logical control. As heterotopia, and in the dark, burial grounds were experienced as realms of infinite possibility.

Fear, imagination, and indeed thrills are closely bound up in the identity of the graveyard at night. I have argued elsewhere (Deering 2012) that burial grounds are slippery, multi-vocal sites whose accumulation of death has a potent effect on visitors. In this research I found that the excitement and fear of the cemetery was exacerbated by darkness which deprives the senses, hides and obscures. Darkness impeded sight but enhanced heterotopia. It changed the sense of access to a site, changed perception of time and was in juxtaposition to the norm of daylight. By escalating the qualities of heterotopia, which I argue accounts for why cemeteries are so rich for storytelling and legend, the stories become more important, the fear more potent and the sense of the forbidden intensifies. Foucault argued that societies need heterotopias. This research suggests that graveyards at night may also be needed by society in order to provide a place where people can safely play with taboo, play with fear, and play with notions of death.

Note

1. In this chapter I use the words cemetery, graveyard, burial ground and churchyard interchangeably to reflect the fact that my research took place in several settings. For a definition of the actual differences between these terms, see Rugg 2000.

Bibliography

Allor, M. 1997. 'Locating Cultural Activity: the "Main" as Chronotype and Heterotopia', *Topia* 1: 42–54.

Aries, P. 1994. *Western Attitudes toward Death from the Middle Ages to the Present*, 2nd edition. London: Marion Boyars.

Berg, A.E., van den, Heijne, M. ter. 2005. 'Fear versus Fascination: An Exploration of Emotional Responses to Natural Threats', *Journal of Environmental Psychology* 25(3): 261–72.

Berridge, K. 2002. *Vigor Mortis: The End of the Death Taboo*. London: Profile.

Bird, S.E. 1994. 'Playing with Fear: Interpreting the Adolescent Legend Trip', *Western Folklore* 53(3): 191–209.

_____. 2002. 'It Makes Sense to Us: Cultural Identity in Local Legends of Place', *Journal of Contemporary Ethnography* 31: 519–47.

Breslin, T. 1995. *Whispers in the Graveyard*. London: Mammoth.

Cascone, A.G. 1997. *Grave Secrets*. Mahwah, New Jersey: Troll Communications LLC.

Cloke, P., P. Crang and M. Goodwin. 2005. *Introducing Human Geographies*. London: Hodder Arnold.

Cohen, S., D. Janicki-Deverts and G.E. Miller. 2007. 'Psychological Stress and Disease', *Journal of the American Medical Association* 298(14): 1685–87.

Deering, B. 2010. 'From Anti-Social Behaviour to X-rated: Exploring Social Diversity and Conflict in the Cemetery', in A. Maddrell and J. Sidaway (eds.), *Deathscapes: Spaces for Death, Dying, Mourning and Remembrance*. Farnham: Ashgate Publishing, Ltd., pp. 75–94.

_____. 2012. 'Over their Dead Bodies: a Study of Leisure and Spatiality in Cemeteries'. Unpublished PhD thesis, University of Brighton.

Dunk, J. and J. Rugg. 1994. *The Management of Old Cemetery Land: Now and the Future*. Crayford: Shaw and Sons.

Ellis, B. 1994. '"The Hook" Reconsidered: Problems in Classifying and Interpreting Adolescent Horror Legends', *Folklore* 105: 61–75.

Foucault, M. and J. Miskoweic. 1986. 'Of Other Spaces' , *Diacritics* 16(1): 22–27.

Gorer, G. 1965. *Death and Mourning in Contemporary Britain*. London: Cresset Press.

Hall, L.E. 2004. 'Sitting Down in the Square: Indigenous Presence in an Australian City', *Humanities Research* XI(1): 54–77.

Hanyu, K. 1997. 'Visual Properties and Affective Appraisals in Residential Areas after Dark', *Journal of Environmental Psychology* 17: 301–15.

Holloway, J. 2010. 'Legend Tripping in Spooky Places: Ghost Tourism and Infrastructures of Enchantment', *Environment and Planning D: Society and Space* 28: 618–37.

Holly, D.H. and C.E. Cordy. 2007. 'What's In a Coin? Reading the Material Culture of Legend Tripping and Other Activities', *Journal of American Folklore* 120(477): 335–54.

Johnson, P. 2006. 'Unravelling Foucault's "different spaces"', *History of the Human Sciences* 19(4): 75–90.

Jones, K.M. and J.L. Nasar. 1997. 'Landscapes of Fear and Stress', *Environment and Behaviour* 29(3): 291–323.

Linden-Ward, B. 1989. 'Strange but Genteel Pleasure Grounds: Tourist and Leisure Uses of Nineteenth-century Rural Cemeteries', in R.E. Meyer (ed.), *Cemeteries and Gravemarkers: Voices of American Culture*. Michigan: University Microfilms, pp. 293–328.

Lyng, S. 1990. 'Edgework: A Social Psychological Analysis of Voluntary Risk Taking', *The American Journal of Sociology* 95(4): 851–86.

McNamee, S. 2000. 'Foucault's Heterotopias and Children's Everyday Lives', *Childhood* 7(4): 479–42.

Meyer, M. and K. Woodthorpe. 2008. 'The Material Presence of Absence: A Dialogue Between Museums and Cemeteries', *Sociological Research Online* 13(5). Accessed on 1 May 2010, http://www.socresonline.org.uk/13/5/1.html

Morris, N.J. 2011. 'Night Walking: Darkness and Sensory Perception in a Night-time Landscape Installation', *Cultural Geographies* 18(3): 315–42.

Pink, S. 2008. 'An Urban Tour: the Sensory Sociality of Ethnographic Place making', *Ethnography* 9(2): 175–96.

Rigor, S. 1985. 'Crime as an Environmental Stressor', *Journal of Community Psychology* 13: 270–81.

Robinson, C. 2009. 'Nightscapes and Leisure Spaces: an Ethnographic Study of Young People's Use of Free Space', *Journal of Youth Studies* 12(5): 501–51.

Rugg, J. 2000. 'Defining the Place of Burial: What Makes a Cemetery a Cemetery?', *Mortality* 5(3): 259–75.

Saldanha, A. 2008. 'Heterotopia and Structuralism', *Environment and Planning A* 40: 2080–96.

Shackley, M. 2001. *Managing Sacred Spaces*. London: Thompson.

_____. 2002. 'Space, Sanctity and Service; The English Cathedral as heterotopia', *International Journal of Tourism Research* 4(5): 345–52.

Somers, M.R. 1997. 'Deconstructing and Reconstructing Class Formation Theory: Narrativity, Relational Analysis, and Social Theory', in J.R. Hall (ed.), *Reworking Class*. Ithaca, New York: Cornell University Press, pp. 73–106.

Stine, R.L. 1999. *Attack of the Graveyard Ghouls*. London: Scholastic Children's Books.

Tuan, Y. 2008. *Space and Place: The Perspective of Experience*, 6th edition. Minneapolis: University of Minnesota Press.

Walter, T. 1991. 'Modern Death: Taboo or Not Taboo?', *Sociology* 25(2): 293–311.

_____. 1994. *The Revival of Death*. London: Routledge.

Warner, M. 2007. *Monsters of our Own Making: The Peculiar Pleasures of Fear*. Lexington: University Press of Kentucky.

Woodthorpe, K. 2010. 'Private Grief in Public Spaces: Interpreting Memorialisation in the Contemporary Cemetery', in J. Hockey, C. Komaromy and K. Woodthorpe (eds), *The Matter of Death: Space, Place and Materiality*. Basingstoke: Palgrave Macmillan, pp. 117–32.

15

SCENARIOS OF DEATH IN CONTEXTS OF MOBILITY
Guineans and Bangladeshis in Lisbon

Clara Saraiva and José Mapril

In recent decades, the transnational dimensions of migration have assumed increasing theoretical and ethnographic importance. By 'transnational' we mean the concept first proposed by Basch, Schiller and Blanc in 1992 and 1994, that implies the multiple and permanent ties sustained between the sending country and the country of reception, in its economic, political and cultural aspects. One of the consequences of such an interpretative shift is the acknowledgement that such ties and mobilities – real or imagined – are frequently accompanied by the social and symbolic construction of places of belonging. As Karen Olwig (2007) and Clifford Geertz (1996) have shown, global mobilities and flows are accompanied by everyday processes of place making. In transnational migratory contexts, these processes are produced through the sending and use of remittances (in capital and goods) and in the performance of certain rituals and ceremonies.

In this chapter, death will serve as a metaphor to think about the production of places and spaces of belonging in transnational contexts. In the study of migrations, death and dying are good examples of the circulation of symbolic universes in which the notion of process is extremely important. Such arguments will be explored through two case studies: Bangladeshis and Guinean migrants in Portugal.[1]

In social anthropology, the conceptions of death and dying have attracted wider attention from several authors such as Frazer (1890) , Hertz (1960) and Evans-Pritchard (1976) or Gable (2006) and De Boeck (2008). Approaches to the topic include studies on the symbolism of several ceremonial elements and the liminality of funerary rituals (Pina-Cabral 1984).

In the present chapter, we want to explore the relationship between funerary ceremonies and the (re)production and symbolisation of places of belonging, places which include among many others a local community,[2] a space of diaspora or the belonging to a nation-state. Additionally, we will discuss the relationship between the notions of belonging to a place and the idea of 'good death'.

One of the most important books on death is certainly *Death and the Regeneration of Life* by Maurice Bloch and Jonathan Parry (1982b) in which several authors reflect on the presence of fertility symbols in funerary rituals. Among a vast set of themes, two approaches assume particular importance for the present chapter as they explore the relationship between funerary ceremonies and place and the notions of 'good death'. In the last text of this collective work, Bloch (1982a) resumes an argument previously explored in his main ethnographic work – *Placing the Dead* (1971) – in which the author draws our attention to the relation between funerary rituals and the identification with a place, a land. Based on a study of the Merina of Madagascar, Bloch's argument is that the funerary rituals imply two burials. The first one takes place in the vicinity of the place of dying, and aims at cleansing the body of all impure substances. Two years later, the body is moved and buried again, but this time into the grave of the ancestors. There is a link between the grave and the group of kin and thus to be buried in the homeland signifies a reunion between present, past and future kin. This burial in the ancestral land is the celebration of the union of family networks and victory over the division and separation that everyday life entails. This second burial, also known as *famadihana*, repositions the Merina who died far away from the ancestral land in the society of their ancestors.

The relation between death, funerary ceremonies and places of belonging is visible in other ethnographic contexts linked to migrations and diasporas. A recent article by Eric Gable (2006) is a clear example. Based on his research on Manjack migrants in the cities of Guinea-Bissau, Gable argues that funerary ceremonies are occasions to demonstrate personal success and claims of belonging in the rural communities left behind. The funerals are events where Manjacks appeal to their cosmopolitanism, as migrants and urbanites, to legitimise their belonging. A similar argument has been presented by Peter Geschiere (2005) in his work on funerals in the South of Cameroon.

Another example is the work of Françoise Lestage (2008) on Mexican migration in the US and the processes of repatriation of bodies. The author analyses the creation of an industry of repatriation where several funerary agencies and state institutions are the main actors. Such processes reveal, once again, the relation between migrations and place making but this time in relation to nationalism. For the Mexican state the migrants have assumed a role of principle agents of economic development and thus they have access to unprecedented rights and privileges: dual nationality and the right to rest close to their ancestors.

Finally, in his recent historical ethnography on the Yemeni diaspora in the Indian Ocean, Engseng Ho (2006) shows how graves are the nodes in the transnational circuits that link the Arabian Peninsula to the South of China. The Hadrami graves represent generations of Yemenis that have worked on the commercial routes of the Indian Ocean and thus represent and materialise the secular memory of displacements in colonial and post-colonial times. The graves mark the places of belonging of this vast diaspora.

In all these examples, the main idea that emerges is precisely the telluric dimension of death and its importance and role in many different migration and diasporic contexts. Further, they also reveal how the maintenance of ties to a specific place implies a notion of 'good death' and good relations between the worlds of the living and the dead.

In order to explore this argument, we will firstly contextualise the migration flows that link Guinea-Bissau and Bangladesh to Portugal.[3] In the two following sections, we will focus on the discourses and practices regarding death and funerary ceremonies in these two contexts. This comparative exercise will lead to a fourth section dedicated to migrant transnationalism and death and dying.

People from Guinea-Bissau in Portugal

People from Guinea-Bissau have a long tradition of migration, and there are Guineans scattered throughout Senegal, France and Holland (Machado 2002), but Portugal is a preferred destination, due to the ties connecting the two countries.[4]

The first migrants started to arrive in Portugal after the official independence of Guinea-Bissau which followed the Portuguese military coup of 25 April 1974. However, it was mainly after 1984, with the opening of the country to more Westernised economic and social models, that immigration increased (Machado 2002; Saraiva 2008; Quintino 2004). Portugal is seen as a paradise, where one can have a job and send remittances to the families back home (Saraiva 2008: 256).

Guinea-Bissau is a small country, with about 1.2 million inhabitants, but with a large ethnic diversity, involving more than twenty-three ethnic groups (Einarsdottir 2000). Most groups in the interior are Islamised, and the coastal ones are animistic, but religious affiliation does not always follow ethnic division (Jao 1995), and there are multiple combinations of animistic and Christian religious options.

Bangladeshis in Portugal

Migrants from Bangladesh first arrived in Portugal in 1986 but it was between 1995 and 2003 that this population increased significantly: from 47 to a little more than 2,000 (legally registered persons in the Portuguese immigration services). In spite of these official numbers, other sources, namely the Bangladesh Honorary Consul, identify more than 4,500 Bangladeshi citizens.

Like Bangladeshis in Italy and in Spain, the majority come from the capital Dhaka. With a high level of education, they belong to what in Bangladesh have been described as the new and affluent middle classes. For these groups, coming to Europe is not a way of escaping poverty but a strategy to access what in Bangladesh is called *adhunik* – the modern (Mapril 2007). Many Bangladeshis first came to Portugal in the context of the legalisation processes carried out by the Portuguese authorities in 1992, 1996 and 2001–2004 or to reunite with family and friends already living here. Several arrived on their own but during our fieldwork – between 2003 and 2007 – we witnessed many family reunifications.

Having said this, it is important to understand that this population is divided according to migratory generations. Thus, on the one hand, we have the pioneers, who arrived at the end of the 1980s and beginning of the 1990s; they began working in the most underprivileged sectors and are today owners of several businesses. They have constituted their own households and are examples of success. On the other hand, the recently arrived, also called *bachelors* or *freshies*, continue to work in the most precarious sectors or in the labour market created by the pioneers and, in most of the cases, are still single. For these, the future of the migratory project is very uncertain.

In these migratory contexts, how is death and dying managed?

The *Mala* of the Deceased: The Case of Guinean Death

In her book on immigration from Guinea-Bissau to Portugal, Quintino mentions a trans/identity, constructed around the permanent relations between the immigrants and the host community, the original home territory and the desire to one day be able to return home (2004: 35).

People from Guinea-Bissau have a strong associative movement and in Portugal there are over fifty Guinean NGOs. Most of them give support to immigrants in matters of administration and legalisation of their status, but they also promote solidarity initiatives, such as collecting funds for public facilities and improvements back home or cooperation programmes. They are also in charge of the organisation of all aspects of rites of passage and cyclic religious or profane feasts, in which Catholic, Animistic and Muslim practices come together, and which are moments of intense intra/ethnic sociability. One of the principal functions of these NGOs is to financially support the shipment of the deceased, or, at least, to help to arrange for members of their families living in Portugal or valuable goods to be sent back home. The fundamental idea behind this movement of people and goods is to be able to maintain links with the places of origin.

Let us see how this works in practice. Most of these organisations require the payment of a membership fee that reverts to the common fund. This fund contributes to the expenses related to sending back the corpse, if this is the wish of the family. Due to the high cost involved, sometimes a symbolic shipment is organised to replace the sending of a real body. The *mala* (suitcase) and the *toka chur* (funeral ceremonies) are the two most important significant elements to be sent back home.

One such organisation, the Associação dos Naturais do Pelundo residentes em Portugal, founded in 1992, is particularly active in maintaining the relationship with the place of origin. It is a Manjack-based organisation, Manjacks being one of the ethnic groups that has the longest immigration tradition, also with large numbers of immigrants in France, where a sister organisation exists. One of its major activities is the support of its members in case of illness or death. According to the established rules, in the event of a death in the family, the members are entitled to economic support to enable them to perform the funerary rituals. Most individuals (ninety per cent) are buried in Lisbon cemeteries, and the organisation pays the costs of the funeral. If the body is sent back to Guinea-Bissau, the organisation gives the same amount of money and the rest of the expense (around 5,000 euros) has to be borne by the family. Most families do not have the economic means to send the body back home. In the face of such an impossible task, the emphasis is placed on the ritualisation of the bonds with the place of origin and with the family back in Guinea, in order to attain the ideal 'good death'.

One of these rituals, which surpasses ethnic or religious diversity as it is used by Catholics, Muslims and Animists alike, is the *mala*. After the funeral, the close family organises the suitcase of the deceased. This suitcase is filled with the person's most important belongings, mainly clothing, jewellery and textiles or cloths, especially *panos penti*, the hand-woven cloths which are highly prized in Guinea and all over West Africa (Saraiva 2008). Beyond the funeral costs, the organisation gives 250 euros which may be supplemented with family donations. This money is placed inside the suitcase and sent back home by a family member. It is the duty of the immediate family to fulfil these obligations, and in doing so, they may benefit from the protection of the deceased; if they do not ensure that the rituals are performed correctly, they may instead face a vengeful ancestor. This act confirms two fundamental ideals: firstly, the continuity of the family beyond national borders and the members' mobility. Secondly, when one's physical mobility ends with death, the belongings symbolising the person must return home and close the cycle of the connection to the home ground, the *tchon*.

The goods placed in the suitcase either belonged to the individual or were gifts offered at the funeral. No one comes to a funeral without a gift. It is believed that the deceased will need such things in the other world. Also, all that the living offer to the dead will ultimately revert in their favour, as these are goods that enrich the other world. Although they may seem contradictory, these two assumptions complement each other. What belonged to the deceased goes to the living family, both in the diaspora and in the place of origin; all that is offered by those coming to the ritual is symbolically given to the spirit of the deceased and to the world of the spirits in general.

The organisation of the suitcase takes place immediately after death, in the house of the deceased or of a family member. Songs are sung and drinks are poured in the ground for the spirits (*darmar*); in the case of Muslims, the ritual also includes the sacrifice of an animal. *Darmar* has the ultimate meaning of communion between humans and ancestors: the idea is that ancestors surround us, and we need to share with them what is going to be drunk or eaten. This is especially important at the moment when communication between the worlds of the living and of the dead is open, due to the new death. The dead ancestors live in a totally mobile world, and thus they are present in the ceremonies in Portugal and in Guinea.

In the same way, if someone dies and is buried in Portugal, ceremonies must also take place in Guinea, and vice versa. Eating, drinking, giving gifts and the sacrifice of animals as offerings for the dead are all part of the ceremonies in both Portugal and in Guinea. All such instances are part of what Quintino (2004) calls the 'ethnic package' of Guineans in Portugal. By this, Quintino means a group of instances which show not only the origin of the individual, but also proof of his/her connection to both the physical world of the home lands as well as to the invisible world of the ancestors. It is part of the (moral and real) expectations of any family back in Guinea-Bissau that emigrants contribute and help the family back home. Besides the fact that being an emigrant means having succeeded in life, the funerals are events of high social value, in which one can exhibit the success achieved in one's migration trajectory, as Eric Gable explains. Following the same logic, and given the high cost involved, it is mainly highly successful immigrants who have their bodies repatriated. Another case when a body should be sent back home is when the deceased was one of the elders (*omi garandi*)[5] who hold important social, political or religious roles in the community.

The hegemony of the elder over the young continues beyond death. As Kopytoff (1971) explains, an elder is already considered a potential ancestor, and his/her death is a feast, a celebration of his/her entrance into the world of the dead and thus becoming a protective ancestor. An elder is someone with prestige which he/she carries to the other world. The death of an elder must therefore be sumptuously celebrated.

This is the logic behind the various offers that take place during the funerary rituals of the coastal Animists in Guinea-Bissau, such as the Pepel, Manjacks, Mancanhas, Bijagós and Balantas, and also individuals who consider themselves

Catholics but also practice *uso6* ceremonies. In the case of the Pepel, the first part of the ceremony includes the wrapping of the body in cloths for several days. The cloths are offered by those attending the funeral; they are offered to the bereaved and to the deceased and are thus symbolically taken to the other world. A prestigious elder must take plenty of clothes, which will be redistributed by the ancestors who live in the other world. In the second part of this ceremony (*toka chur*), the blood of sacrificed animals is offered to the ancestors (Saraiva 2003, 2004a, 2004b, 2008). The celebration of the *toka chur* is essential for the spirit to reach its place in the other world and thus conclude the process of a 'good death' (Saraiva 2008). With the Pepel, the *toka chur* must take place in *tchon* Pepel; a *toka chur* taking place in Portugal has no value whatsoever. This takes us back to the relationship between elders and youngsters, since the younger ones must work and be successful enough to pay for their elders' funerals.

In Portugal, since burying a body wrapped in hundreds of cloths is not allowed, a few cloths are placed inside the coffin, but they count symbolically as hundreds. What we have here is a transnational network of spirits, individuals, bodies and goods that circulate between two parallel worlds: the physical, concrete worlds of the two national contexts – the country of origin and the country of diaspora – and the two universes that exist beyond any spatial distance or frontier, the world of the living and the world of the dead (Saraiva 2008: 267).

Here No One Prays For You: The Bangladeshi Case

In the case of Bangladeshi migration the management of death and burial of migrants is directly linked to reciprocity and the moral responsibility that connects kin in Portugal with those in Bangladesh. The migration project implies the obligation to send money for the members of the family back in the *desh* (the Bengali word for Bangladesh or home). This obligation is intimately linked to the corporate nature of the migratory investment, in which several members of the domestic unit participate. If the migrant dies, the return of the body to the country of origin symbolises the telluric and kinship connection.

Between 1986 and 2006, fourteen Bengalis died in Portugal and, except in one case, all were buried in Bangladesh. The expenses and the organisation behind the transfers were mainly the responsibility of the pioneers. They frequently assume the role of community leaders (reminiscent of the Guinean 'big man') and are hence called upon to resolve such situations. It is they who organise the funerary ceremonies in close collaboration with Portuguese Islamic institutions, namely the Lisbon Central Mosque and the *Hazrat Bilal* mosque in Oporto. The bodies are usually sent to one of these two institutions according to proximity and convenience.[7] It is in these institutions that the management of the funerary rituals among Bangladeshis is partially carried out: the ablutions (*wuzu*), the cleansing of the body (*ghosul*) and the wrapping in the *kafan* – the white cloth also used by the pilgrims during the *hajj* – is undertaken by the staff of these mosques.

The body is then embalmed and the coffin is sealed in order for it to travel back to Bangladesh. Before sealing it, the body is taken to the prayer room, or in the case of the Lisbon Central Mosque, to the inner courtyard where the *salat-ul-janazah*, the funerary prayer, is performed. According to the people we interviewed, the number of participants in this prayer must be significant because the merit (*sowab*) received by the deceased depends on the number of participants. On such occasions, it is usual to see Bangladeshis coming from various parts of the country in order to participate in the funerary prayer, even if they are not connected to the deceased by kinship or friendship ties. It is important to be present as in the future everyone will need the participation and commitment of others. This is usually an exclusively male congregation. The wife of the deceased (in the case of a man), whether in Portugal or in Bangladesh, should remain at home, with minimal outside contact for at least forty days. During this period, she receives visits from other women but it is frequently said that she should be kept away from men who do not belong to the patrilineage.

During the daily prayers in the Bangladeshi mosque, in central Lisbon, on the days that follow, the deceased is remembered and the *imam* asks the congregation to pray for him. The process of repatriating the body begins as soon as possible and involves a funerary agency that usually works with the main representative institution of Islam and Muslims in Portugal – the Islamic Community of Lisbon (ICL). All the expenses – the airplane fare and the fees of the funerary agency – are financed by informal collections of money by the pioneers and by the existing regional associations. For the former, it is vital that they contribute and redistribute their wealth to the 'community'. These donations are seen as good deeds (*waqf*) and thus as something that allows the accumulation of merit or sacred capital. Simultaneously, they legitimise their authority as central figures.

The collection of money also takes place in the eighteen regional associations that have emerged in the past years. One of the main characteristics of this migratory flow is its significant diversity in terms of places of origin in Bangladesh. Therefore, several associations have been founded to represent these regional identities and to cater for their members through savings and loans of economic capital. This capital is not only used for commercial investments but also in cases of need, such as the death of one of its members. In these circumstances it is up to the remaining members to help to finance the sending of the body to the *desh*. There is no obligation in terms of the amounts given but the majority of the money is usually given by the more successful members. These quotas usually include a set amount to be delivered to the family or the widow in Bangladesh and in one of the cases exceeded 5,000 euros. It is then up to the family to collect the body at the airport. In some cases an ambulance is hired to carry the body to the cemetery and the next step is to organise the funeral procession and the burial. Just before the proper burial, the coffin is again opened and a new *salat-ul-janazah* is performed.

Other possibilities include burying the body in family lands, together with other relatives, or close to the *mazaars* of famous *pirs*, i.e. the places where saints were buried (Gardner 1998, 2002). In Northeastern Bangladesh, where the historical importance of pirism is essential to understanding the dynamics of the Islamisation of the Bay of Bengal (Eaton 1993), this practice is considered auspicious since the deceased is protected by the charisma of the holy man.

But why not bury the body in Portugal? After all, and as some members of the Islamic community of Lisbon argue, there are several Islamic plots in the country.[8] According to these members, sending the bodies to the countries of origin is considered a non-Islamic practice. This critical perspective is also shared by some of our Bangladeshi interviewees, especially those with migratory experience over several generations. They argue that not only is the repatriation of the body an unnecessary expense but it also fails to take into account the 'appropriate' theological orientations which ask for the body to be buried as soon as possible.

This concern with burial in Bangladesh is related to the widespread belief in the mandatory 'return' to the *desh*, to one's own relatives (*atyio*). Ali, one of our interviewees, made this point quite clearly: 'here no one prays for you because nobody knows you. In Bangladesh, whenever people pass by in the cemetery they might remember you and make a *du'a*, a supplication, in your name'.

What Ali meant was that every prayer made in the name of the deceased reverts to him in the future, when one's actions are judged by God, and thus it is essential to bury people in the vicinity of their closest social affinities. These social networks are essential for the ultimate journey that death represents and when the final judgment comes, everyone will be held accountable for their actions on earth. In this sense, having relatives who offer prayers and/or devotional collective prayers on behalf of the deceased is a way of gaining and accumulating merit.

This idea is related to the conceptions of death shared by many of our interviewees and has striking similarities with what has been described in various contexts in contemporary Bangladesh (Kotalová 1994; Gardner 1995). For many, one's actions have consequences not only in life but also after death. Everyday actions are often measured – in terms of meanings and moral charges – according to the consequences they might have after death. This is related to the notion that people can perform certain acts in order to acquire merit and sacred capital that after death will be essential to determine if one will enter paradise (*janna*) or suffer the torments of hell (*jahannam*). Charity (*lilla*), in the form of donations and gifts, as well as good actions (*waqf*), such as the personal sacrifice of economic resources in favour of the broader 'community', are two examples of merit making. Furthermore, during the annual religious calendar there are occasions, such as the night of revelation, also known as *Shab-e-Qadr*, which correspond to unusual moments of accumulation of merit. The idea is that the prayers performed on the night of *Shab-e-Qadr* are 'better' than the prayers held at any other time because the accumulation of merit is equivalent to a thousand prayers made on other occasions.

After death, the acquisition and accumulation of merit is done through the prayers, supplications and devotional assemblies performed on behalf of the deceased by family and friends, hence the need to be buried close to them. This relationship between the burial in Bangladesh and *sowab* has been interpreted by Katy Gardner (1993) as follows. Gardner showed how, for many Bangladeshis, *bidesh* (the Bengali term for foreign lands) implies an idea of a land of plenty, of unimaginable wealth and success. *Desh*, on the other hand, which refers in Bengali to Bangladesh, the village and region of origin, is closely associated with poverty and lack of opportunities. However, the flipside is that *bidesh* is seen as non-religious and morally threatening while Bangladesh is a place of devotion, piety and values. Therefore, since death is a path leading to God that depends on the religious acts of others, it is better to be buried in a land of pious people than in an amoral and non-religious land. In this context, to be buried in Portugal is often perceived as a sign of failure and of having been abandoned.

Sending the body to Bangladesh is therefore a way of achieving the ideal of 'good death', as Maurice Bloch and Jonathan Parry called it and has been widely documented in several ethnographies on Bangladesh (Kotalová 1994; Gardner 2002; Garbin 2004). The 'good death' is one that occurs among one's relatives – members of the household and the patrilineage – and not all alone or among strangers. Since many still consider Bangladesh as home it is clear that the ideal is to be repatriated rather than buried in Europe.

This view is shared by many Bengali Muslims in London, the most important destination of emigration, and so many feel the need to send the deceased to Bangladesh because the relatives should see the corpse one last time (Gardner 1998). Thus, among Bangladeshis in the UK, between sixty and seventy per cent of bodies are repatriated (Gardner 1998).

This concern has also been raised by the Bangladeshi state itself which has developed specific programmes for the repatriation of the bodies of their expatriate workers. In the context of the general governance of migration flows, in 1990 the state implemented the *Wage Earners Welfare Fund* (WEWF). This fund was set up in large part with the subscriptions of migrant workers, with a percentage of the deposits of recruiting agencies, with ten per cent of the fees of diplomatic representations abroad, and finally with institutional and personal contributions. The objective of this fund is to develop programmes of social support for migrant workers and their families that include the transfer of the bodies of deceased migrants and financial support for their families – it can go up to as much as 20,000 *takas* (ca £157). In total, since its creation, this fund has repatriated the bodies of 5,000 expatriate workers (in Siddiqui 2001). According to several officials involved in this process, the repatriation of the deceased *probashis* (the Bengali term for immigrant) is a way of repaying the sacrifices made by many for the sake of the development of the country. The economic capital accumulated abroad and subsequently channelled to Bangladesh through payments and investments by the 5 million *probashis* in countries such as the UK, Saudi Arabia, the USA, UAE, Malaysia, Italy and many others, is seen as essential for the economic development and 'modernisation' of the country. Therefore, repatriating the deceased and paying compensation to their families is frequently perceived as fair treatment to someone who has made sacrifices on behalf of Bangladesh. But what happens when these social networks disappear, when one's relatives live in the migratory destination?

Alam's case is revealing. Alam had been living in Portugal since 1996 where he had been working as a peddler in different markets. In 2001, he suffered a car accident and was seriously injured. Initially the family wanted to take him to Dhaka but the trip was strongly discouraged by the doctor. Instead, his wife and four children came to Lisbon with the help of the maternal uncle, and bought an apartment in order to take care of Alam. In January 2006, Alam died at home and the family decided to bury him in Lisbon in the Islamic section of the Lumiar cemetery. When questioned about this decision, they explained that he should be buried as soon as possible and also that Alam had no relatives in Bangladesh. His parents had died and the only living relative, his sister who lived in Dhaka, refused any responsibility towards her brother, since some years before the accident relations between her and Alam had deteriorated. Thus, it was unnecessary to send the body to Bangladesh because there was nobody who could pray for him: his family was now in Portugal. His son-in-law and his children participated in the ritual cleaning of the corpse in the Lisbon central mosque. The *salat-ul-janazah* was held in the courtyard of the central mosque, where there were close to thirty Bangladeshis, including some of the most prominent figures of the community, together with friends and acquaintances of Alam's family. The coffin was then closed and the body taken to the Lumiar cemetery and, just prior to the burial itself, the congregation made a new *salat-ul-janazah*. Shortly after, Alam was buried facing Mecca. It was the first burial of a Bangladeshi in Portugal.

Final Notes: The Burial Place and 'Good Death'

In the cases studied, funerary rituals constitute systems of circulation of goods between the living and the dead, and contribute to the reinforcement of the continuum between the two worlds. In the Guinean case, the deceased only become protective ancestors if the rituals are integral and correctly performed (Saraiva 2004a, 2004b, 2008: 259); in the Bangladeshi case, the spirits of the deceased will not be able to enter Paradise without the prayers of the living relatives (Mapril 2010).

Bloch (1982a: 15) suggests that the notion of 'good death' is connected to the human need to control the unforeseeability of biological death. Thus, prototypes of ideal situations are produced in which death is domesticated and transformed into an element in a repetitive cyclic order, which will ultimately result in the regeneration and reproduction of life. Focusing on several examples, namely the Merina and the Lugbara, Bloch specifies that without the burial in the communitarian tomb or close to the ancestral house, not only is a potential source of regeneration for the group lost, but the individual death is terminal. The emphasis put on the place of eternal rest in order to ensure a 'good death' is evident. This is present in the cases described above, either by means of a physical concretisation of such rules – sending the body back home – or by a symbolic transformation and an unfolding of actions that aim at overcoming the impossibility of sending the real, material body. Herein lies the significance of sending the *mala*, the sharing of the ceremonies divided into two spaces (in Guinea and in Portugal) and the *toka chur*, in the case of the Guineans. The devotional assemblies, supplication and prayers performed from a distance do the same for the Bangladeshis. What is assumed in these ceremonial dynamics is precisely the connection between migration, reciprocity, redistribution and 'good death'.

Emigration is normally an enterprise through which one seeks prestige and economic success. If this is realised, it must be shared with the other relatives in a logic of reciprocity and moral co-responsibility, which implies a connection with the home land and the family of origin, and has consequences in the perception of death and dying. Migrants hope that those 'who stay behind', in Guinea or Bangladesh, care for them, and show it in the reception of the dead bodies and by performing the ceremonies that will help them to have a 'good death'. After all, they also once sacrificed themselves by going abroad for the sake of a common good. A successful migrant also has an obligation to care for his/her relatives back home by paying for the funerary rituals. This also guarantees a continued connection with their place of origin.

What these two cases reveal is that, in a globalised world, the notion of 'place' continues to exist and is reproduced within social life (Olwig 2007). There is a homology between places of belonging and notions of relatedness (Carsten 2000) that have their *oxymoron* in death and dying. Through territorialisation of death, a union with the places where the deceased relatives are buried. This union signifies a victory over the separation implied by migration. In fact, in the diaspora, where one is buried is more important than one's place of birth

(Ho 2006), and the funerary transits between Portugal, Bangladesh and Guinea-Bissau are good examples of such telluric dynamics.

To return to Bloch's premise on 'good death' as a potential for group regeneration, what we intended to show is the way in which, in two diverse ethnographic contexts, and in two different diaspora situations, the notion of relatedness acts. In these transnational networks we have strong relations between the afore-mentioned parallel worlds – the physical and concrete worlds of the national origin of the migrants, i.e. Guinea-Bissau or Bangladesh, and the foster country – amongst which the dead bodies circulate, as they are taken care of by their relatives. This first circulation of bodies lies under the responsibility of migrants themselves, who are fulfilling their duties not only towards the dead but also towards their families in their homelands. But, beyond these, symbolic goods and spirits also circulate, making it possible to fulfil the duties of the living towards the spirits of the dead. Such dynamics send us back to the notion of relatedness, in the sense that the 'community' (of Guineans or Bangladeshi) exists at the intersection between the world of the living and the world of the dead. Such 'communities' are thus constituted of both the living and the dead, and it is expected of the living (migrants) that they contribute to maintain the dead, even when away from home. At the same time, this reveals that the death of a person is never terminal, since it functions as a true source of regeneration, in this case, regeneration of life even in the enlarged scenario of migration, since it is death that triggers the re-inscription of the relationship with the place of origin.

Notes

This research was done within the project sponsored by FCT PTDC/CS-ANT/102862/2008, 'The invisibility of death among immigrant populations in Portugal: vulnerabilities and transnational managements'.

1. Fieldwork was done in Portugal, Guinea Bissau and Bangladesh and included participant observation, in-depth interviews, life histories, and archival and bibliographic research.

2. As well as the vast literature on cemeteries as spaces of collective memories (Ariés 1989; Vovelle 1983; Thomas 1975, 1982), there are also several texts that deal with the role of funerary rituals and graves in the construction of local community and the relation between the living and the dead, such as the classic *Death in Morelega* (1969) by W. Douglass.

3. The two cases we analyse in this text have very distinct immigration stories. Guineans are one of the most important immigrant groups in Portugal, whereas Bangladeshi migration is recent and represents a minority within the immigration scenario. Their position in the labour market is also totally different: the former are associated with less privileged sectors, while the latter are active entrepreneurs.

4. Guiné was a Portuguese colony until 1974. Both countries are part of the CPLP (Community of Portuguese speaking countries) and Portuguese is still the official language of the country.

5. Literally: big man, meaning, someone who must be respected or even feared.

6. Kriol expression meaning 'tradition'.

7. The central mosque of Lisbon was created in 1985 and is linked to the Islamic Community of Lisbon, the first association of Muslims founded in 1968 (Tiesler 2000; Vakil 2003). The *Hazrat Bilal* mosque, also known as the Oporto central mosque, was inaugurated in 2001 and is the main representative institution of Islam in the North of the country.

8. There are currently three Islamic sections of cemeteries in the Lisbon Metropolitan Area, namely in Lumiar, Odivelas and Feijó, created as part of an infrastructure for Portuguese Muslims (Kettani 1996).

Bibliography

Ariés, P. 1989. *Sobre a História da Morte no Ocidente desde a Idade Média*, trans. P. Jordão. Lisbon: Teorema.

Basch, L., N. Schiller and S. Blanc. 1992. 'Transnationalism: a New Analytic Framework for Understanding Migration', *Annals of the New York Academy of Sciences* 645: 1–24.

_____. 1997 (1994). *Nations Unbound: Transnational Projects, Postcolonial Predicaments and Deterritorialised Nation-States*, 2nd edition. Amsterdam: Gordon and Breach.

Bloch, M. 1971 . *Placing the Dead: Tombs, Ancestral Villages, and Kinship Organization in Madagascar*. London: Seminar Press.

_____. 1982a. 'Death, Women and Power', in M. Bloch and J. Parry (eds), *Death and the Regeneration of Life*. Cambridge: Cambridge University Press, pp. 211–30.

Bloch, M., and J. Parry (eds). 1982b. *Death and the Regeneration of Life*. Cambridge: Cambridge University Press.

Carsten, J. (ed.). 2000. *Cultures of Relatedness: New Approaches to the Study of Kinship*. Cambridge: Cambridge University Press.

De Boeck, P. 2008. 'Danças com os mortos: os jovens em Kinshasa e a ordem da desordem', *Distância e Proximidade Conference*, Lisbon, 27-28 October.

Douglass, W. 1969. *Death in Murelaga: Funeral Ritual in a Spanish Basque Village*. Seattle: University of Washington Press.

Eaton, R. 1993. *The Rise of Islam and the Bengal Frontier, 1204-1760*. Berkeley: University of California Press.

Einarsdottir, J. 2000. *'We are Tired of Crying': Child Death and Mourning among the Pepel of Guinea-Bissau*. Stockholm: Stockholm University Press.

Evans-Pritchard, E. (1976) Witchcraft, Oracles and Magic Among the Azande, Oxford, Oxford University Press

Frazer, J (1890) [[1993] The Golden Bough, London, Wordsworth

Gable, E. 2006. 'The Funeral and Modernity in Manjaco', *Cultural Anthropology* 21(3): pp. 385–415.

Garbin, D. 2004. *Migrations, Territoires Diasporiques et Politiques Identitaires: Bengalis musulmans entre 'Banglatown' et Sylhet*. PhD dissertation. Tours: Université François Rabelais.

Gardner, K. 1993. 'Desh bidesh: Sylheti Images of Home and Away', *Man* 28(1): 1–15.

_____. 1995. *Global Migrants, Local Lives: Travel and Transformation in Rural Bangladesh*. Oxford: Oxford University Press.

_____. 1998. 'Death, Burial and Bereavement amongst Bengali Muslims in Tower Hamlets', *Journal of Ethnic and Migration Studies* 24(3): 507–21.

_____. 2002. *Age, Narrative and Migration: The Life Course and Life Histories of Bengali Elders in London*. London: Berg Publishers.

Geertz, C. 1996. 'Afterword', in S. Feld and K. Basso (eds), *Senses of Place*. Santa Fé: School of American Research Press, pp. 259–62.

Geschiere, P. 2005. 'Funerals and Belonging: Different Patterns in South Cameroon', *Africa Studies Review* 48(2): 45–64.

Hertz, Robert (1960) Death and the Right Hand, London, Routledge

Ho, E. 2006. *The Graves of Tarim: Genealogy and Mobility across the Indian Ocean*. Berkeley: University of California Press.

Jao, M. 1995. 'A questão da etnicidade e a origem étnica dos Mancanhas', *Soronda. Revista de Estudos Guineenses* 20: 19–31.

Kettani, A. 1996. 'Challenges to the Organisation of Muslim Communities in Western Europe: the Political Dimension', in W. Shadid and P. Koningsveld (eds), *Political Participation and Identities of Muslims in Non-Muslims States*. Kampen: Kok Pharos, pp. 14–35.

Kopytoff, I. 1971. 'Ancestors as Elders in Africa', *Africa* 41(2): 129–42.

Kotalová, J. 1994. *Belonging to Others: Cultural Construction of Womenhood in a Village in Bangladesh*. Dhaka: University Press Limited.

Lestage, F. 2008. 'Apuntes relativos a la repatriación de los cuerpos de los mexicanos fallecidos en Estados Unidos', *Migraciones Internacionales* 4(4): 217–28.

Machado, F. 2002. *Contrastes e Continuidades. Migração, Etnicidade e Integração dos Guineenses em Portugal*. Oeiras: Celta.

Mapril, J. 2007. 'Os sonhos da "modernidade": migrações globais e consumos entre Lisboa e Dhaka', in R. Carmo, R. Blanes and D. Melo (eds), A *Globalisação no Divã*. Lisbon: Tinta da China, pp. 65–88.

———. 2010. '"Aqui ninguém reza por ele": trênsitos funebres entre o Bangladesh e Portugal', *Horizontes Antropológicos* 15(31): 219–39.

Olwig, K. 2007. *Caribbean Journeys: An Ethnography of Migration and Home in Three Family Networks*. Durham: Duke University Press.

Pina-Cabral, J. 1984. 'A morte na Antropologia Social', *Análise Social* XX: 349–56.

Quintino, C. 2004. *Migrações e Etnicidade em Terrenos Portugueses. Guineenses: Estratégias de Invenção de uma Comunidade*. Lisbon: Universidade Técnica de Lisboa-Instituto Superior de Ciências Sociais e Politicas.

Saraiva, C. 2003. 'Rituais funerários e concepções da morte na etnia Papel da Guiné-Bissau-Parte I', *Soronda, Revista de Estudos Guineenses* nova série 6, Bissau, INEP: 179–210.

———. 2004a. 'Rituais funerários e concepções da morte na etnia Papel da Guiné-Bissau-Parte II', *Soronda, Revista de estudos Guineenses* nova série, Bissau, INEP: 109–34.

———. 2004b. 'Embalming, Sprinkling and Wrapping Bodies. Death Ways in America, Portugal and Guinea-Bissau: a Cross-cultural Study', *Symposia. Journal for Studies in Ethnology and Anthropology*, Craiova, Center for Studies in Folklife and Traditional Culture of Dolj County: 97–119.

———. 2008. 'Transnational Migrants and Transnational Spirits: an African Religion in Lisbon', *Journal of Ethnic and Migration Studies* 32(4): 253–69.

Siddiqui, T. 2001. *Transcending Boundaries: Labour Migration of Women from Bangladesh*. Dhaka: University Press.

Thomas, L.-V. 1975. *Anthropologie de la mort*. Paris: Payot.

———. 1982. *La mort africaine*. Paris: Payot.

Tiesler, N. 2000. 'Muçulmanos na margem: A nova presença islâmica em Portugal', *Sociologia: Problemas e Práticas* 34: 117–44.

Vakil, A. 2003. 'Muslims in Portugal: History, Historiography, Citizenship', *EuroClio Bulletin* 18: 9–13.

Vovelle, M. 1983. *La mort et l'Occident de 1300 à nos jours*. Paris: Gallimard.

16

KARAOKE DEATH
Intertextuality in Active Euthanasia Practices

Natasha Lushetich

The Lingering Calvinist Tradition

I was invited to an unusual party in Amsterdam in autumn 2005 – a dying party, organised by a friend and former colleague of mine in honour of his terminally ill partner. The partner, who had been suffering from cancer for over two years and had spent the previous ten months either in unbearable pain or unconscious due to the large doses of morphine he was taking to alleviate the pain, had decided to celebrate the end of a long but nevertheless victorious battle against the medical and bureaucratic apparatus in the Peter Sellars style. Contrary to common belief, the request for active euthanasia, which differs from its passive variant in that it requires the patient's anaesthesiologist to perform the deed rather than simply to stop administering life-sustaining medication, is a long and emotionally exhausting process with no certain results. The procedure has become considerably more bureaucratised in the recent years despite the fact that there was no discontinuity in the law regarding active euthanasia between 1991 and 2005. Indeed, 1991 was the year of the controversial Remmelink report which brought to light that 19.61 per cent of all deaths in the Netherlands were physician-assisted thus causing an uproar in the international medical community and triggering heated public debates about what constitutes an 'explicit and persistent' request for euthanasia. Not only did the patients' requests have to be repeated several times at clearly specified intervals as well as in a state uninfluenced by medication, they also had to prove a steadily deteriorating, rather than stagnant condition.

To celebrate the fact that he had finally overcome this Kafkaesque entanglement and obtained his 'dying license', Jan Bokma's last farewell was to be a distinctly festive affair just like the proverbial comedian's funeral at which the mourners danced, made merry and consumed large quantities of champagne. Family, friends and colleagues, but also neighbours, the local baker and the local pub owner, were invited to a sing-along evening with good food and drink. Upon acceptance the guests were carefully instructed in the dramaturgical requirements of the event. We were to come to Jan's house dressed in any combination of white, red and black anytime between 7.30 and 8.30 P.M., then proceed to eat, drink, dance and mingle until 10 P.M. At 10 P.M., Jan was scheduled to make an appearance, address the gathered company, distribute small gifts; sing a song, then retreat to his bedroom where he was going to be injected with a lethal dose of potassium chloride. The party was to go on, however, until such a time as Jan's anaesthesiologist emerged from the bedroom to pronounce him dead. At this point, only close family would remain. In keeping with the Calvinist tradition, they would bathe and dress Jan's body.

Despite the fact that overt religious practices – at least of the Christian kind – have long lost currency in the Netherlands, the influence of Calvinism can still be palpably felt. Among the most widely spread examples of this subtly continuing tradition is the fact that the majority of Dutch homes have no curtains. Like other brands of Protestantism, Calvinism discourages practices which bestow the power of mediation between God and the individual on other individuals, as is the case with the Roman Catholic confession. In the Calvinist tradition, the individual is held accountable before God and, importantly, before fellow humans all the time, not only at designated times, in designated places and before designated church figures. The windows on Dutch houses, which are usually fairly large on account of the 'low skies' and the chronic lack of light, are curtain-less so that any given member of the anonymous community of 'fellow humans' may peer in at any given time. By the same token, the inhabitant of a curtain-less house indicates an impeccably clean conscience by showing a willingness to be observed, and thus also judged, twenty-four hours a day. Nudity is no exception in this respect either. Rather, it is thought to be part and parcel of the human condition, as is, indeed, death and dying.

This is very different from the practices prevalent in the UK and the US where the facts of death are usually carefully avoided. Not only do the majority of deaths occur in hospitals, where the fiction of likely recovery is maintained until the very end, but the body of the deceased is usually removed from the hospital without the aid of close family or friends. The latter see the body again only under special circumstances, after it has been washed, shaven, coiffured and made up to appear as if asleep. The premises of the death specialist, the mortician – whose name indicates the same level of professionalism as that of the paediatrician, beautician or politician – are described with cosy-sounding words such as 'funeral home'. In the Netherlands, however, it is often considered the children's duty to wash their deceased parents' body. The same unabashed, one could even say 'concretist' relationship to the materiality of existence can also be observed in 'birthing parties'. Unless faced with potential complications, such as a Caesarean, it is customary for the pregnant woman to give birth at home, surrounded by family and friends. Although a midwife is invariably present, it is the father who is supposed to cut the umbilical cord. If this is successfully performed, the baby is often greeted with a round of applause from the gathered company, habitually located in one of the adjacent rooms. This practice, which, like that of assisted suicide, is semi-public, engages the notion of performance on three different levels: performance as execution, as an act of carrying something out; performance as attainment of a certain effect, state, status or standard which is observed, as well as judged, by others; and, performance as a form of play, a playful and/or aesthetic execution of a staged action. All three of these levels are present in ritual as well as in theatre or entertainment. This is why the two categories are neither pure nor separate but, as the performance theorist Richard Schechner suggests, 'form the poles of a continuum' (2003: 130). The important difference between the two, however, is that ritual is always participatory and postulates an authoritative representation of the social world, whereas theatrical performance does not. In other words, ritual is *conspicuously constitutive* and its constitutivity – its ability to actualise that which it symbolises (127), to inaugurate a new reality and in this way affect social relationships – derives from the ritual's adherence to three elements: a special ordering of time, a reliance on a set of predetermined rules, and the use of symbols (8). It is the combination of these three elements that creates performance efficacy.

Performance Efficacy and Intertextuality

As the anthropologists Sally Moore and Barbara Myerhoff (1977) reveal in *Secular Ritual*, performance efficacy is not a monolithic term. The reason for this is that there is a palpable difference between doctrinal and operational performance efficacy. Doctrinal efficacy refers to religious ritual and operates in an explicit manner, by 'postulating a cosmic order and simultaneously *affect[ing]* the spirit-world [as well as] *demonstrat[ing]* the postulated validity of the explanations it offers' (Moore and Myerhoff 1977: 12, emphasis in original). If we take the Catholic Mass as an example, or, more specifically, the communion, in which the host represents the body of Christ, the taking of the host both unites the congregant's physical body, his or her mortal existence with the immortal body of Christ, and reasserts the immortality of the Christian soul, which is to say that it reasserts the symbolic validity of the ritual.

Operational efficacy, on the other hand, is less clear-cut; it can be both explicit and implicit since it is concerned primarily with 'social/psychological effectiveness' (Moore and Myerhoff 1977: 12). If a participant's worldview is changed as a result of a particular ceremony – regardless of whether this effect was overtly targeted, subliminally targeted, or not targeted at all – the ceremony is said to have been operationally efficacious. Furthermore, if a ceremony is performed in the form of a ritual, its efficacy is tradition-constituting. Moore and Myerhoff explain:

> the work of ritual is attributable to its morphological characteristics. Its medium is part of its message. It can contain almost anything, for any aspect of social life, any aspect of behavior or ideology, may lend itself to ritualization. And once used in collective ceremony, whether performed for the first time or the thousandth, the circumstance of having been put in the ritual form or mode, has a tradition-like effect. Even if it is performed once, for the first and only time, its form and content make it tradition-like. (8)

This is of particular relevance to intertextual dying ritual which emerges as a reaction to the bankruptcy of religious institutions, and, implicitly, doctrinal performance efficacy. Formerly, in a religion-governed and thus also mythological universe, death was integrated into daily existence; it was seen as a part of life, leading to a better, purer, more peaceful or more sacred way of living. It was an important transition with a clear mytho-poetic dimension; the dying were seen as the protagonists of a cosmic drama and were, as such, treated with utmost respect. However, in contemporary society, preoccupied with accumulation and consumption, death has no value, as it can be neither accumulated nor consumed. Worse still, death is that final consumption which puts an end to all possibilities of 'having fun'. Consequently, the dead and the dying are seen as a class of the 'less fortunate', a 'bunch of losers' and any association with them is regarded as best kept to a minimum.

In *Symbolic Exchange and Death*, Jean Baudrillard (1993) elaborates the idea of the dead no longer being partners in symbolic exchange. Essentially, symbolic exchange is an exchange of values assigned to an object by a subject in relation to an/other subject or other subject/s. This differs vastly from the purely functional or economic value concerned solely with the extraction of a thing's or event's consumptive potential. Baudrillard writes:

> At the very core of the 'rationality' of our culture [...] is an exclusion that precedes every other, more radical than the exclusion of madmen, children or 'inferior races', an exclusion preceding all these and serving as their model: the exclusion of the dead and of death [...]. [T]here is an irreversible evolution from savage societies to our own: little by little, the dead cease to exist. They are thrown out of the group's symbolic circulation. They are no longer beings with a full role to play, worthy partners in exchange. (1993: 126)

What Baudrillard is suggesting here is that non-industrial societies respond to the rupture and the uncertainty of death by engaging in ritual practice and that, within this practice, gifts and promises are made to the dead and the dying which are just as binding as those made to the living and that this marks the moment when the dead enter the arena of symbolic exchange.

In its essence, ritual is an enactment of the symbolic in the temporal dimension. Even if it only involves movement and/or chant as opposed to making incisions on the body, ritual *binds* the body. The more often or the more intensely a ritual is performed, the stronger the symbolic bond between the performer, that which is performed, and the purpose the performance is hoping to fulfil, or, in other words, performance efficacy. Every ritual is therefore a gift and an asking of a return, even if performed only once. In this sense, dying rituals not only 'present' to the gathered company the community member's exit from the scene, as it were, they also mobilise the mytho-poesis of symbolic exchange. This would seem to establish a clear distinction between consumerist and symbolic relations and place ritual incontestably in the latter category. However, such a clear-cut distinction is not possible for at least two reasons. First, we are living in a postmodern universe which is that of bricolage, citationality, and, most importantly, contagion. I use the term postmodernity here despite its contested status, not only to designate the collapse of modern culture's temporal-material framework of linear progress, but to designate the shift in incidence from face-to-face modes of subject-constitution to those that include ubiquitous broadcast media and networked computing. As both Baudrillard and the media theorist Lynne Joyrich (1996) have argued – albeit to very different ends – ubiquitous broadcast media and networked computing bring consumer desires to the individual with an immediacy that undermines the separation of subject and object, agent and event, virtuality and materiality, simulacrum and reality. They produce simulacra that bear no relation to a prior reality. They uncouple the signifier from the signified and the sign from the referent and in doing so expand the semiotic field and open a new space of cultural production.

The second reason is that the steady evolution of the society of the spectacle, to use Guy Debord's term, has culminated in the commodification of all or most human relations. In this universe, the individual is no longer a mere spectator but has become an active collaborator, an extra of the spectacle, so to speak. The most obvious example of this is reality TV in which the individual acts as a stand-in for personal freedom by sporting a 'liberating', 'just-got-out-of-bed' hairstyle, wearing 'liberating' 'I-don't-care-what-I-look-like' clothes and speaking of the therapeutic effect of the 'survival holidays' in the Sahara whilst simultaneously not only conforming to the spectacle-dictated, pre-fabricated notions of freedom, but, in fact, advertising these very notions. It is at this point that the individual begins to function as a signifier in the universe of floating signifiers, and becomes a stand-in for a stand-in.

The question thus arises whether intertextual dying ritual functions in the same way, by adding value and enhancing the individual's social prestige, which is to say that it functions as a form of extended consumerism and a continuation of spectacularised relations. Or can intertextual dying ritual be seen as entirely apart from these relations on account of its performance efficacy, as Moore and Myerhoff seem to suggest? And, furthermore, is intertextual dying ritual efficacious despite the fact that it operates in the universe of floating signifiers, purely because it is performed in ritual form, or is the floating signifier universe somehow a part of its performance efficacy?

It is important to note at this point that ritual 'binds' on two levels. It binds the biological and the ideological, usually by means of symbols which act as palpable condensations of a vast field of references. It also binds the individual and the communal, either by creating or by reaffirming communal conceptions and strengthening social bonds. But in order for this double binding to function, ritual actions, chants, costumes and/or symbols have to display a structuralist relationship between signifier and signified. In other words, in order for the communion with the body of Christ to have performance efficacy and inaugurate a new reality, the host cannot signify anything else but the body of Christ. It cannot refer to Christ, Mohammed and Elvis in equal measure.

What occurs in many contemporary symbolic practices, such as tattooing and body modification, is that they do not point to specific signifieds, but, rather, operate as floating signifiers. An example of this is the tears tattoo, usually worn on the outer corner of the right eye, which formerly signified that the tattooee had killed someone. These days, the same tattoo denotes the tattooee's resourcefulness in identifying the self-referential semantic prestige borne of the association with the daring and the dangerous, as well as with other members of the 'in' circle for whom the tear tattoo operates as a fashion accessory. Baudrillard is once again instructive when he says that fashion is 'a universalisable sign system which takes possession of all others, just as the market eliminates all other modes of exchange' (1993: 92). What Baudrillard is referring to here is the equivalence between the semantic and the economic in which the quality of any given good, in other words its specific and unique value, is turned into a quantity, commensurable with the quantities of other abstracted qualities. However, unlike the market which retains a general equivalent, money or gold, fashion is itself 'the form of general equivalence' (92). This makes fashion its own system of reference and a 'flotation of signs' (92), which, whilst diverging radically from the economic, in the sense of diverging from the calculating and the restrictive, is, in Baudrillard's words, its 'crowning achievement' (93).

This closed, semantic-consumerist universe in which the consumer is, in fact, the residue of the spectacle – as in the recent fashion of wearing T-shirts with designer sweat marks, the purpose of which is to provide the consumer with a ready-made image of a dynamic, physically active person, or, indeed, the habit of cruising around in designer-mud-splattered Jeeps which provide the owner with an instant image of the Marlboro-man-type adventurer – is inextricably intertwined with the emergence of the experience economy. As theorised by B. Joseph Pine and James Gilmore, this economy treats experience as a 'genre of economic output' (1999: ix) and is a logical sequitur in the progression from the commodity to the service and finally the experience economy. Within this framework, the latter is defined in the following way: 'when [a consumer] buys an experience, he pays to spend time enjoying a series of memorable events that a company stages – as in a theatrical play – to engage him in a personal way' (Pine and Gilmore 1999: 2). This is done by 'inging the thing' or 'experiantializing the goods' (23–24), which is to say by branding the prospective buyer's experience as in the case of a recent Nike campaign in which the consumers of the 'Nike experience' – the prospective buyers of Nike shoes – play basketball with a laser projection of Michael Jordan. Seeking to achieve active participation, multi-sensorial interaction and total immersion, these experiences are geared towards creating a fictitious world woven of three different elements: entertainment, aesthetics and escapism. In this universe, consumers do not buy commodities, services and experiences to *express* who they are but to *create* a referential sense of identity. This further creates a 'fused sign' culture in which the extras of the spectacle form a single sign system with the objects, services and experiences they consume which further means that they communicate predominantly through purchased messages thus forming a complex network of floating 'stand-ins' for lived experiences. It is interesting to see how this vortex of 'stand-ins' reflects on the dying ritual.

The Concretist-Absurdist Disruption of the Symbolic

The setting for Jan's dying party was nothing short of astounding. Full of exuberant floral arrangements, crimson velvet tablecloths, antique vases and aboriginal masks reflected in the glamorous floor-to-ceiling mirrors, the setting resembled a private view or a 'cast-only' premiere do. Most of the guests were conspicuously jovial and gregarious, too. The DJ was mixing 1980s funk such as *Ring My Bell* and *Daddy Cool* to which a group of scantily dressed men were dancing with a mixture of humour and abandon. At 10 P.M. sharp Jan appeared wearing a long red dress, a wig and elaborate make up. Despite the fact that he was very frail and had to be led around the room by his partner, he shook hands and kissed each of his guests, looked deep into their eyes, exchanged a few words, patted them on the hand and gave them a present. I got a beautiful white orchid. After enquiring how my work was coming along, Jan told me he was sorry he had never had the chance to have a proper, long conversation with me, smiled broadly then said 'hope to see you again but not too soon', evidently alluding to the 'other world'. He then moved on and continued to distribute presents, simultaneously resembling an impeccable host, a kinky father Xmas and a dying person from an altogether different epoch. Indeed, as the anthropologist Philippe Ariès notes in 'Death Inside Out':

> in the Middle Ages, people were expected to detect the imminence of their death and prepare for the event. The preparations were spiritual as well as social. The drama took place in a room crowded with people – kin, workmates, neighbours, even casual passers-by. The dying person played the central role, striving for the same dignity that they had previously witnessed at similar scenes. Each visitor was bade adieu, asked for his or her forgiveness and given a blessing. After the event, the close kin gave themselves over to uninhibited grief. With this cathartic release they soon returned to normal life. (Ariès 1974: 3–4)

A re-mixed or 're-appropriated' variant of this practice was evident in Jan's slow and dignified present-giving rounds. This was syncopated by the guests' excited examination of each other's presents – photographs, little boxes with sand and seashells, locks of hair, CDs and letters. Jan had recorded messages and hand-written letters for his friends and colleagues.

The present-giving ritual was thus also a trace-leaving ritual. In his seminal *The Gift Forms and Functions of Exchange in Archaic Societies* – which plays a crucial part in the formation of Baudrillard's notion of symbolic exchange – Marcel Mauss suggests that '[t]hings are not inert objects' (1980: 48) but were formerly considered a part of the family: 'the Roman *familia* comprises the *res* as well as the *personae*' (48). In Mauss' analysis all things are partly people which is why gifts mobilise social obligations and why their exchange requires a thorough consideration of the temporal, material, contextual, social and emotional processes involved in producing or, indeed, choosing a gift. I was given a living plant by a dying man. Despite the fact that I did not know Jan very well it was immediately clear to me that I was going to do my utmost to keep the orchid alive for as long as possible, that the only way to reciprocate this gift was to let it exercise its relational pull on me. However, it was also immediately clear to me that there was a discrepancy between the orchid's delicate petals and the sixty-year-old's wrinkled and heavily made-up face. The performance efficacy of the orchid was thus simultaneously symbolic because it inaugurated a new life – that of a plant suffused with the personality of a dying human being – as well as concretist because it inaugurated a lived temporality within which this symbolism was to come into effect. It was also slightly absurd since the signifier did not quite reach its destination but seemed to have performed a U-turn instead. An example of such a U-turn would be the failure of some or all of the twenty-one guns involved in a twenty-one-gun salute to fire. Such a technical inefficiency would fail to inaugurate the targeted symbolism of awe-inspiring heroism – often called for in military funerals – and would instead point to the signifier's inability to transcend its own limitations. Instead of inspiring respect, admiration and gratitude, this type of failure entices laughter. But this is only so if the failure to fire is not intentional. If the failure to fire is intentional, as in the case of the American artist Robert Watts' funeral which took place in Pennsylvania in 1988 and used guns that shot out plastic balls, firecrackers and flags with the word 'bang' written on them, then it operates in a paradoxical way, both through the force of citationality and in spite of it. The reason for this is that the gesture both indicates the 'need' for a twenty-one-gun salute and engages in a simultaneous derision thereof; it both draws attention to the reference and highlights the comical failure to cite the reference properly. In a similar manner, the white orchid's symbolism – habitually associated with virginity, youth, beauty and delicacy – was rendered operational on account of its incongruity. The orchid's performance efficacy functioned precisely because it mobilised a convention which had been cited countless times before but without citing it accurately, without 'hitting the target' so to speak.

After Jan had finished his present-giving round, he made his way to the microphone and a smooth transition to what had been announced as the pivotal moment of the evening ensued. Within seconds, I recognised the opening phrase of Aretha Franklin's *You Make me Feel Like a Natural Woman*. As anybody who has ever been to a gay club knows, *Like a Natural Woman* is an iconic song, an anthem of sorts, often played at closing time. Jan's voice was weak and frail but his pitch was perfect. Despite the song's dramaturgical placement, which was reminiscent of smash hit musicals, such as *Cabaret*, or indeed *All That Jazz*, in which the protagonist states his/her case in a proud, brave and sexy 'I am who I am' manner, this was a moment of unprecedented performance efficacy in which a sixty-year old man became a 'natural woman'. Here, I am not referring to the guests' willingness to suspend their disbelief as a token of support for the dying man's wishes. Rather, I am referring to the concretist-symbolic-absurdist effect derived from the timing of the song within the ceremony, the performer's frailness and his evident exhaustion, in other words, the liminal state from which the song was performed.

Liminality is the time-space of transformation; it is an ambiguous, marginal and transitional state between the participant's hitherto inhabited state, status or social role and the social role the participant is about to adopt. In many non-Western cultures, such as that of the native Indian Mohave, it is the initiation rite that confers gender. For example, the Mohave recognise four genders: male, female, *alyha* and *hwame*. As Michael Kimmel explains in *The Gendered Society* (2003), if a boy shows a preference for feminine behaviour he undergoes an initiation at puberty and becomes an *alypha*. He does so by painting his face and performing a female ritual dance (Kimmel 2008: 69). After this, the boy lives as an *alypha*, wearing female clothes and eventually marrying a man. Jan's song functioned as a ritual transition which not only emphasised the already existing horizontal *communitas*, rooted in the reinstatement of condensed communal content shared by the members of the gay community present at the party, but created a vertical *communitas*, borne of the disruption of the signifier-signified chain. Once again, the signifier could be said to have performed a U-turn since Jan's ritually acquired identity had no temporal horizon in which to come into effect. Furthermore, this ritual was a part of a larger ritual full of intertextual cross-pollinations. Bearing in mind the original meaning of the word 'text', which derives from the French *tisser* and means to 'weave', Jan's dying party created a rich fabric of ambivalent references.

Embedded in the Calvinist framework, which is of a predominantly concretist kind, rooted in the suchness of things, it proliferated references to gay iconography and the myth of Narcissus evident in the floor to ceiling mirrors. It also highlighted the universal association of the colours the guests were asked to wear with the human body: red being associated with blood, white with semen or milk, black with decay and the loss of consciousness. The vigorous dancing referenced anything from fertility, pride or defiance and funk nostalgia to kitsch and camp which accompanies the reframing of cultural codes. There was even a humorous recoding of Christmas – a patriarchal festivity par excellence. All this indicates a swarm of floating, redirected and U-turn-performing signifiers. But does this indicate that however intertextual a ritual is, its performance efficacy, which, by definition, operates beyond the horizontal *communitas* to create a vertical one, depends on the sheer irrevocability of death, on its high stakes, as it were? Furthermore, does this mean that if a person were willing to die on the cross for a designer-mud-splattered Jeep, the floating signifier would be restored to its linear, structuralist function?

It is clear that intertextual ritual functions through internal repetitions of form, rules and symbols and that it is these repetitions that mobilise cross-referential impregnations, a cultural marinade of sorts. It could therefore be argued that the performance efficacy of such a ritual derives from the mixing of past performative sedimentations, whilst creating new and, importantly, ambivalent or even contradictory connections. What occurs in intertextual dying ritual is a double disruption – a re-mixing of past sedimentations and a dispersion of the field of reference. Singing *Like a Natural Woman* prior to retreating to one's bedroom to be injected with a lethal dose of potassium chloride is a re-mix of past sedimentations, a cultural re-appropriation of an Indian initiation rite. However, this re-appropriation is not carried out as a statement of some long-lost primordiality. Rather, it is simultaneously a critique of the Judeo-Christian gender regime, and one of the most 'tattered', most used and abused karaoke songs in the world. Its cultural status is both iconic and McDonaldised, so to speak, and it is the latter that creates a contamination of signified and signifier as well as breeding other cross-contaminations.

Among the most obvious examples is the singer's Aschenbach-like appearance, which can, once again, be associated with the Olympic cult of youth as well as with paedophilia, depending on the view one takes of Luchino Visconti's or Thomas Mann's *Death in Venice*. It would therefore be fair to conclude that intertextual dying ritual functions in an expanded semantic field by, paradoxically, both hitting the mark and missing it and that the failure to inaugurate an unequivocal reality is, in fact, its success. In other words, it is the purposefully embroiled citation of past conventions that points to a closed semantic-consumerist universe and by this very reference disrupts the literalness of consumerist-spectacular relations.

Bibliography

Ariès, P. 1974. 'Death Inside Out', *Hastings Center Studies* 2(2): 3–18.

Baudrillard, J. 1993. *Symbolic Exchange and Death*, trans. I. Hamilton Grant. London: Sage.

Joyrich, L. 1996. *Re-Viewing Reception: Television, Gender and Postmodern Culture*. Bloomington: Indiana University Press.

Kimmel, M.S. 2008 (2003). *The Gendered Society*. New York and Oxford: Oxford University Press.

Mauss, M. 1980. *The Gift Forms and Functions of Exchange in Archaic Societies*, trans. I. Cunnison. London and Henley: Kegan Paul.

Moore, S. and B. Myerhoff. 1977. *Secular Ritual*. Assen: Van Gorcum & Comp.

Pine, J.B. and J.H. Gilmore. 1999. *The Experience Economy Work is Theatre & Every Business is a Stage*. Boston: Harvard Business School Press.

Schechner, R. 2003 (1978). *Performance Theory*, 2nd edition. London and New York: Routledge.

PART V

PERSONAL REFLECTIONS ON DEATH

17

DEATH IS NOT WHAT IT USED TO BE
A Comparison between Customs of Death in the UK and Spain. Changes in the Last Thirty-Five Years

Lala Isla

Before I begin, I would like to explain my place in this volume. I am a writer and have spent a good part of the past fifteen years researching for my current book, a sort of sequel of my first one *Londres, pastel sin receta* (2002). It is a personal commentary about London, with anthropological, historical and social contents and one of its four parts contains three long chapters on funerary customs. After the death of my mother in 2003 and after the shock I received when I realised how much things had changed in Spain since I came to live in London more than thirty-five years ago, I decided to continue researching funeral customs in both the UK and Spain. This chapter presents some of my personal experiences and insights during that research. It is the result of a personal journey rather than an academic study. In the course of my research, I read many books and articles on funeral customs and led several interviews: in 1998, I started my research and interviewed the Miller Brothers, undertakers in the London borough of Islington, as well as my father Alfredo Isla García, my mother Angeles Ortiz de La Fuente, my aunt Lucila Isla García, and my cousin Luis Santos Isla; in 2010, I interviewed several times Josefina Alonso, a ninety-one-year old woman from La Bañeza, Spain, whose sister's remains appeared in a mass grave from the Spanish Civil War in Izagre, in the province of León. Since 2010 I have also held several interviews with the researcher Jose Cabañas, who, alongside the archaeologist Alberto Martí, is involved in the opening of mass graves from the Civil War in several places across Spain, including Izagre; in 2011, I also interviewed Maruja Delgado, a housewife from La Bañeza who had several relatives killed in the Civil War.

When I arrived in Britain in 1976, one of my first surprises was to find out the extent to which death was a taboo. The attitudes towards death I had grown up with in Spain until I came here were very, very different. Spain has had a cult of death that makes us see her (in Spain death has feminine gender) as something scary but also very familiar and sardonic. In how many other countries are women named after death? In Spain, the name Tránsito – shortened to Transi – is not uncommon. In translation it means 'transition' and is associated with the death of a saint, and in particular the death of the Virgin Mary.

During the thirty-five years I have lived in London, I have witnessed considerable change in the customs of death both in Spain and the UK. In Spain, the changes are due to the general and remarkably rapid transformation the country has experienced since the death of the dictator Franco in 1975. Attitudes towards death are an intrinsic part of those profound social changes. The same thing happened with sexual customs as Spain went from being a very repressed society to one of the first European countries where gay marriages became legal.

Spain started to leave behind its identity as an agrarian country in the 1960s and 1970s and the transition to democracy and the prosperity that followed Spain's joining the European Community have modernised the industry of death. In the process, death has been taken from the family home and put into the hands of professionals. As in so many other countries, in Spain, too, technological development has also led to increasing escapism and a denial of death as part of life.

In Britain the same process began much earlier, i.e. between 1930 and 1950. The last changes in Britain have happened partly to the influence of AIDS-related deaths of young men, which brought a sense of humour to funerals and a need to personalise them. Another example of the changes in the UK are the farms which closed due to European Community regulations and which in some cases have been turned into ecological cemeteries. In any case in both countries death is a very profitable business run mostly by international firms.

Something else that had a very big impact in British society was the death of Princess Diana which cut through firm taboos. I visited the three central sites in London where tributes were placed after she died and what I saw had nothing to do with Protestant restraint but was more an explosion of Mexican baroque. Until that time, a burial like that of Spanish flamenco artist Lola Flores in 1995, where the people of Madrid clapped and shouted their appreciation to the coffin in the streets, had never been seen in Britain.

Although I had a very protected life as a child, death was very present because as well as the type of Catholicism we have in Spain, we lived under Francisco Franco's[1] political regime that was born around a crazed cult of death. Some Nationalists fascists in the Spanish Civil War used to shout: ¡Viva la Muerte! (Long live Death!). Even if one was not a practising Catholic one could not avoid the images of Catholicism, especially in the 1940s and 1950s because Franco used the Catholic Church to legitimise his dictatorship and the Church was very happy to go along with anything he did including horrendous atrocities committed during and after the war. Furthermore, the Christian religion is based on the death of a man who supposedly believed that he came into the world to sacrifice himself in order to save human beings: therefore the ultimate Catholic image is of a dead man hanging from a wooden cross. This meant that death was seen everywhere because crucifixes were in each class in each school, religious or not, in each room of a hospital and in every public place along with the portrait of the dictator. The images of the Spanish Catholic Church are much more bloody than in other European countries, especially the ones that were sculpted during the baroque period. Blood is in our culture, the blood of bulls, of bullfighters, Christ, of some images of the Virgin Mary whose chest is stabbed by seven knives.

I was born in Astorga – a town in the province of León in Northwest Spain – but I never lived there. I was brought up in Barcelona and every July we would cross the whole of the Peninsula from Barcelona to Astorga – 900 kilometres – to spend the three months of our school holidays there. Astorga is situated in Old Castille, far from the sea, and was much more backward at that time than Barcelona. My maternal family had lived there and the house was preserved and used only in the summers. The comparison between these two tremendously different parts of Spain was a constant source of family stories and death was part of it.

During various summers some relatives in my father's family died while I was in La Bañeza – their hometown 23 km from Astorga – and I became a witness of all the rituals that were performed. I was a child but nobody obliged me to do anything or stopped me from doing anything either and so I was around watching what happened. This helped me understand the different stages of death well before I studied anthropology or researched customs of death.

In those years the families washed the bodies (they still often do this in Spain when relatives die at home) which were exposed in the houses for twenty-four hours because in Spain the custom is to bury the dead twenty-four hours after they die. Here, customs are similar to those practiced by Muslims and Jews, maybe because Islam and Judaism also originated in hot countries, where bodies decompose quicker. In Spanish wakes – wake in Spanish is *velar*, from *vela*, candle – men drank coffee and a glass of spirits in one room while the women were in another praying the rosary the whole night or day around the coffin. If the houses were big, as was the case in my family, people were scattered in different rooms talking to each other but the genders tended to be separated, men on one side and women on the other, normally around the coffin. If the wake was during the night the silence was broken only by the praying of the rosary. When dawn arrived everybody was exhausted. When the undertakers came to collect the body they nailed the coffin shut: the hammering made a sinister and profoundly sad and terrifying noise which increased the grief as it signified the crucial moment of total separation. Today there are ways to close the coffins in silence. Once the coffin was closed everybody went to church where the funeral was celebrated.

The funeral was always Catholic because at that time it was the only religion permitted by Spanish law to be practiced in public (this lasted for quite a while after Franco's death). In 1996 (more than twenty years after his death) I organised the transportation to the UK of the body of Patience Edney – a British woman who had been a volunteer nurse during the Spanish Civil War – who died during the homage to the International Brigadiers in Madrid. I asked the insurance undertakers to look for a coffin without a crucifix on top and they told me that there was no such thing in Madrid. I asked them to remove the cross and the coffin arrived with the screw holes and the shape of a crucifix still visible in the wood because it was darker all around it.

Living in Barcelona in a solid middle-class area, the few funeral processions I saw consisted of big black hearses pulled by horses and covered in big crowns of flowers, which are the typical Spanish funeral floral tribute. At that time only men walked behind the hearse and if they were relatives of the deceased they wore a black band on the upper part of their jackets or coats. A woman once told me that when her father died in the 1970s she decided to accompany the men to the cemetery in a village near Alicante and was heavily criticised. Now all the women in that village go to the cemetery too.

In small towns like Astorga and La Bañeza death was publicly acknowledged by the tolling of church bells which sounded very tragic and melancholic when somebody had died. The custom of ringing bells or letting off rockets at funerals, as happens in México and Goa, or the widespread custom of firing a cannon when somebody really important dies, comes from believing that people drive away bad spirits with noise.

In my childhood after the burial people came to the house of the deceased to give their condolences and the family prepared themselves for a whole afternoon receiving anybody who decided to pay a visit. This could last a month or more. One of my uncles died two years ago and the family closed the house door and only very intimate friends and family came during the first week. This would have been unthinkable only a few years ago, even more so because he and his family were very well known in their town. His body was laid out for a few hours before burial in the *tanatorio* (funeral parlour) and his widow and sons were there to receive anybody who wanted to come and pay their respects.

As a child and later, as a young adult, I was present in my grandparents' house when funerals still happened the old way and people came to visit. Apart from hearing constant details of the deceased, I marvelled at the most amazing stories about everything under the sun, because some of the women were great storytellers. I remember well seeing an aunt who had just been widowed trying not to laugh at some hilarious story. This constant reminder of the dead person helped the relatives to get used to the idea of death little by little and the initial shock left space for the beginning of the healing process. When I first lived in London I heard cases of social workers visiting people to talk to them about a deceased relative because they did not have anybody to talk to and I was stupefied.

Wakes and talking to friends about death are important ways of getting used to the new absence. This is why the opening of mass graves in Spain, and in other countries with a history of brutal repression, is so important; only then can the wound be closed, otherwise the dead put obstacles in the road of the living. But this is not well understood, sometimes out of ignorance and sometimes due to political ideas. The argument used against this is that it is better to leave the dead where they are otherwise wounds will be opened, it will create disturbance and problems, it will divide people again like in 1936. I will never forget the expression of satisfaction of Josefina Alonso, the ninety-one-year-old woman whose sister's remains appeared in the mass grave of Izagre, León (Spain), when they gave her the box of bones to be buried in the cemetery. Josefina said to me: 'Now I feel that the war is finished. All those years living with the anxiety and the pain doubting if María was buried there are finished. If only my mother could see it. She died with María's name on her lips'. This is, according to the researcher Jose Cabañas and the archaeologist Alberto Martí, both involved in the opening of mass graves, what all the relatives of people found in mass graves say.[2]

Another important aspect of mourning when I was a child and a young woman was the colour of the dresses; some were dyed black immediately and some were made new. There was also special black jet jewellery because you could not wear anything else. The process of death causes a social fragmentation, a temporal chaos, breaking the established order that mourning tries to minimise. The problem is that this control has been directed traditionally against women. Therefore it is no wonder that to dress in black for long periods of time is today an anomaly in developed countries. The time of mourning varied considerably depending on who the deceased was and was of a fixed number of years, more for a husband or parents. After a certain time, a bit of purple or grey was introduced in the clothes and this was called *alivio* (alleviation). Some women in the Spanish countryside were always in black because one death followed another and they could never get out of the dark colour. In the case of young girls, in some parts of Spain a death in the family could be a disaster because they were 'locked' inside the houses where they could not open the outside windows, sing or hear the radio and this stopped them meeting boyfriends, thereby jeopardising their chances of marrying them. *La niña de luto* (1964) [*The Girl in Mourning*] directed by Manuel Summers, is a film which deals with this issue, as does the play *The House of Bernarda Alba* (1936) by Federico García Lorca.

There were conversations that I heard as I grew up that have contributed to my seeing death as something than can be jolly and sardonic. Angelita – the mother of a friend of my mother – used to say: 'I just bought a plot in the cemetery of the Almudena (Madrid) and it is fantastic. I have the sun all day long and I am near Marañón (a famous doctor and writer) near X, near Y... (other celebrities). I am really well situated'. With this sentence she was expressing something that a lot of people only achieve in death: to be near important sections of society that otherwise she/he could have never achieved. Hearing her, one felt a strong desire of being with her in that very comfortable grave.

In Spain there is not the same taboo as in the UK of moving bodies from one grave to another. One day my brother was in the cemetery of Almuñecar (on the coast of Granada) and saw a woman in black who started to talk to him showing him very proudly the grave of her husband: 'You see, he used to be a bit further back but he did not have any sun and I changed him to this one. Look, he has a good view of the sea'. My brother said to me: 'She was talking to me as though describing a flat and I almost expected to be invited inside the grave to have a cup of tea'.

Spain is a big and extremely varied country therefore the customs of death can be different from one part to the other. In Galicia, in Northwest Spain, the customs of death are quite particular and they share with León, Zamora and Salamanca a belief in the *Santa Compaña*, a group of souls dressed in white that go in procession after midnight and roam the country visiting the houses where a death is imminent. A cousin of mine who lived in the Galician town of Lugo told me that there the funerals are announced in the local paper or at 12.30 in the radio because they are considered as very good occasions to do business. The families of the deceased even pay for buses to take the people to the funeral – like they do in the UK for weddings – because some tiny villages do not have public transport and are only accessible by car.

My first contact with death in the UK was shortly after I arrived in London. One morning I woke up and looked at the houses at the other end of the garden wall where there was a small Council property with different doors, and on the bottom of one of them bouquets of flowers had been left on the floor. I thought this must be a funeral custom: it seemed exquisite, something done in silence and with so much respect. I do not remember how long it took me to realise that all this was part of a fear of confronting sentiments and feelings. It took me a long time to realise that in London I could not continue to deal with death as I had done in Spain. To start with, people here did not say 'he/she died' but 'he/she went' and at the beginning I always asked where. It took me ages to internalise the meaning of 'went'. Once I read on a grave in Stoke Newington cemetery 'he fell asleep', and my first instinct was to think they had buried him alive. When I started to have contact with the Natural Death Centre, I heard the story of a Welsh woman who had a friend, Mary, who was not very *compos mentis*. One night she received a phone call from Mary's husband who said: 'Mary has gone' and the friend thought: 'Where can this mad woman be at this time of night?' When she arrived at the house it did not take her long to realise that Mary was in fact dead.

When my mother-in-law lost her sister, who died of a heart attack, I started to ask her questions and she became visibly disturbed. After a while she told me: 'You see, darling, I have never spoken about death with anybody' and I was left totally speechless. The funny thing was that at the end she opened herself to me and it was like a catharsis, she started to speak about death and brought out an incredible amount of repressed feelings.

One day the sister-in-law of a very close friend of my ex-husband died in very tragic circumstances. I spoke with that friend and asked him the date of the funeral to put it in my diary. I noticed that he reacted in a very uncomfortable way and wondered why. Later on, I asked my ex-husband how we were going to go to the funeral and he looked at me amazed that I had any intention of going there: 'We have not been invited', he explained. This sentence stuck forever in my heart and made me understand the profound differences between Spain and the UK and the importance of intimacy in the UK. Today, of course, we have in the UK more and more funerals which are celebrations of life. Here, you aim for privacy and in Spain, the more people attending a funeral the more proud you feel. This is well described in the Almodóvar film *Volver* (2006) when the aunt of the protagonist dies and she cannot attend the funeral. Somebody tells her afterwards: 'The whole village came'. And this is the greatest tribute anybody could have paid.

But modern customs and a greater emotional detachment are creeping into Spain. Before, the family used to stand in line side by side after the funeral and shook hands or kissed anybody who had attended the religious service; I heard negative comments from relatives of the deceased who were exhausted after a night without sleep and nevertheless had to greet and kiss lots of people, many of whom they did not know. The traditional sentence to say to the relatives was: 'te acompaño en el sentimiento' ('I share your feelings') and something that has become a joke: '¡qué bueno era!' ('he/she was so good!'). Today, in some places, people stand in the church and bow their head to anybody who approaches them to offer their condolences.

One of the most enormous changes that people of my age have noticed in Spain concerns the cemeteries. In small villages there used to be just a few marble tombs and the rest consisted of simple ones with iron crosses. In Spain today, lots of them are made in marble and small cemeteries, such as the ones in Jimenez de Jamuz and Castrillo de los Polvazares in León and Venialbo in Zamora, look totally stuffed with ostentatious pieces of marble that leave almost no space between the tombs. This is one more example of the country's prosperity. At the same time lots of *nichos* (burials in walls which are cheaper than in the ground) seem to be empty in big cemeteries like the one in Seville due to the number of cremations. In Britain people are buried the traditional six feet under in coffins without the holes that are found in Spanish coffins and so the organic matter takes much longer to be recycled. In 1994 the journalist Sarah Bosley took a trip to Spain with British undertakers who reported: 'Decomposition, made speedier by good air-flow through the coffin, is more environmentally friendly, they [the Spanish] claim, than burning' (*The Guardian*, 19 November 1994).

The big change in customs of death came in Spain with what we call *tanatorios* which are buildings where the cadavers are deposited during the hours before burial or cremation. According to the information service of Tanatorio Irache in Pamplona, Navarra (Spain), the word 'tanatorio' is new, invented around 1975 when the first *tanatorio* was inaugurated in that town and derives from the Greek noun *thanatos* (death). Although the Catholic Church started to allow cremation in certain circumstances in 1963, the reactionary Spanish authorities only agreed to allow it in 1975. In Astorga, people started to take their dead to the *tanatorio* in 1990, which shows how recent the changes have been in small towns. The *tanatorios* are a sort of an extension of the undertaker's facilities, a space hired for a day to allow the families to mourn outside the home.

The *tanatorios* are in my view a very strange institution. They are very different from the British undertakers which tend to be small and intimate. According to the Millers, Islington funeral directors (as the undertakers like to be called), in Britain not many people see the dead in their coffins or stay near them for hours as in Spain. The *tanatorios* couldn't be less intimate though; they are big buildings with divisions inside containing something like modern hotel suites, individual cubicles in the style of VIP waiting rooms, with a lavatory and two rooms, one at the back for the coffin, and another at the front for the family and visitors who can sit on comfortable sofas and talk to each other without having to see the dead person in front of their eyes. The *tanatorios* resolved a problem of space in small modern flats. In the 1970s there were occasions when somebody died in a new high-rise flat and the undertakers could not fit the coffin in the lift. The solution was to bring it down with a pulley outside the building.

There is a great difference between having the wake in one's own home with just family and friends and facing the upheaval of death in the public space of a *tanatorio* with people who have not met before. In *tanatorios*, death becomes a compartmentalised thing, very convenient for our society of speed. I may be wrong but I do not think they or the niche-graves in cemetery walls would be successful in Britain. In *tanatorios*, which are a sort of warehouse of mourning, the human relationships are taken out of any familiar context. *Tanatorios* work as an antidote against intimacy because although you can close the door and be with the loved ones, sometimes the space is very crowded and one needs to go outside. Then there starts an emotional competition because in the communal space there are big groups that look at each other and inevitably compare numbers.

Some groups are gigantic and some are not. Some people cry noisily and others restrain themselves. The final result is the minimisation of death, another modern depersonalisation.

Some big *tanatorios* like the ones I know in Barcelona, close at 9 P.M. and people cannot mourn near the body during the night. This does not happen in small towns as I was told by one funeral director in Astorga whom I interviewed when I researched the new customs of death in the area. In the big *tanatorios* there are restaurants or bars (in *Las Corts* in Barcelona it is in the basement of the building) where people eat, drink and blow their noses in a strange atmosphere of coldness and generally not very nice decoration.

When my father died, I had not seen the interior of any *tanatorio* before and I was horrified when we entered into our cubicle and saw him in the coffin covered by a crystal dome, like Lenin. That made it impossible to touch him or give him a last kiss. I found the whole thing most inhuman. The service was in a beautiful chapel in the middle of a pinewood belonging to the crematorium and after the service my sister and I were called to testify which one was his coffin to avoid giving us the ashes of another person. We arrived in an open space where several coffins were on the floor and an employee asked us which one was our father. I felt I was in IKEA organising the delivery of some furniture. It was so awful I wanted to write to them afterwards to complain but I never did. I do not know if they still do the same today. I was aware all the time of being part of new procedures that could easily change in practice as time went on. Being used to funerals in Britain run by the Humanist Society, I spoke about my father in the church, something that was totally new to all the people there and some friends did the same when their parents died afterwards. This was totally unknown in Spain because the Catholic Church runs all the services. However, this will change gradually over time, as there are many non-believers in Spain now who are not afraid to show in public what they think.

In Britain, when young men started to die of AIDS they made specifications about what they wanted in their funerals and many were funny and all highly personalised. This changed customs little by little and influenced society in the way in which we see death. I have been to several funerals in Britain and due to the ideology of my friends they have been mostly non-religious and run by the Humanist Society. The traditional ones I have seen in London have struck me by their coldness and awkwardness. Proof of the new preoccupation towards death in Northern Europe came in the exhibitions where artists used human material, sensitivised maybe by the precariousness of human life, nuclear threats, the wars, epidemics. I thought that the new funerals started in the UK and United States after the AIDS epidemic. However, as the historian Pilar Salomón explained in a seminar at the London School of Economics, anarchists and socialists already had secular mass funerals in the Spanish Republic before Franco won the Civil War. Here the secular funeral was also a way of celebrating that one more person had escaped the repressive power of the Catholic church. As such it worked as anticlerical propaganda.

Some years ago, I thought that the UK had to learn from Spain how to confront death but now I see that the opposite is the case, because Spain has modernised itself at great speed and in the UK, at least in the sector of society where I move, it seems as if death is starting to be born again and now we wish to look it directly in the eyes. Regarding death I could almost say that they are at the opposite ends of the spectrum, with Spain taking death outside the home and dehumanising it, and Britain personalising it and, in some cases, bringing it back home.

Spain is fast becoming more secular, but most of the time it does not know what to put in place of the church. Regarding death the new non-religious services are still cold and a bit clumsy for lack of tradition. In the future, I suppose Spain will have to create a Humanist Society, as nothing of the kind exists so far. Before the economic crisis, Spaniards were immersed in modernising their entire society. However, the present conservative government (Partido Popular) is trying to reverse this process. Regarding rituals of death, as the Catholic Church loses its grip on society, people will start to create new personalised rituals and maybe one day, mourners will get together for a meal after a burial or cremation as the British do. This ancient and pagan custom is totally unknown in Spain now, so much so that when I tell Spanish friends what happens here, they are horrified. It is very probable that things will swing back the other way as the process of depersonalisation evolves beyond what people deem acceptable. You never know with Spain: before the death of Franco, nobody could have predicted what the country would be only two years later.

Notes

1. The Spanish Civil War started in 1936 and lasted three years; as a result Nationalist General Francisco Franco was the dictator for nearly forty years until his death in 1975.
2. The opening of the mass graves in Spain since 2000 is another one of the areas I have been investigating but it is not possible to develop it further here due to lack of space.

18

THE DAD PROJECT

Briony Campbell

Three months after my Dad died, I found myself hanging photos on a gallery wall that revealed the story of our relationship and of his death. We had recorded it together through photography and film during his last six months, and it became 'The Dad Project'. He was sixty-five, I was twenty-nine, and two years have passed since.

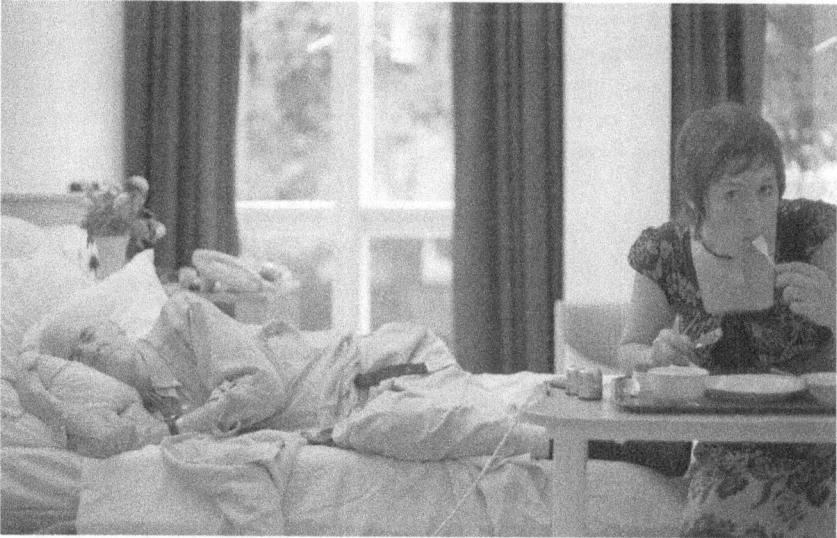

Figure 18.1 At our family dinner table Dad had always been called, 'the dustbin'. As his appetite disappeared, Mum couldn't bring herself to finish his food. But I could. By this point, upholding the waste-not-want-not values he'd instilled in me felt more worthwhile than hoping he might eventually force down enough food to regain strength.

While I was stumbling through the process of recording our experience, I had fleeting moments of speculation that if this eventually manifested as something coherent, perhaps it would help me cope with Dad's absence. During my most optimistic periods I daydreamed that others might even see it, and maybe it would help them too. I never imagined that in the end it would feel so right to share it, or that it would provoke such overwhelming responses. Today The Dad Project has been seen by tens of thousands of people around the world.

In approaching this essay I'm reminded of something that the artist Lasse Johansson said. He was talking about his project 'I am here' which was a response to the fact that his home was to be demolished, and he said 'the context of the work was a dragon to slay not a piece of clay to mold'. Slaying the dragon is a reactive process rather than a proactive one. A project approached as 'clay molding' can be well reported within an academic structure, but my project took form as it occurred. So this essay will simply be an account of the journey that my responses to dad's immanent death took me on, both as a daughter and a photographer.

Cancer Came Along

My dad got sick in December 2007 and had a major operation the next February. In the run up to it I assumed, as I always do, that everything would be fine. The highly specialised, and somewhat risky, eight-hour 'Whipple procedure' actually took twelve. And while we waited the extra hours I began to feel that perhaps, just maybe, there was a chance things wouldn't go our way. But eventually he came out, came round, began the fight to recover, and my naïve optimism returned; how did I ever doubt my instincts – nothing bad could happen to my dad.

I had a conversation about optimism with dad in the Royal Marsden Hospital. He chose to go there for drugs trials after the doctors found, in October 2009, that the Whipple had not, in fact, whipped out the cancer and there was no further treatment for his very rare, and terminal, type of bile duct cancer. Dad seemed to feel the need to justify why he had continued to paint a rosy picture for us all. In his own words:

> Some people will always assume the pessimistic position: that the glass is half empty, and some will take the optimistic one: that it's half full. I like to take the half full position because I think it's a waste of energy and goodwill to assume the negative... unless it's actually proven. Some might consider that naive, but I'd guess those people prefer pessimism, which is fine, but that's not my position.

Figure 18.2   Rose-tinted glasses.

He described it as a glow inside him that had always been there, and that reassured him everything would be ok. (When I thought back on his description I realised how much it sounded like a spiritual reference. Many people draw the equivalent inner-strength from their faith in God's presence within them, but he didn't mean it that way.)

To Photograph, Or Not?

Hearing Dad's description of 'the glow' was very affirming for me because I have it too (though I'd never really articulated the feeling), and this was a huge influence on my desire to photograph Dad's journey towards death. Firstly, because he gave it to me. I don't think there are many greater gifts you can give your child, and I wanted to thank him somehow. And secondly, with the glow inside me, I knew that by doing The Dad Project we could look at the half-full-glass together. That seemed to me the best we could do with our little time.

I had just begun a Masters in documentary photography at the London College of Communication, and my tutor John Easterby gently encouraged me to try to photograph. He was sensitive to the complexity of the decision and I knew that I'd have great support from him if I went ahead. My desire to undertake this challenge was not followed easily by the decision to go ahead... far from it. I've never deliberated so heavily over anything. For a while this decision became the most agonising aspect of my grief. My initial plan was that this would be a collaboration, so Dad's encouragement was crucial. This was his response when I suggested the project:

> When you first asked me about doing this project, I thought about what it would mean for me to share my feelings with you, and whether it was going to make you feel sad or upset, or whether it was going to make me feel sad or upset. And then I thought more about what it would mean to you, and I thought, this is an opportunity for me to learn a little bit more about you as my daughter, and more about what it will mean for you to be without a dad someday, sooner or later. And the uppermost thing in my mind is to try to be a good dad to you for as long as possible, and to understand what it means to be a good dad to you.

I was most worried about upsetting my mum, and found it much harder to open conversations about the idea with her. This inhibited me significantly in the early stages. In retrospect, I think I could have involved her much more, but that's how it occurred. (I am trying my hardest to avoid dwelling on regret. When you live beyond someone you love, there is always room for regretting what you didn't share. Just as when you undertake the documentation of a story, there is always room for regretting what you didn't capture. Regret, which is to the past what pessimism is to the future, seems a waste of goodwill and energy.)

However, as we walked out of the room, having said our final goodbyes to Dad's dead body, Mum asked me 'Have you got all the photos you want? Do you want us to take one of you with Dad?' I was quite amazed.

I became aware that by undertaking this project I would be obliged to experience my dad's last days from the self-critical position of a creator, and this made me doubt it was a good idea. So I found myself seeking confirmation of this doubt, and it wasn't hard to find:

Did I really want be thinking about the rigours of creating a cohesive visual product while my dad was dying? It's a taxing enough task at the best of times.

I had never had any desire to tell my own story through my work. Indeed, I'd often regarded self-referential photography as embodying a level of narcissism that I'm not comfortable with.

We're not a photo family. None of us like having our pictures taken. This was a pretty weird way to try changing that.

My photography takes me away from grief to a happy place; it's a positive and productive distraction. If Dad was my work, how would I escape?

More importantly, my work gave me things to tell Dad about. He was uplifted by knowing that we were proceeding with our usual lives, and not wallowing in sadness. The only thing I could do to make his end happier was to show him that I was going to be fine, and to be fine I needed to pursue my ambitions.

Then I always came back to how it would be for Mum. She was already struggling against so much. Doing anything that might make things harder for her wasn't an option.

For a short time all these considerations put me off the idea entirely. I felt resolved that I wouldn't proceed.

Of course, I talked at length with many people – friends, family and near strangers. I wasn't shy about it. Nobody knew what to advise:

'You should definitely do it if you think you can, but I can't tell you to.'
'I know I couldn't do that, you'd need to be so brave.'
'It could be amazing, but only if it's right for all of you'.

These ambiguous responses made my head spin, but just through trying to make the decision, conversations opened that enriched me hugely. Discussions about the ethics of creative documentary practices became more relevant and purposeful than they'd been before. But more significantly, people would always share their own closest experience of death, or sickness, or family struggles, and often said that they rarely talked about it. I realised that I'd joined the majority of humanity who knew the feeling of great loss. This wasn't something to keep quiet about. If just the possibility of The Dad Project could open all these dialogues, how many more people would be reached if I were actually to do it? The project could be as universal as it was personal.

Figure 18.3 Sitting in the garden became an event, then a day's activity, and eventually a strain that he endured only to comfort us. Or was it to comfort himself? I wondered endlessly, but really there was no difference.

This realisation re-opened the possibility again. And there were two more clinching factors.

Every documentary photographer is seeking to reveal truths, but telling another's story truthfully is essentially impossible. If I chose to tell the story of losing my dad I would be telling our story; my dad and me – therefore it would be true. Maybe I would be liberated from the eternal and integral problem of the documentary photographer...

Purely as a daughter, this was my first and last chance to work with my dad. I had to take it.

Beginning to Shoot

During these months of indecision, I'd only been taking photos that I thought my family would like. Mum wanted a nice photo of the two of them before Dad began to look too ill. The more meaningful photos occurred slowly around springtime. At the beginning I made it easy on myself. I took photos that made me happy on sad days. I found myself making photos reminiscent of those I used to make in my 'honeymoon period' with the camera, when I was learning through playing. They were free from the constraints of purpose, and they pleased me. Whenever I was consumed by the bleakness of the cancer, I took photos. If I couldn't sleep, I took photos. If the morning light hit my bed in a way that erased the gloom, I took photos – and it made me happy. I was seeing a narration of my moods occur.

But I knew that these photos would only speak back to me, and not beyond, and that was the impetus for me to take another step forward. How could I show explicitly what I was feeling? Turn the camera around? So I photographed my face when I was sad. It seemed a ridiculously obvious idea. I wouldn't have even called it an idea. It was the only thing I could think of to move myself on. I assumed the images looked clichéd and I felt strange about doing it. This was another sort of self-indulgence that I never thought I'd embrace. It felt dangerously close to narcissism. I didn't show the photos to anyone for a while.

Then, I began to shoot the details of Mum and Dad's house. These images felt sadder. I still wasn't quite brave enough to turn the camera on my dad, but my photos were beginning, very cautiously, to hint at the real story. A crucial moment for me was the first time I witnessed a startling manifestation of Dad's deteriorating health.

He walked into the kitchen carrying a glass of the energy-milkshake that was intended to fatten him up. He lost his balance and it smashed on the floor. Although my camera was around my neck I couldn't bring myself to photograph the moment as it occurred. It would have felt like a cruel and detached response. The duality of my role was suddenly explicit; is it actually possible to be a

Figure 18.4 Me, Tears.

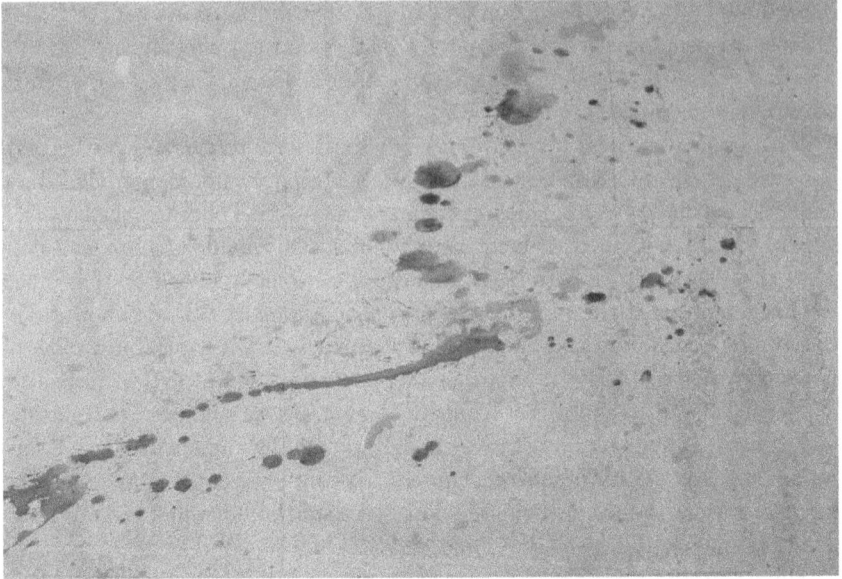

Figure 18.5   Milkshake moment.

daughter and a photographer at once? After I'd cleared up the broken glass (all the time thinking 'that was a photo – I'm missing the story') I managed to take a picture. Although I was slightly disappointed by my initial hesitance, on reflection I realised that what I hadn't captured was as relevant to our story as what I had. This photograph felt like a turning point. The fact that I couldn't shoot everything was the story. And so I became more comfortable with telling it.

Grappling for a Plan

The more I felt the project was underway, the more aware I became that I didn't really have a plan. I thought some good photos were occurring, but wasn't sure if they were enough. Would I just end up with a pile of gentle images about a dad dying a little too early of an all-too-common death; images too sad for my family and too ordinary for an audience? Maybe I needed words to reveal the weight of the story outside the frames. I tried writing but my thoughts never flowed on the page. Should I impose a conceptual methodology on my picture taking? I thought of many plans, but never stuck to them. How could any one approach be the right way to document my dad's ending? I was always waiting for the 'right time' to work it all out with Dad. I wanted to impress him with my plan and to find one that brought clarity to both of our positions. I'd never felt Dad completely understood my photographic motivations, and I hoped perhaps The Dad Project could change that. But I was fumbling. The moment where everything fell into place never happened.

Understanding the Illness

It wasn't until May when I spent a weekend caring for Dad that the magnitude of his situation hit me. Until then I had always been the 'cheer-er up-er', bringing light into the gloom with stories of normal life. I'd help out while I was there, always cook a meal, try to give Mum a moment of rest. But it was only a moment. I didn't really lift the burden. And I was aware that they didn't really want me to know the burden. On this particular weekend I offered to stay with Dad so Mum could go to the country with friends. I thought it'd be nice; I'd cook his meals, fetch his pills, we'd have lots of time to talk together, and all while making pictures. But it didn't go that way. Dad wasn't capable of more than short conversations between sleeps, meagre mouthfuls of food and confused negotiations over pill schedules. I was surprised by my reaction. It wasn't as if I didn't know what stage he was at, but being solely responsible for his wellbeing shook me. So I decided to make more time for him. Neither he nor Mum had ever actually asked me to, and I was just realising how generous that was of them. But I wanted to be part of the struggle now. I couldn't continue to pretend there wasn't one. We wanted to record more conversations and the project motivated us to explore subjects that would've been easier to leave alone.

Space to Focus

When the summer came and term ended, I felt at once glad that my schedule would clear, and anxious that I wouldn't have my tutor's encouraging voice pushing me onwards. Of course my schedule didn't clear, and life was as pressured as usual. I'd been postponing jobs so now had to juggle them with 'dad-time'. When you're consumed by a poignant situation, it's strange how everything else you encounter seems to relate to it. I found myself viewing my client jobs through 'Dad Project spectacles'. The youthful energy of music festivals captured in the 'aspirational' style required by my client felt more hedonistic than ever. While fathers reading to their under-5s for the government's SureStart scheme felt more important. Although I never really managed to clear the decks as I'd have liked to, I began to treat everything else as secondary. The Dad Project became my priority, my normal life worked around it, and it felt right.

Now I began to reflect on the tone of my images, something I hadn't found the objectivity to do until this point. I knew I wanted to make gentle, quiet

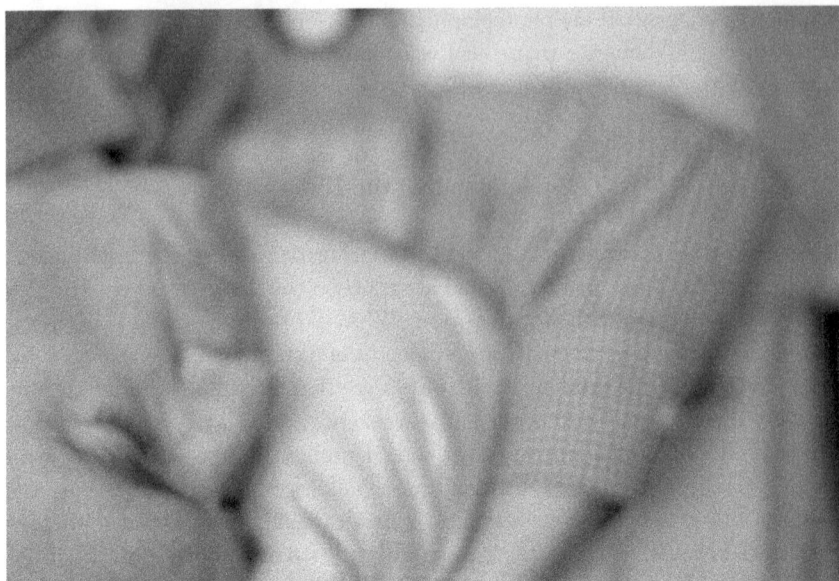

Figure 18.6 Sleeping again.

photographs, and for their message to be open and unselfconscious. I knew I did not want to make gloomy pictures that highlighted suffering. When I tried to view my images objectively I thought, though they looked rather 'safe', they were at least honest.

I asked the photographer Leonie Hampton if she would give me some feedback on the work at this point. Leonie's long-term work is on her mother's mental illness, and I found it raw, elegant and honest, so her opinion was very valuable to me. She told me my photos were strong and touching, and this felt to me like a great validation. I realised how integral external validation would be to my willingness to share the story.

When I asked what other pictures I should look for (as I felt I was beginning to repeat myself), she said 'try to photograph love'.

The End Came into View

I was only just 'finding my feet' in the project, when the immanence of Dad's death came into view. I still don't know, and probably never will, whether this was the natural progression of my creative process or whether my 'feet finding' was a response to the immanent ending. I think both must've played a part. Throughout the year I'd been trying to draw a map for the project, but as my emotions became more fragile it became my map. The more involved I became with Dad, the more involved I became with the camera. As The Dad Project got stronger, I got stronger.

It wasn't even two weeks before Dad's death when I realised it was coming. It wasn't a thunderbolt – it just became apparent. I wondered how long he had known it was around the corner. At this time we tried to talk about his funeral. We wanted to know what he'd like to happen, but we also knew he didn't want to have the conversation. Dad maintained his optimism until the end. When friends came to visit they seemed to know they were saying goodbye, despite being met by Dad's brave and generous spirit. Now I started to wonder: at what point did optimism become denial?

One of the hardest moments for me came a few days before he died. It was his first day with the hospital bed in the living room. We'd managed to get him to the kitchen for dinner with the help of the wheelchair, especially as my aunt was here from America. She knew she was coming to help him die, but Dad wanted to celebrate her visit as normal. When he sat down, he cried and told us he was frightened. He was frightened of not knowing what was happening around him. He was frightened about how Mum would cope without him. We talked about 'letting go', something he'd been struggling with, quite openly, since the diagnosis. When we got him up to go back to bed, he fell. He lay flat on his back in his family kitchen for minutes before he could stand. The camera was part of this heartbreaking evening and nobody seemed to mind.

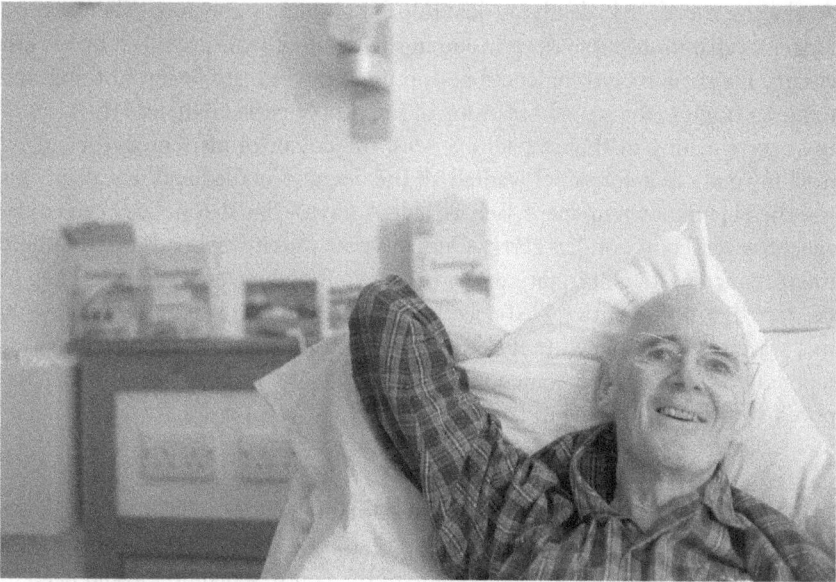

Figure 18.7 Looking at the end.

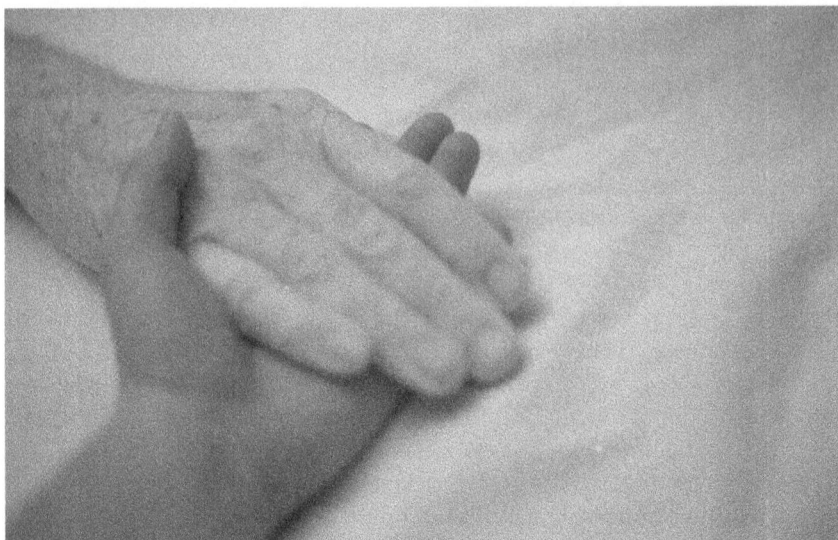

Figure 18.8 When we said goodnight on his last lucid day, he said; 'Think about what we should shoot tomorrow for the project'. By tomorrow his shine was gone and just his shape remained – His unconscious contribution.

Death

At the instant of Dad's death my dual role felt absolutely concrete. There was no longer a separation. From deep inside in the cloud of tears provoked by his last breath, I wished everything could be captured; the sad and beautiful things my mum was saying; the stilted breathing of the people beside him, and the faces of the others aching in their separate spaces, the colour of his skin as it changed from my dad's to a corpse's. I wanted all the details recorded and revealed. This was the big unknown moment, one we will all have – one that nobody can envisage, but everybody wonders about. Ours was now, and it would be gone, but here was a chance to share it in future. As we came out of our clouds, I felt resigned to the fact that documenting Dad's death was as instinctive to me as experiencing it. I was at once ashamed that I was thinking so objectively during the rawest moment of my life, and somehow proud that I was able to – that being the photographer had become innate.

Productive Grief

Dad died on 25 August 2009. According to the course schedule I would need to present my finished 'major project' in late November. Given my situation there was no pressure on me to comply with this schedule, but since the project had become something of a crutch to me, I felt that the process of editing the work might be a sustaining way to embrace my immediate grief. After a few weeks of taking comfort in the company of friends and family I returned to my studio and begun a phase of intense focus, unlike any I've known before.

I spent countless hours rating photos of my dying dad on a scale of 1 to 5, sometimes through tears and sometimes with the efficiency of an editor. It was a simultaneously horrible and wonderful task. When I described the process to a friend he told me I should let the joy and the pain be so intertwined that I can't tell the difference … and that is how it was.

An Outcome

The pressure to commit to an outcome provoked doubt, indecision and procrastination. 'What's life all about? Tough decisions.' Whenever I sought Dad's advice on a problem this simplistic phrase would precede the slow and thorough discussion that followed: an exploration of the relevant factors, each one considered from all possible perspectives. In realising The Dad Project I made a lot of tough decisions. Without my dad, but very much with him.

I found the most difficult aspect was that I couldn't represent our story from every possible perspective. It's my inherited instinct to understand any situation this way. So I took comfort in another of Dad's ideas here: the idea that we need

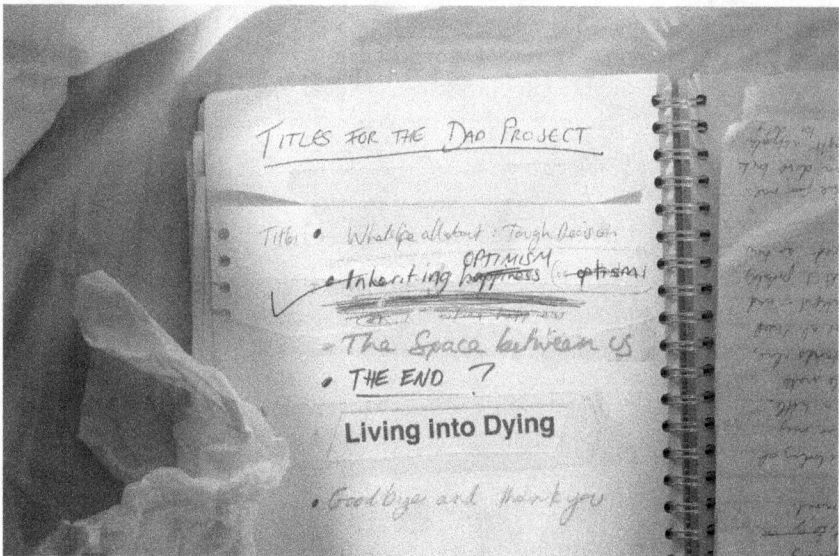

Figure 18.9   No caption.

to 'take positions' ourselves, in order to understand other positions. We hesitate from doing so for fear of being tied to that position. This was an idea he had developed professionally as a family therapist, but when he explained it to me in layman's terms, he used the analogy of shoes: we shouldn't feel tied to one pair of shoes just because we have stepped into them. We shouldn't worry that we'll become known as someone who wears only that type of shoe, and have to wear them forever to maintain our identity. But we should choose a pair and walk around in them for a while. Once we've gained an understanding of what the world looks like with these shoes on, we'll be better equipped to try on another pair, and to understand that what we see wearing the second pair is richer for having worn the first pair. Unfortunately, we can't wear all the shoes at once, but if we chose one pair to start with, we can begin to see.

So with his voice in my head, I decided this initial manifestation would be called 'The First Edit', and that felt like a comforting resolution. I designed a book of images with captions. I wasn't ready to deal with editing the interviews we had recorded, for emotional reasons but also for technical ones. I'm not (yet) a filmmaker, and I didn't want to rush into this highly skilled process. Just watching all my footage was exhausting, so I resolved to return to this at a later point. The book was 7" x 9", printed on a soft matt paper, and beautifully hand-bound with a grey velvet cover. It was, and still is, to my mind, the most perfect work I have done. I didn't imagine that I would get to that stage so soon with The Dad Project, if ever.

The Masters course also required that we hang an exhibition, so shortly after completing the book I designed an exhibition of the photos. I built a small white booth and hung the photos that reflected my story on one side and dad's on the facing side. The photos were in simple white frames ranging from 6" x 4" to 8" x 10", and the layout was broadly chronological but also tonal. I wrote the previous paragraph titled 'Death' by hand on the central wall, and I showed six video clips in their raw state on a screen below it. Again, I was very satisfied with this presentation of the story.

Initial Reflections

At the time of first exhibiting The Dad Project, I wrote the following:

The Dad Project has put my heartache to such positive use. Though this small furry book isn't much of a substitute for Dad's presence, the journey I've been on to make it has been my most inspiring yet. Most significantly because I've been on it with my dad – every day since he died.

There is, of course, a small but incredulous voice in the back of my head saying 'don't think you're going to get away with it that lightly'. Occasionally I worry whether I'm postponing my grieving. But I've been so thoroughly ensconced in grief during this productive phase, that I can't possibly be in denial. I feel sure that if everyone had an equivalent way to unravel their own bereavement, loss wouldn't weigh so heavily on so many.

The emotive responses the project has provoked already have given me glimpses of the bigger dialogues I was hoping to create. My dad was very concerned, both personally and professionally, with understanding relationships, so if The Dad Project helps that occur on some level, I'll feel I've done him proud.

So to answer the first question I posed here to my future self: 'am I postponing my grief?', I don't think I did, but rather the life of the project enabled me to spread it, so that it has become a continuous presence, but never a heavy one. The life of the project is defined by its audience now, and as they continue to send me wonderfully heartfelt messages of appreciation, this continuous presence is very affirming for me. So, with regard to the second question of opening dialogues that help people understand their relationships, Dad would certainly be proud of the extent to which that has happened. I only wish he could read some of the emails I have received from people who have been touched by the work.

Publishing The Dad Project

I now see the project as having two distinct chapters. During the first it belonged to Dad and me. Once it had been exhibited and published the second chapter began, and The Dad Project belonged to whoever saw it.

Having the opportunity to exhibit our story within the supportive environment of the MA course provided a reassuring way to begin sharing it. The responses that came back gave me the confidence to take it further. The next publication was dramatically wider: in *The Guardian Weekend Magazine*. When I showed my book to the Photo Editor she cried, and said immediately that she would like to publish it. I felt I was in safe hands. It's not usual for a photographer to be consulted on the layout of their work, but they agreed that in this case it would be a collaborative process, and the article was very sensitively done. So when they suggested their film department could edit my footage into a short film I was glad to collaborate again. However this was a more stressful experience. While the editors tried to be sensitive to my preferences, I didn't feel I was firmly in the driving seat. The time frame we had to work with was so pressured that I couldn't take the time to consider every choice in the slow and thorough way that I am used to. In the end I was satisfied with the ten-minute film we produced, but it was such an all-consuming experience that after walking out of the edit suite I didn't watch the film for some months.

Following these two publications I received over a hundred emails from readers (and when the work was published in Spain's *El Mundo*, my website received 8,000 visits to The Dad Project pages). They were incredibly intimate and detailed. Many people recounted similar experiences of their own, and often described visual details that they kept stored in their mind's eyes. Others talked about how it had made them think about their relationships with their parents, or their children. Some said what a wonderful man my dad seemed to be, and they always thanked me for sharing our story.

A month later the work was exhibited in The Photographer's Gallery as part of a group show of recent graduates. I hung it in a similar way to my original design and again received heart-warming responses. Some of them were from photographers considering doing something similar. It felt good to be able to encourage others to record their own stories of love and loss.

I learnt a difficult lesson about the editorial process through working with Germany's *Die Zeit*. They proposed to publish the story over eight pages with a detailed interview, so I was pleased when the writer wanted to discuss my journey very thoroughly and sensitively. However, in this case they declined my request to see the text before it was published, that being their editorial policy. Because my previous experiences of sharing the work had been so positive I was feeling quite relaxed about letting others interpret the work, so I didn't argue. When the published piece was translated for me by a German friend, I was quite distressed by a number of significant additions that the writer had drawn from his own imagination. The most glaring being that he wrote, 'Briony calls it The Dad Project, as in Dad, but also Dead'. Whether this was a poor attempt at word play in his second language, or a chance to add some drama to the title, I was amazed that he had made such a clumsy statement. It felt to me that he couldn't have understood my intentions to tell a gentle story emphasising life rather than death, as I trusted he had done.

Considering My Audience

For each of these, and subsequent manifestations of the project I have made different edits. Sometimes they have been influenced by the space available, or by the potential audience, but always defined by my own feelings at the time. I don't feel my relationship to the photos has changed dramatically over these two years, but the on-going reassurance of audience appreciation has coaxed me to feel more comfortable with sharing the most painful imagery. In 'The First Edit' I chose not to include photos of Dad after he died, but earlier this year, when Odee, a new photo book publisher published 'The Dad Project – one year on', I decided to include these images.

In a reflection on her own work, Sally Mann (another photographer who has documented her own family) referenced an Emily Dickinson poem. It seemed to express so beautifully something another filmmaker had advised me. Before I got involved with the Guardian film department, I showed this filmmaker the footage from the moment after Dad died and he told me that if we were editing it for broadcast we would have to cut it half way through. I was surprised that he thought it too raw for a television audience, as I assumed that if I, as the creator, were willing to share it, then it would be considered rare and valuable television content. It was an interesting perspective to consider as I returned to edit and re-edit The Dad Project.

Tell all the Truth but tell it slant
Success in Circuit lies
Too bright for our infirm Delight The Truth's superb surprise
As Lightning to the Children eased with explanation kind
The Truth must dazzle gradually
Or every man be blind

Emily Dickinson

In the early stages of sharing the story I had some unique encounters with viewers. There were many times I was approached by someone with tears in their eyes. These emotional responses were as unexpected to the viewers as they were to me, and that would be apparent in our exchange. I was deeply affected by each person. However, I didn't find it difficult to play the comforting role when I sensed that was what they needed. It offered me a chance to honour Dad's values, and felt like another wonderful validation of the project. While my own grief, and my attempts to cope with it were still so new to me, these mutually enriching encounters were very much a part of my journey.

But as time passed, and I experienced many similar moments, my responses to the intimate thoughts strangers were compelled to share with me became less emotive. I felt I might be disappointing them. I have occasionally had to remind myself that people are still seeing the work for the first time, and that their initial reactions will continue to be charged, even if my own have been diluted by familiarity. I worry that I may come across as flippant because I am so comfortable talking about the whole experience now.

Moving on

I did an interview for the BBC World Service a few months after Dad died and as I was leaving, the interviewer asked me 'Is it hard to talk about the experience and then just get on with a normal day? Do you feel the project is stopping you

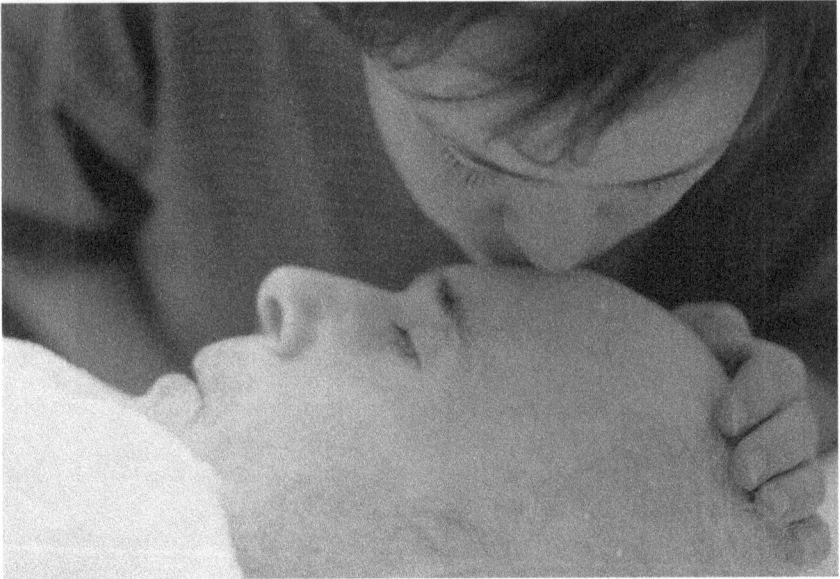

Figure 18.10 25 August 2009.

from moving on?' Her question stuck in my mind. I didn't find it hard to get on with my normal day at all, as my dad and the project were very much a part of my normal day. I had no desire to 'move on' as I felt no disadvantage to staying with the memories. I have the process of The Dad Project to thank for this.

When we are weighed down by our memories we have to be careful not to access them at inappropriate moments, for fear of exposing our fragility. I consider myself fortunate that my memories of the death of my wonderful dad enrich me rather than depress me, and fortunate for feeling comfortable talking about it. It means I can do it as often as it may be relevant, thus keeping his memory ever present. I am so grateful to my dad and for giving me a way to keep moving forward with him, and to photography for making it possible.

Endnote

All that remains to say is how grateful I am that I was on the London College of Communication MA course during Dad's last year. Without John Easterby's support, I probably wouldn't have managed to do The Dad Project – and that's an awful thought.

INDEX

www.ingramcontent.com/pod-product-compliance
Lightning Source LLC
Chambersburg PA
CBHW060031030426
42334CB00019B/2277